I'll Be Right Back

Memories of TV's Greatest Talk Show

Mike Douglas

with Thomas Kelly and Michael Heaton

SIMON & SCHUSTER

SIMON & SCHUSTER

Rockefeller Center

1230 Avenue of the Americas

New York, NY 10020

Designed by Karolina Harris

Manufactured in the United States of America

10 9 8 7 6 5 4 3 2 1

Library of Congress Cataloging-in-Publication Data

Douglas, Mike.

I'll be right back : memories of TV's greatest talk show / Mike Douglas ;

with Thomas Kelly and Michael Heaton.

p.   cm.

Includes index.

1. Mike Douglas show. 2. Douglas, Mike. 3. Television personalities

—United States—Biography. 4. Singers—United States—Biography.

I. Kelly, Thomas. II. Heaton, Michael. III. Title.

PN1992.77.M55 D68 1999

791.45'028'092—dc21

[B]   99-46415

ISBN 0-684-85437-6

Endpaper photographs courtesy of Eyemark Entertainment and Michael Leshnov/

Lost Archives © 1999, and Bernie Rich/Score Photography Collection © Bernie Rich.

Acknowledgments

FIRST, last, and always, my thanks go to my bride of fifty-three years, Genevieve Purnell Douglas. I look back now and realize it was hardly less than a miracle that a teenage kid from Chicago walked through the door of a modest home in Oklahoma City and gazed on the best his future would hold. I have thanked God every day since. Gen has been my flower, my rock, my heart, and my soul.

This book is the story of *The Mike Douglas Show,* and it took almost as many people to make it happen as the show itself. Thomas Kelly and Michael Heaton are not just co-authors, they are my friends. Kelly Dowd Douglas is not just the photo editor, editorial consultant, and administrative assistant, she's my daughter. Michele Dowd and Christine Dowd Voinovich are like two of a kind when it comes to inspiration, dedication, and loyalty. No wonder. They are my lovely and loving twins.

Thanks to Ron Konecky for making it happen, Frank Campana for holding the fort, Joe Petito and Gus Janos for getting it started, David Rosenthal at Simon & Schuster for believing.

And thanks to so many of my favorite guests for helping me remember the moments: Bob Hope, Muhammad Ali, Billy Crystal, Burt Reynolds, Don Rickles, Ann-Margret, Dom DeLuise, Phyllis Diller, Jay

ACKNOWLEDGMENTS

Leno, Arnold Schwarzenegger, Aretha Franklin, Ray Charles, Muriel Humphrey, Steve Allen, Ed McMahon, Diana Ross, Tony Orlando, Steve Martin, Stevie Wonder, and many, many more. Forgive me, I'm older now, I forget.

Most of all, thanks to the fans who still stop me in restaurants, on airplanes, and on street corners every day to say they liked our show. What a bargain for Gen and me. We tried to make your days a little brighter. You made our dreams come true.

This book is dedicated to all those who were so dedicated to *The Mike Douglas Show*. From the gaffers and cameramen to directors and producers, these wonderful people made my day, every day, for over twenty years. They were not just top-flight professionals, they were intrepid pioneers, daring to go where no one in television had gone before, and they did it with creativity, endurance, and class. Over the years there were hundreds of them, so I can't begin to mention names . . . except one.

As a contributor, counselor, advisor, and crisis manager whose name never appeared in the credits, my wife, Gen, was an integral part of the show from Day One. As for titles, she never had one, so let's just call her the executive producer of my life.

Contents

Introduction
by Rosie O'Donnell

Look, I'll just admit it: the plain fact is that when I was a kid, school just marked time between Mike Douglas shows. It was simply something to get through until I could get home to tune in with my nana and sister.

Sitting there, sharing my stack of Ritz crackers and peanut butter, I watched as plain old entertaining conversation flowed. With a twinkle in his eye and a kindness to his being, Mike was my ideal of graciousness. He knew how to talk, but almost even more importantly, he knew how to listen. He put guests at ease and made them feel comfortable enough to be themselves. As a result, all of us out watching in TV land got to feel intimate with the biggest stars of the day. No one got hurt; everyone had fun.

It was an imprint that lasted. A quarter century later, when I got a chance to do my own show, there was not a moment's hesitation about what I wanted to do. The spirit and style of Mike and Merv guided me the whole way through,

To say I was very nervous when I actually got a chance to meet Mike is not an exaggeration. But just like the guests in those chairs in Philly, I felt my anxiety put to rest by his charm, grace, and kindness. Getting to know him was as much of a joy as I ever imagined it could be.

I know I'm not the only one who holds such a trove of memories of

Mike. When I asked him to do my show, he was characteristically modest, but on top of that, he honestly could not understand why I would want to book him. Maybe the standing ovation he got cleared up the mystery.

If a genie granted me three wishes, I know one of them would be five hours on a boat with Mike where he would tell me all his stories. In the meantime, this book is no sorry substitute.

For me there is no doubt, Mike is one of the most delightful men in this little girl's life.

Foreword

I'M not a namedropper. Honest. I'm a name*dripper*. After fifty plus years in the show business spotlight, the names just ooze out of me. Like John Wayne told me, "No brag, just fact." Oops, there I go.

Starstruck from day one, I loved to be around them. The stars. Hear them sing, watch them dance, laugh at their jokes, listen—really listen—to their stories. And I've been lucky enough to spend a good part of my life doing just that. Over ten thousand stars appeared on *The Mike Douglas Show*, give or take a constellation or two, not to mention thousands more lesser lights—meteors and comets streaking past. If show business was astronomy, I'd be Carl Sagan.

I still consider myself the world's luckiest fan. Looking back, there are times when it all seems like one long, wonderful dream. Was that really me, at age nine, crooning "Mother Machree" for spare change in a Chicago saloon? Was that me in my teens, touring the country's fabled nightclubs, singing for my supper? Was I really the "boy singer" for Kay Kyser's Kollege of Musical Knowledge, the biggest of the big bands?

Talk about a charmed life. Thanks to Walt Disney, I sang the role of Prince Charming himself for *Cinderella*.

And was that my television show that started in a tiny Cleveland studio and ended up being broadcast all over the world for two decades? It doesn't seem likely, hardly even seems possible, but I remember it all so clearly, just as if it were real. Was that really me singing duets with Barbra Streisand? Dancing with Fred Astaire? Running roadwork with Muhammad Ali? Trading barbs with Bob Hope? Doing bits with Jackie Gleason and Jack Benny? Playing straight man for Bill Cosby and Billy Crystal? Chatting with presidents, kings, and goddesses?

If it was, thanks. Thanks to the stars for sharing their talents and the stories of their lives. Thanks to Woody Fraser and Roger Ailes and Ernie DiMassa and Larry Rosen and Rick Rossner and Burt Dubrow and Brad Lockman and Ernie Sherry and the greatest production staff and crew ever assembled on the show. And thanks to all of you out there who turned us on every day and said, "Yes, we enjoyed that, come on back again tomorrow, Mike."

And if it wasn't, please—don't wake me up.

1

A Million to One

PEOPLE ask me how I became a star. That question still floors me. I never thought of myself as a star. Still don't. If you want to know the truth, I fell into the American Dream. I didn't have lofty ambitions or a Master Plan. I liked to sing and entertain people, and the only reason I became (wince) a star is because, by the early 1960s, there weren't enough joints left for a ballad singer like myself to make a few hundred bucks a week and support a growing family. I was in danger of becoming obsolete, a typewriter salesman in Silicon Valley.

It's not like I hadn't already had more than my share of success. I had been singing for my supper since my teens, featured vocalist on some of the nation's best radio stations before I was twenty. I had paid my dues, toured the country with some big bands, and learned some licks from some of the biggest names in the business—Count Basie, Duke Ellington, Harry James. I listened, I watched, I learned.

I had starred with America's favorite radio musical show, and later the first hit musical program on television, *Kay Kyser's Kollege of Musical Knowledge.* With Kay, I had even scored two number-one records in two years. "The Old Lamplighter" was my first hit—still a special song to me—then "Ole Buttermilk Sky" topped *Billboard*'s chart for eighteen weeks. Those were sweet days.

But by the early 1950s, night was falling for the big bands. In spite of banner ratings, Kay's prime sponsor withdrew and the old maestro closed the Kollege forever. For us, it was the beginning of hard times.

In spite of my credits, work was scarce. The buzzword at the record companies was "rock 'n' roll" and that wasn't me. Most of the night-clubs that had welcomed me in the 1940s no longer existed, torn down to make way for malls and fast food stores. The few that were left were struggling. I worked for months at a time at the Bar of Music and Dick Whittinghill's club in Sherman Oaks, doubling as house singer and MC. Some in-studio jobs at infant KTTV helped pay the bills. Once or twice a year, we would hit the road. A week in Chicago, two weeks in St. Louis, three nights in Boston, a week in New York. But the writing was on the wall. In every city, we'd hear the same sad refrain. Crowds thinning out. Band musicians were scarce. Money was scarcer.

My wife, Gen, and I managed to maintain a decent lifestyle, but show business wasn't paying for it anymore, real estate was. My bride had a wonderful sense of value when it came to houses and I had learned enough watching show biz agents to negotiate good deals. We bought our first home in Burbank on the G.I. Bill for under $8,000 and sold it a few years later for double that. We moved up, found another bargain in the Valley, then doubled our money again a few years later. I wouldn't recommend it today—it reminds me of the old Detroit saying, "You can live in your car, but you can't drive your house"—but it worked for us time and again. In the leanest years, we lived off the profits from flip-ping homes in the flourishing L.A. market.

That was a hobby. In comparison, my vocation was producing dismal results. I was thirty-five years old and still wondering what I was going to be when I grew up. I looked at my beautiful girls, all four of them, and said to myself, "This is no way to live. I'm no quitter, but I've got to let it go." I was into my third day of scanning the want ads when a letter arrived, the old Air Mail Special Delivery.

It was a note from Woody Fraser: "Dear Mike, Please contact me right away. I need you in Cleveland."

It came as a complete surprise. I hadn't heard from Woody since our days together at a WMAQ, an NBC-TV station in Chicago, where Woody was a kid on the production staff and I was staff singer. He re-membered me from our time together and my short stint as host of a lo-

Mike and Edward Arnold on "Hi Ladies"

cal show on WGN-TV called *Hi, Ladies!* An afternoon afterthought, the show was formatted for me to do a little song-and-dance, then ask some nervous guest questions about women's issues (which, back then, were limited to subjects like "Baking with Yeast" and "Cleaning with Ammonia"). It garnered a decent audience and, looking back, it was way ahead of its time. That may sound impressive, but it's not. In television, being ahead of your time is deadly. Besides, the budget was so small we had to choose every day between ordering a pizza or doing the show. In spite of a good response, the station wouldn't budge on the dollars. After six months, we insisted on raises and a bigger budget. The station said no. Goodbye, ladies. Just a footnote in early TV talk history, but Woody remembered.

I remembered Woody was an energetic youngster with some brash ideas about how to make television into something a lot more than what it was back then, radio with pictures. No one was listening yet, but that didn't stop Woody. In our time together, we spent hours every day talking about the vast potential of this amazing medium that was hardly more than an unruly child.

It had been a few years, but we had established a nice rapport and it was great to hear his voice again. Woody was excited. Woody was always excited.

"Mike! You gotta come to Cleveland!"

Woody had moved on to a position in program development for the modest Westinghouse cluster of TV stations. He was at KYW in Cleveland, where he had finally convinced Ralph Hansen of Group W to roll the dice on his concept for a live, talk-entertainment daytime show. With a green light from Hansen, Woody had firmed up a format and went about trying to find a host. He was still looking when word came down that Hansen was no longer with the company. It looked like the end of Woody's short-lived concept, but Chet Collier, the new director of programming at KYW, picked up Hansen's mantle. He needed an afternoon show to compete with the success of *The One O'Clock Club,* an informal chat show featuring Dorothy Fuldheim, an octogenarian legend in Cleveland news circles, and affable radio personality Bill Gordon. They were killing KYW in the ratings and Collier directed Woody to stop the bleeding. Woody said he had a show in the works, but he hadn't had any luck finding the right host in the local talent pool and needed to reach out to New York or L.A. to find someone who could pull the whole thing together. Bringing in a host from the Coast wasn't in the budget. "Damn the budget," said Collier (God bless him), "full speed ahead."

*

The Mike Douglas Show premiered on December 11, 1961.

I know time is compressed in memories, but it seems like I went to bed that night and never woke up from the dream that became a life. In a few weeks, we were a local hit. Less than a year later we were syndicated. At the time, I didn't even know what that meant because there was no such thing as a syndicated talk show. Before the weather changed, we were on in several major markets. By the end of 1963, we were blanketing the nation with an unprecedented, live, ninety-minute talk-variety show with big-name guests every day. By 1964, we were number one in daytime all over the country.

For the next twenty years, I spent most of my time chatting, joking, singing, and dancing with the most famous, most talented, most interesting, most powerful, and most beautiful people in the world. I didn't deserve it. I didn't ask for it. I didn't dare even wish for it. It just happened.

You want to hear complaints? You want to hear "get even" stories about the people that double-crossed me or let me down? You want to hear gripes about performers that got on my nerves or executives that got in my way? Read another book, my friend. The complaint window is closed. If Jimmy Stewart hadn't already made *It's a Wonderful Life* such a famous title, you could put it on the front of this book.

I'm Not Merv

Can I take a moment to clear something up that's been a problem for many years? I'm not Merv Griffin. Although sometimes I wonder if the two of us weren't separated at birth.

The first time I heard of a young fellow named Merv Griffin, I was singing with Kay Kyser's band. I heard a song called "Lovely Bunch of Coconuts" with Merv featured as the vocalist. He was of Irish descent, about my age, some say he even looked a bit like me, and he was singing with a big band. Like me.

I didn't think much about it. A few years later, I was offered a contract with a major movie studio in Hollywood. While I was in L.A. to discuss the proposal, an old friend asked me if I knew Merv Griffin. No, but I had heard his "Coconuts" song. Well, as soon as I turned down the studio deal because I couldn't get a release from my contract with Kay Kyser, Merv signed an identical contract with the same studio.

A few years later—this is the mid-1950s now—I did a stint as host of a local television show in Chicago. The next time I heard Merv Griffin's name, he was into television, trying his hand as a host. Now it was starting to get a little spooky.

Believe it or not, several years after *The Mike Douglas Show* cranked up, hit the national airwaves, and started its long run at the top of the ratings, *The Merv Griffin Show* appeared, with a strikingly similar format. For years, if I was watching TV in the afternoon and grew weary of seeing my own mug, I could flip over to the closest channel and see Merv's. More often than I care to count, a guest would appear on our show and would pop up on Merv's program a short time later. There weren't any stalking laws on the books back in the 1960s, but if there were, I had a pretty decent case against this guy, this Merv.

Merv Griffin

Fact is, I think the world of Merv Griffin. He's about as likable as people get, his show was a class act, and I like to think we were brothers in the Exalted Order of Pioneer Daytime TV Hosts. There are only two more items I have to mention with regard to the Mike-Merv confusion.

First, I don't mind at all when people come up to me on the street and say, "Ohmygod. Merv. I just loved you and your show. Would you give me an autograph?" I have no qualms about scribbling Merv's name, either. But I will never forget the ultimate example of this mixup. I was at the Beverly Hills hotel several years ago, crossing through the lobby, when an elevator door opened and a lovely woman stepped out, saw me, and exclaimed with arms open wide, "Merv, darling, it's wonderful to see you!" She gave me a big hug and asked what I'd been doing. I had seen her before but I couldn't come up with a name. She was so genuinely concerned and ingratiating, I couldn't help but spend several minutes exchanging pleasantries. Then, with a kiss on the cheek, she was gone. Never asked for an autograph. It wasn't until a few minutes later I stopped dead in my tracks, realizing who she was. The elegant woman who had mistaken me for Merv was Merv Griffin's former wife, Jewel

Anne. I had to take out my wallet and check the driver's license. I am Mike Douglas, aren't I?

And finally allow me a moment for a personal message to Merv. I become a singer, you become a singer. I get a gig with a big band, you get a gig with a big band. I get some hit records, you get hit records. I get my own smash daytime show, you get your smash daytime show. I finally get to spend time with my family, play some golf, and enjoy life. You keep working hard and get *Jeopardy* and *Wheel of Fortune*.

Some people might see a little inequity there and I have to admit, with my loving family and this lucky life, I guess they're right. So give me a call sometime, Merv, old buddy, and I'll treat you to a round of golf. It's the least I can do to make up for the fact that I've been so blessed in so many ways and you're down to your last billion dollars.

Oh, and one more thing. I was about to tell you how I got started on *The Mike Douglas Show*. Well, the truth is, Merv played no small role in opening the door.

When Chet Collier gave Woody permission to expand his search, he headed to Chicago in search of the elusive perfect host. After three days, countless interviews, and no results, he found himself in a little downtown tavern called Henrici's. It was late afternoon and a TV was droning behind the bar. Woody glanced at the screen and his eyes lit up.

Mike! Mike Douglas! There he was, hosting some quiz show.

Woody suddenly realized that Mike Douglas just might be the answer to his prayers. He could talk—the two of them had spent endless hours in conversation in Chicago about every conceivable topic under the sun. He could sing—a big bonus for a ninety-minute, daily show that would gobble up bits, segments, guests, and material like a hungry lumberjack at an all-you-can-eat breakfast. He had TV experience—a rarity in the early days.

That's him! That's the guy I want! He was so excited, he shouted out my name.

"Mike Douglas!"

The bartender looked up, looked at the TV, then gently corrected him. It wasn't me. It was Merv Griffin on *Play Your Hunch*.

Didn't matter. Woody didn't know Merv, he knew Mike. And he didn't have Merv's address, he had Mike's.

A few days later, I was on my way to Cleveland.

Thanks, Merv. Thanks a lot. Make that two rounds of golf.

*

I flew to Cleveland and did the audition. I don't know why, but I wasn't the least bit nervous. It seemed like no big deal. Sing a little, talk a little, make some introductions, smile at the camera. I had already done some time on local and national television. Add that to fifteen years on the road and everything that could happen to a performer had already happened to me.

One night in Columbus, I was working a club that was owned by the mob. I had been booked for several weeks as the "host-singer." I would do the warm-up, sing a couple of songs, and introduce the feature act. Just as I was about to walk on stage one night, the manager buttonholed me behind the curtain.

"Hey Mike—we gotta problem."

"What problem?"

"Cancellation. Ain't gonna be nobody but you tonight. You gotta do ninety minutes."

"What? But I've got a set twelve minutes. I can't do an hour and a half."

He took a step closer and poked his cigar at my chest.

"We got four hundred people out there. I said you gotta do an hour and a half. Don't let us down."

I stared at him for a long moment. He didn't smile, didn't even blink.

"You know," I said, "ninety minutes are really not that much more than twelve."

*

One camera in a little studio in Cleveland didn't scare me much. I breezed through the audition, headed back to California, and waited to hear the outcome. It wasn't long before Woody called with the good news.

"They flipped over you in New York."

They flew me back into Cleveland to do some pilot shows. The Group W brass liked the first batch and loved the second. I returned to Cleveland a third time to negotiate a contract. A day later, I went home to Gen with a deal that I thought was the worst of both worlds.

"It's done, sweetheart. And I have to tell you straight off, these Westinghouse people are brutal."

Gen asked about the terms.

"Well, the good news is, we got a three-month guarantee."

"Three months? That is good news."

"For a television show? Honey, that's not exactly a marathon. It's a sprint."

"What's the bad news?"

"The most they'll give me is four hundred a week."

"Four hundred dollars a week? Every week? That's wonderful, Mike."

"But Gen, it's a ninety-minute show! Every day! I can get that for one night!"

"Not every week, honey. You know there's nothing out there."

"How are we gonna live on four hundred a week?"

"Look at it this way—if it works, you can be on all five of their stations. That'll be more. And who knows, maybe somebody'll see it and you'll get a show from a network."

"C'mon, Gen, that's a million to one."

"It'll be all right, Mike. They'll come around when they see what you can do."

One month later we were on our way to the Midwest.

I'm going to have to confess to something here for the first time. We had a small sum from Westinghouse for moving expenses. It was nice to have, but it wasn't much. The biggest outlay was going to be for the moving company that hauled our worldly possessions from Los Angeles to Cleveland.

We hired Bekins to handle the move. We went through those dreary weeks of sorting, boxing, and packing and the day finally came. The Bekins movers arrived and transferred everything out to the front lawn. Just as they started loading everything on their moving van, I got a call from my agent, Vinnie. We talked about the show a bit, then I mentioned I had to go—the movers were there. Chet Collier surprised me with some good news. He thought he had told me. Westinghouse was sending Mayflower at their expense. That was part of the deal. The Mayflower truck was on the way.

I told him I would call back, hung up the phone, and rushed outside.

Several hundred dollars was a fortune to us in those days. I had to do something and do it quick. I went into my John Barrymore routine and sadly informed the Bekins movers that there had been a problem with the contract. We didn't know if we would be going to Cleveland after all. Sorry, fellas.

They were kind enough to ask if I wanted them to put everything back in the house before they left. I felt terrible. No, I said, just leave it in the garage. We'll take care of it. And thanks anyhow.

The Bekins truck literally passed the Mayflower truck as it drove away. I'm sorry, Mr. Bekins, but Gen and I needed that extra money for milk and diapers in Cleveland.

*

It wasn't exactly smooth sailing when we got there. Woody had signed a talented pianist, Ellie Frankel, and a couple musicians as a minimal band for the show and started assembling a bare-bones staff and crew. Even that was a problem because the local unions got wind of it and raised a ruckus.

Cleveland was a union town from way back. When the business agent for the Stagehands Local heard that Westinghouse had no plans to pay union scale for the crew, they threatened to picket and shut down the entire station. Westinghouse didn't want to talk about it. The standoff went on for weeks while we waited to hear if there would even be a show. They finally reached some sort of compromise. I was relieved to hear the show was on, but not very happy with Woody's comment: "We're a go, but now we've got less money than we had before, and that wasn't near enough." I marked off thirteen weeks on my calendar and started preparing myself for the move back to California.

As the start date drew closer, another problem became apparent. Guests. Cleveland was not exactly the center of the entertainment universe. It wasn't going to be easy to get enough prominent names to fill twenty to thirty slots a week. That chicken came home to roost when we learned that, ten weeks into preproduction, we still didn't have enough guests for the first show. I wondered if the Cleveland audience would enjoy a daily, ninety-minute monologue by your lonely host, Mike Douglas.

There were some bright spots. The people at KYW and the people of Cleveland couldn't have been any nicer. I had never spent any time in Cleveland and had only a vague impression of the city as an old, Midwestern industrial center, down on its luck and plagued by dreary weather. I discovered that none of that was true. It was a working-class town, all right, but full of vitality, interesting characters, and pleasant surprises. I was born in Chicago, I love Chicago, but Cleveland is where really good things started to happen for Gen and me, and it became our adoptive hometown. Some of the finest human beings I have ever met are Clevelanders, and they were kind enough to take me under their wing.

One of them was Linn Sheldon, a top all-around talent who hosted a kids show on KYW that was the perennial favorite program on local television. And "Barnaby," as Linn was known on the show, was the most popular TV personality in Cleveland. I was astounded when he took me to lunch one day. As we walked a few blocks to a restaurant, every other person would wave, wink, smile, or run up for an autograph.

"Barnaby!"

"Hey, Barnaby, how ya doin'!"

"We love you, Barnaby!"

Linn took it all in stride. I was in awe. I remember thinking, if I could

Barnaby

only be as famous as that someday—what a great life. Many years later, after Gen and I had been jostled hard by a crowd of fans at a theater in Miami who had almost knocked her down and ripped my shirt to grab a cuff link, I remember thinking, "If only nobody knew me—what a great life."

Woody took us to football games at mammoth Municipal Stadium and we learned what ferociously loyal fans Clevelanders were. Gen discovered the wonderful museums, lakefront parks, and open-air markets. We found a little apartment overlooking the lake. The fall brought magnificent colors. We began to settle in and we liked it. Cleveland had a comfortable feeling about it. We started to think that maybe, just maybe, everything would be all right.

*

D-Day was scheduled for early December. Momentum started to pick up. Woody Fraser was the producer and we managed to get a fine young director, Ernie Sherry. Another fortuitous draft choice was the selection of Launa Newman as talent coordinator. To this day, I don't know what kind of background or experience qualified her for the job, but she proved to be the best in the business from Day One. Working with no budget, no time, a bad location, and no track record, she came up with quality guests day after day, week after week. After a few weeks' rehearsal, the Ellie Frankel Trio started to sound like a ten-piece band. Assistant producers, cameramen, lighting technicians, boom operators—everybody that came on board seemed to meld together like they'd been doing *The Mike Douglas Show* all their lives. Don't ask me why, the pieces just fit.

And Woody had a few other tricks up his sleeve. For weeks before the show debuted, the station ran spots that just said "MIKE DOUGLAS," day in, day out. No voice-over, no hype, no details, just "MIKE DOUGLAS." It piqued people's interest and they tuned in to the first week of shows in droves, just to see what the heck "MIKE DOUGLAS" was all about.

We went into full rehearsals, every day, run-throughs that looked and felt like the real thing. By the end of November, the energy levels were sky-high and all systems were go. Maybe we were fooling ourselves, but there was something in the air, a heady feeling that hey, we just might have something here.

*

December 11, 1961. John F. Kennedy was in the White House talking about New Frontiers. People were driving Edsels, DeSotos, and Ramblers. The average family income in the U.S. was under $9,000. The number one television show was *Gunsmoke*. The number one daytime show was *General Hospital,* followed closely by another half a dozen soap operas. The only remotely comparable show on national television was Jack Paar's *Tonight Show,* a thoughtful and eminently watchable program, but hardly the concept we had in mind. Jack Paar was an intelligent and erudite host, but Jack had little performing background himself, which led to a show long on interesting conversation and short on active entertainment. We wanted to go another way and raise the excitement level by emphasizing performance. The problem was, performance meant production values, rehearsals, and a lot more hard work than impromptu talk. We were confident we could do it, but the big question was: could we do it every day? Westinghouse had given us ninety days to make it happen or we were gone. It wasn't much of a chance, but it was a chance. Maybe, just maybe . . .

"Three . . . two . . . one . . ." That ominous little red light flickered on.

"Now, ladies and gentlemen, here's your host for *The Mike Douglas Show* . . . Mike Douglas!"

When we started, we didn't have any demographics or target groups or viewer profiles or test audiences. There wasn't a single lawyer or accountant anywhere near the studio. KYW was technically owned by Westinghouse, but the corporate giant's entertainment empire was limited to five local stations back in '61. They were still more comfortable around light bulbs than klieg lights, and they pretty much left the programming decisions up to the local managers after plugging in the network lineup, while the Group W bean counters tried to figure a way to make money from this frivolous new industry. They didn't know it and neither did I, but the first major entertainment profit center of the Westinghouse corporation had just opened shop in Cleveland with a budget of a couple of thousand dollars a week.

One of Woody's greatest talents, and one that he imbued in our staff so that it perpetuated beyond the Woody Years and became an inherent part of the show itself, was his concept of "The Mix." The object wasn't just to get enough guests to fill ninety minutes of live TV, nor was it to have me carry the ball all day, every day. That had been tried before and a hundred times since, only to prove, time and again, that it doesn't necessarily work.

It's "The Mix," and Woody knew it. A full-length, daily, unscripted entertainment show has to become something sooner or later, and it just doesn't make it to turn it into a endless stream of stand-alone interviews, skits, or songs. That seemed to be the logical way to go—you could hardly do anything else with the time and budget constraints when you were due up to bat again in less than twenty-four hours. But it was entirely wrong. What you had to do, and Woody realized it more clearly than anyone in the business, was make every show a show of its own, good or bad, memorable or forgettable, but completely unique. And the way to do it consistently was to keep creating strange brews of diverse talents and personalities, launching them into orbit for ninety minutes around a central figure that provided some semblance of stability and continuity, then sit back and watch what happens. It was an intentional daily hurricane, with Woody's old pal Mike Douglas sitting there in the middle of the eye, trying to hold on. What a ride.

*

It started with the first show. We had scored a big coup when Launa lined up Carmel Quinn, nationally known as a leading vocalist on Arthur Godfrey's shows, as our very first co-host. For a local show in Cleveland, this was pretty impressive. Not as impressive as we had hoped, because Carmel didn't show up. She canceled when her schedule was revamped and she was summoned back to New York. We hadn't even been up yet and we were 0 for 1.

Somehow, Launa managed to get Gretchen Wyler, then playing the lead in the road show of *Bye Bye Birdie,* as a last-minute replacement. Gretchen sang "Lola" and "Spanish Rose," talked about the play and introduced her co-star, Dick Patterson, who couldn't have been more accommodating on short notice. He sang, talked, joked, even did a little soft-shoe. Trombone player Kai Winding joined us and did a nice number with Ellie Frankel and the band. Great, I thought to myself, good, tight first show. We're off. Then I looked at the clock and saw that we had sixty-five minutes to go. I felt like I had crossed into another dimension where minutes are hours and hours are days. Rod Serling would have been an appropriate next guest. I'm sorry we didn't have him booked. The best we could do was a press agent promoting a new movie—agents are difficult enough in real life but on television they are lethal—and a priest who played the banjo. There's a limit to the enjoyment one can get from quasi-religious sing-alongs led by members of the clergy. I suppose we passed that somewhere between "Kumbaya" and "Michael, Row the Boat Ashore."

Okay, maybe it wasn't the show I'd put in the TV Hall of Fame, but it was a start. We did it! Exhausted but encouraged by the fact that we had made the show a reality, I dragged myself back to my dressing room. Finally, time to relax.

Not quite. We had another, brand-new ninety-minute presentation due in twenty-two and a half hours. Oh, that's right. We're going to start over from scratch and do this every day. I needed to talk to Woody. Could we maybe cut back a little? Say, a half hour a day? But Woody

The Ellie Frankel Trio, Fr. Joe Dustin on banjo, Gretchen Wyler, and Dick Patterson

wasn't there. He had jumped on a plane to New York to beg Carmel Quinn to reconsider—we were still short a co-host for the rest of the week. Meanwhile, Launa and the rest of the staff had flooded me with notes, comments, background, songs, and schedules for Tuesday. What had I gotten myself in to?

I suppose it was a blessing in disguise. With the pressure of such a relentless schedule, there was no time to worry about "Can we do this?" The clock was ticking. Just do it. The next few weeks are a blur. All I remember is, my most frequent comment was, "Really?"

Woody returned after conning his way into a meeting with Carmel Quinn's New York producer. Somehow, Woody managed to convince him to free up Carmel Quinn for the rest of the week. We rolled up our sleeves and plunged back into the work. Ernie Sherry's first comment was, "We have to pick up the pace."

Really?

He wanted me to spend less time with each guest, move it along faster, compress the bits and sketches and crank the energy up higher. That meant we would need more guests, more concepts, more material—every day. Launa made that possible by producing guests like a magician yanking an endless supply of rabbits out of a hat—Joe E. Brown, comedian Jerry Lester, Johnny Desmond, musician Tony Pastor, opera singer Elaine Malbin, Morey Amsterdam—names, big names, kept popping up on our show like we knew what we were doing.

Really?

We filled in the gaps with local performers, comedians, polka bands, tap dancers, dog trainers, short-order cooks—whatever. We learned that if you had a couple of recognizable names on the marquee, you could get away with squeezing in a few lesser lights (or no lights at all) to fill up the bus. The one thing for certain was that we left the terminal on time every day at one o'clock sharp and didn't stop until two-thirty. Ready or not, here we go.

*

A minute is a long time. You don't think so? Ask the ad people that fork over two million bucks for sixty seconds on the Super Bowl. Better yet, ask a stand-up comic who's dying a slow death on national TV, with the flop sweat dripping and the studio audience as quiet and respectful as mourners at a state funeral. I've seen it. Lived through a few myself. A minute can be like a stiff sentence from a merciless judge. And we did over half a million of them. Every one an adventure.

Don't get me wrong. Most of them were good, some great, more than a few unforgettable. But if there's one thing I want to get across in this modest little book, it's how much work went into every single one. Time, effort, planning, and coordination by dozens of people, too many of whom you never heard of.

Woody Fraser was—and is—the greatest "live action" program producer ever. Live action isn't just difficult, it's downright dangerous. Up on the high wire with millions watching and no net. Don't look down. By the 1960s, live action was already a thing of the past, except for us. Once in a while, one of the Big Three would feature a heavily promoted, star-studded "live" hour special. It would take months of preproduction and a staff the size of a small army. When it was over, everyone involved would collapse, spent from the effort. We did ninety minutes live every day for years. Up at six, into the studio, meet with the staff, digest the information, greet the guests, rehearse the skits and songs, make last-minute changes, get into wardrobe, then makeup, warm up the audience. Three . . . two . . . one . . . theme music, red light—go! Ninety minutes straight. The two-minute commercial breaks were a real-time two minutes. Change sets. If you're three seconds late, you lose. There's a stagehand carrying a stool on national television.

Okay, that's a wrap. Then, as soon as it was over, we'd go right into the postmortem: this worked, this didn't. That guest was great—bring her back. The second skit was a little flat. Move the band mike closer. Soften the baby spot on stage left. Move Camera Two back for a wider angle. Good job, thank you all very much.

Take one deep breath. Now, let's talk about tomorrow—a brand-new show: new guests, new material, new songs, new jokes, new sets. Who do we have? Bob Hope, Marvin Gaye, Tab Hunter, and Kreskin. What happened to Ozzie & Harriet? Wednesday? Okay. Good. Let's go over the time sheet . . . time's up—three . . . two . . . one . . . red light, go!

Whole years are homogenized in my memory into a sea of famous faces, handshakes, hugs, and one endlessly recurring phrase. "We'll be right back." I felt like that Truman character in the Jim Carrey movie—my life was one long, continuous show, interrupted by occasional commercials. I'm sure I must have eaten and slept, but I don't remember when.

It may sound like drudgery but it was just the opposite, strangely en-
ergizing and rewarding. Sixty, seventy, eighty hour weeks—it didn't matter. The more intense the schedule became, the more vigor we seemed to
have to deal with it. I believe the key to our stamina was success. Before
any ratings verified what we already knew, the buzz was hot. At the station, on the street, we were the talk of the town.

Really?

That was good news because television is about communication and
connecting with a mass audience, but, above all, television is about
money. For the viewer, TV is an entertainment miracle—accessible, continuous, and free. The only minor irritant are those insipid commercials.
For the guys in the front office, TV is a selling machine, an endless series
of magnificent commercials interrupted by loathsome but necessary
blocks of programming. If they could only get you to watch ads, back to
back, twenty-four hours a day, they would never both to show so much
as a rerun of *My Mother the Car*. And they're trying. The genius who invented the infomerical is considered a god by some in the executive
suite. A sixty-minute commercial: heaven on earth. But until they have
everyone completely lobotomized, they will reluctantly run some entertainment to keep the customers happy.

A successful show means more viewers responding to more ads for
more products and that means money. The insignia of our show was
that oversized asterisk in the background of the main set. No reason,
just a cute symbol that gave the set some pop. It didn't take long for the
big boys to see it as an oversized dollar sign. The phones at KYW
started ringing off the hook with sponsors and agencies clamoring to
buy time on *The Mike Douglas Show*.

*

Don McGannon was president of Westinghouse the day I came on
board in 1961. He was a shrewd businessman with one eye on the clock
and one eye on the checkbook. He knew hundreds of Westinghouse em-
ployees by name, had hired many in upper management, and fired more
than a few. Don ran a tight ship, and everyone knew it.

He was also a gentleman, a sentimental Irishman, consistent, fair, and
good on his word. I loved him like my older brother.

Don McGannon taught me a lot. When Westinghouse decided to
commit to broadcasting *The Mike Douglas Show* in 1961, I was guaran-

teed the impressive amount of four hundred dollars a week. Not exactly a record contract for the host of a ninety-minute television show, but Mr. McGannon had insisted that was all they had in the budget. Period.

A few months later, the show was a monstrous local hit. The reviews were great, the audience was huge, and, far more important to Westinghouse, we had a backlog of sponsors and the commercial fees were "off the book," meaning that the sales department guys charged according to what mood they were in on any given day.

In the meantime, I felt as if the Douglas family was still living like the Joad family in *The Grapes of Wrath*. I had mentioned the possibility of a token raise or a merit bonus or something—anything—at a few production meetings, but the horrified glances of the corporate guys encouraged me to change the subject.

One day at rehearsals, Woody, who loved to surprise me with fun facts on a regular basis, happened to mention that Ellie Frankel was getting four-fifty a week. I don't remember who we had on the show that day, but it wasn't my best effort. I was distracted. I know it's tight, but how come the piano player's making more than the host?

The next day, I had lunch with my friend, advertising guru Mark Wyse. I shouldn't put this in a book because he might send me a bill, but Mark made me a rich man that day for a four-dollar lunch. He probably forgot about it long ago, but I never will.

He's the one who told me I should make sure to "get what you're entitled to as long as the TV deal lasts."

"Thanks, Mark, but getting a dime out of Westinghouse isn't easy, and they think the piano player would be harder to replace than me."

"I don't think so. Do you know what they're charging for premium spots?"

"What's a premium spot?" (I wasn't very sophisticated about advertising yet.)

"Feature the host."

"Sure. Those are my spots. I do a lot of those."

"Premium. Costs extra with you."

"How much extra?"

"Didn't they tell you? Usually, double. But you—five, six . . . ten times the going afternoon rate. Whatever they're asking for, they're getting."

"You think that's because of me?"

"Your name's on those contracts, my friend. It doesn't say 'the Host.' It says 'Mike Douglas.' If you don't do the spot, there's no premium."

As soon as I returned from lunch, I placed a call to Westinghouse headquarters in New York and asked for Don McGannon. They put me right through. That was a good sign. And Don was as chipper as a squirrel in a field of acorns. Another good sign.

"Michael, me boy, and how's my favorite TV host?"

I told him I wasn't feeling very well and didn't know if I could go on with the show. I might not be able to do the scheduled premium spots either. I couldn't say exactly what the malady was, but I started getting nauseous every time I looked at my paycheck. Disoriented. Woozy. I loved doing the show, but I was starting to worry that it could develop into something serious unless I got some relief. I knew he wasn't a doctor, but I was hoping he could write me a prescription.

Dr. McGannon flew to Cleveland the next day. He made the proper diagnosis and gave me what I needed to cure my ills. No hassles, no hard feelings. For the next seventeen years, I dealt with Don the same old-fashioned way, man to man, come to terms and shake hands. He was the most honorable man I ever met in this business. I miss him. I miss doing business that way.

For me, he confirmed his sense of fair play by giving me that much-needed raise in 1962. A few years later, his own ego was sorely tested in the next round of negotiations. This time, I was aspiring to become the highest paid employee in Westinghouse history and that meant Don would have to sign off on paying me an annual sum that dwarfed his own salary and that of all the other ranking executives combined.

Really?

*

That million-to-one shot that Gen and I had talked about in 1961 when we were agonizing over whether or not to accept the paltry four hundred dollars a week from Westinghouse had come home with a vengeance. *The Mike Douglas Show* was the equivalent of a wildcat oil drilling venture. The company had given us a few dollars and a tiny rig, wished us luck, and sent us on our way. We went out and hit the mother lode. A geyser of revenue and profits was spewing all over Westinghouse.

When the time came to renew our partnership and renegotiate the terms, my agent, Vinnie Andrews, Sr., marched off to New York with a steely glint in his eye. Vinnie was not just one of the best and most reliable agents in the business, he was also a former IRS agent, handy experience when it came to checking the numbers.

The Nielsen Book is the Bible of television and Vinnie read them the Book of Revelation. The Nielsen ratings ruled the airwaves then as now. Just the word "Nielsen" struck fear in the hearts of anyone in TV. For us, from Day One, Nielsen was like some magic mantra. Simply invoking the word brought nothing but happiness, recognition, respect . . . and money.

The joke is, I never believed in the ratings game. The logic of it is so contrary, but no one on the executive side of television would dare invoke a phrase like "common sense." How can these people take a flash poll of a couple hundred viewers and tell you exactly how many people are watching every single program on the air on any given day? Hundreds of millions of potential viewers in the most diverse country on earth, and these people make a few phone calls, say, "here's the numbers," and the networks fall to their knees and worship. It's ridiculous. It's pathetic. It's the law.

In my day, it was rough. In the early days, we would pace around the office every month, biting our fingernails, waiting for Mr. Nielsen to tell us if we would live or die. Today, it has gotten entirely out of control. With the technology currently in place, the networks can get ratings on a minute-by-minute basis. It's the difference between the Pony Express and e-mail. My heart goes out to today's talk show hosts. It's so competitive, there's so much money at stake, and all the time, there's some whiz backstage getting a printout of the ratings over a laptop. If you sneeze, your numbers plummet with kids twelve and under and women with allergies. Mention the word "cow" and you get a bounce with farmers and a drop in vegetarian viewers.

I'm surprised you don't see more rattled talk show hosts out on the ledge about forty stories up at Black Rock, screaming, "I can't take it anymore! I can't do any better in the 18 to 34!"

I shouldn't talk. Every month Mr. Nielsen sent us a love letter.

Vinnie headed off to New York armed with all the numbers and returned with a grand tale of anguish and woe, crisis and redemption. The anguish, woe, and crisis was on Westinghouse. The redemption was ours.

Westinghouse had welcomed him like a foreign head of state. They treated Vinnie with the utmost courtesy and respect, lavished praise on me and our show, and proudly announced they wanted to avoid any need for haggling—they were prepared to make Mike Douglas the highest paid performer on television, the first to earn a million dollars a year. The entire entertainment industry, primarily television and sports, has gone through tumultuous financial changes in the last thirty years and a million dollars for a performer, like it or not, doesn't seem like so much anymore. But in 1968, it was an offer no one in his right mind would refuse.

Vinnie turned them down cold. They threw him out of the office.

I have to admit, I had to gasp when I heard he rejected their offer. The total package, including additional premiums for sponsor-related promos and activities, meant I would be receiving over one hundred times my starting salary, a hefty raise by any standards, but I loved it. Go get 'em, Vinnie!

A few weeks later, they raised their offer and Vinnie signed off without further quibbling. We really had no thoughts of leaving Westinghouse in spite of other lucrative offers. They may be tight with a dollar, but they had gotten the whole thing started and this was no time to abandon loyalty for greed. We just wanted to enjoy the game a little bit this time around and even the score. There were never any problems with money or contract negotiations over all the remaining years of the show. They made huge profits and we were paid handsomely. Even net profits were never an issue. By the end of our wonderful fun, they owned half the show and so did we. It was a pretty fair partnership.

Except for one thing. Westinghouse deserved every dime they made on our show. They paid to get it started and covered every nickel of costs. What they didn't know was, *The Mike Douglas Show* was a joy and a dream come true for me. I loved the show so much, I would have gladly done it for free and driven a cab at night to pay for groceries. But as long as a global corporation is giving away tens of millions of dollars, who am I to say they don't know what they're doing?

Don't make me tell you the exact numbers, it's embarrassing. Just don't worry about having to contribute to the Mike Douglas Relief Fund because they found the poor old guy wandering the streets of Cleveland, homeless and penniless. I'll be okay. Enough talk about money. Now, let's get on with the show.

2

Your Hit Parade

With Your Host, Mike Douglas

Allman Brothers * Animals * Paul Anka * Louis Armstrong * Fred Astaire * Burt Bacharach * Joan Baez * Count Basie * Beach Boys * Bee Gees * Harry Belafonte * Tony Bennett * Chuck Berry Eubie Blake * Blood, Sweat & Tears * Pat Boone * James Brown Buffalo Springfield * Sammy Cahn * Cab Calloway * Glen Campbell * Carpenters * Johnny Cash * Harry Chapin * Ray Charles Cher * Roy Clark * Petula Clark * Rosemary Clooney * Joe Cocker * Judy Collins * Phil Collins * Commodores * Bing Crosby Crosby, Stills & Nash * Vic Damone * Bobby Darin * Sammy Davis, Jr. * John Denver * Neil Diamond * Dion * Jimmy Durante * Billy Eckstine * Duke Ellington * Everly Brothers * Fifth Dimension Roberta Flack * Four Lads * Four Seasons * Four Tops * Aretha Franklin * Art Garfunkel * Judy Garland * John Gary * Marvin Gaye * Genesis * Dizzy Gillespie * Benny Goodman * Robert Goulet * Al Green * Guess Who * Marvin Hamlisch * Lionel Hampton * Emmylou Harris * Isaac Hayes * Lena Horne * Engelbert Humperdinck * Mahalia Jackson * Michael Jackson * Jackson

5 * Harry James * Al Jarreau * Billy Joel * Elton John * George Jones * Jack Jones * Tom Jones * Gene Kelly * Stan Kenton Chaka Khan * B.B. King * Kingston Trio * Kinks * Eartha Kitt Gladys Knight & the Pips * Labelle * Frankie Laine * Steve Lawrence & Eydie Gormé * Brenda Lee * Peggy Lee * John Lennon & Yoko Ono * Jerry Lee Lewis * Ramsey Lewis * Liberace Little Anthony * Little Richard * Trini Lopez * Loretta Lynn * Gordon & Sheila MacRae * Mamas & the Papas * Barbara Mandrell Manhattan Transfer * Barry Manilow * Martha & the Vandellas Johnny Mathis * Andrea McArdle * Marilyn McCoo * McGuire Sisters * Sergio Mendes * Johnny Mercer * Ethel Merman * Robert Merrill * Bette Midler * Roger Miller * Liza Minnelli * Melba Moore * Nana Mouskouri * Anne Murray * Jim Nabors * Ricky Nelson * Olivia Newton-John * Oakridge Boys * Odetta * O'Jays Donny & Marie Osmond * Buck Owens * Patti Page * Dolly Parton Carl Perkins * Peter, Paul & Mary * Bernadette Peters * Roberta Peters * Wilson Pickett * Platters * Pointer Sisters * Charley Pride * Louis Prima * John Raitt * Boots Randolph * Lou Rawls Johnnie Ray * Otis Redding * Helen Reddy * Buddy Rich * Righteous Brothers * Lionel Ritchie * Tex Ritter * Marty Robbins Smokey Robinson * Monti Rock III * Kenny Rogers * Rolling Stones * Linda Ronstadt * Diana Ross * Sam & Dave * Neil Sedaka * Pete Seeger * Sha-Na-Na * Dinah Shore * Beverly Sills Carly Simon * Paul Simon * Sly & the Family Stone * Sonny & Cher Spinners * Dusty Springfield * Ringo Starr * Barbra Streisand Donna Summer * Supremes * James Taylor * Temptations * Tiny Tim * Mel Torme * Tanya Tucker * Tina Turner * Jerry Vale * Rudy Vallee * Vanilla Fudge * Sarah Vaughan * Dionne Warwick Grover Washington, Jr. * Muddy Waters * Jimmy Webb * Lawrence Welk * Barry White * Andy Williams * Nancy Wilson * Bill Withers * Stevie Wonder * Tammy Wynette * Neil Young * Frank Zappa

Music is pretty important in my life. That's how I got into this business, how I started. If anyone ever asked me—if you ask me today—what do you do for a living? I don't say "talk show host," I say "singer." That's what I am. I love to sing. I love to hear other people sing and play music. I love orchestras, big bands, rock groups, jazz quartets. After Gen and my girls, nothing has meant more to me in life than music. I promised I wasn't going to do a tell-all autobiography, but if you don't mind, I'm going to go way back for a minute here so you know how music changed my life.

I was nine years old, living in a rental house in Chicago. Dad worked for the Canadian Pacific Railroad and Mom stayed home and took care of us kids. Were we poor? I guess so, but nobody ever told us that, so we never knew. We had clothes on our backs, food in our bellies, friends to play with, and a dime every now and then to go to the movies. Not much more. Traumatic childhood? Heck, no. I thought we were upper-middle-class.

Did we have any problems? A couple, sure. My father was a good, kind, honest, hardworking man, and he was Irish. He drank a bit and he gambled way too much. Call *Hard Copy* if you want, but it wasn't much different than a lot of the families in our neighborhood. In a way, it was an inspiration.

There came a day, after Dad had lost his entire paycheck again betting on arthritic horses, that my mother took brother Bob, sister Helen, and myself by the hand and, filled with righteous anger, herded us over to the local bookie joint, which happened to be the headquarters for no less a Chicago notable than Al Capone's own brother, Ralph. Before any of the button men in attendance could stop her, she marched into the back room and delivered a ten-minute lecture on family values to the Big Guy himself in front of a roomful of double-breasted suits, fedoras, and cigars. She told him her little ones would not eat because of him. He had allowed her husband to fritter away his hard-earned pay and he was ruining our family and many more like ours.

Italians have a soft spot for families and small children. While Bob and I wondered if Mr. Capone would arrange a special St. Valentine's Day Massacre for our family, he calmly counted out the exact amount my father had lost, returned it to my mother, and promised he would never let Dad set foot in the place again.

Mike at fifteen at the State and Lake Theatre in Chicago

That taught me a wonderful lesson in courage and perseverance. It's amazing what you can accomplish if your heart's in the right place and you won't take no for an answer. Yes, you can do what you've always wanted to do. Don't let fear, setbacks, or naysayers get in the way.

I always wanted to be a singer. I loved to sing. My earliest memories are of the Irish lullabies my mother would croon to us as she put us to bed and the haunting Latin chants we would hear at High Mass on Sundays. In the evenings, we would sit around the radio listening to Bing Crosby and Ted Mack. It was all magic to me, beautiful magic.

So I sang. On my way to school and back, at the playground, around the house. I sang along with Bing Crosby on the radio. It was Sinatra who first noted what a wonderful influence Bing was because his songs were so accessible, his easy style a virtual invitation to a duet, and I was there to help him out. My mother picked up on it and encouraged me. "Sing to me, Michael."

When I was nine, I experienced a revelation somewhat akin to St. Paul being struck down from his horse by a bolt of lightning. My buddy, Loren Eminger, informed me that people made a lot of money singing. Of course, I thought it was a joke. You didn't have to lift or carry, use a hammer or break a sweat? Just sing?

"It's the God's truth," he said, "and the famous singers are rich as kings." It was the best news I had received since learning that people gave you presents on your birthday just for being born. Loren was not only cocksure that his sources were correct, he suggested we put it to the test. There was a neighborhood saloon just around the corner called Mickey Rafferty's where the men would gather after work most days, and where the beer flowed most freely on Fridays, when the owner of Rafferty's was kind enough to cash the men's paychecks and save their spouses a trip to the bank. It was Jimmy's idea to test the validity of his songs-for-money thesis by launching my career at Rafferty's.

Not long after my mother made her triumphant entry to the mob hang-out, Loren and I strolled into Rafferty's one Friday evening and worked our way to the corner by the bar, next to the old upright where a weary piano man provided a little background music for the crowd. We waited impatiently for him to take a break. Then, as soon as there was a lull in the talk and laughter, without thinking long enough to allow an anxiety attack, I launched into an a cappella rendition of "When Irish Eyes Are Smiling." The chatter faded. As I finished the last few bars, the place was as hushed as a confessional and I thought I had made a terrible mistake, offended these rough-hewn men with my childish interruption, and was soon to have my skinny Irish behind tossed onto Harrison Street. A moment later, they burst into cheers and applause. The bartender winked and tousled my hair. At the far end of the bar, near the doorway, Loren reached deep into his dungarees and dug out a precious nickel, tossing it my way. As agreed, he was the shill and the nickel was our investment—some start-up money to prime the pump of appreciation.

It worked like a charm. Other nickels, dimes, and even a few dazzling quarters came raining down on the bar like manna from heaven. Loren, my personal Colonel Parker, clapped, whistled, stomped his feet, and shouted "More!" I was only too happy to oblige. After a few more tunes and a handful of silver, I humbly took my leave, not wanting to wear out this prodigious welcome.

I have never forgotten that night. I still remember lying on my bed, wide awake long after dark, counting and recounting the shiny coins in the moonlight. Three dollars and thirty-five cents. It was more than a day's wages for a strong-backed laborer in 1936. I had earned it singing songs. It made me believe: I'm a singer, that's what I am, that's what I will always be.

Mr. Rafferty himself urged me to return for another engagement and we were back, my agent Jimmy and I, a few days later. More songs, more applause, and more silver tokens of appreciation. My mother didn't approve of pubs, so I never dared tell her what I was doing, but I soon became a regular at Rafferty's. Every Friday night, after my fifteen-minute set, Loren and I would skitter out of the bar, race around the corner, and gleefully add up the take, splitting fifty-fifty (apparently, Loren and Elvis Presley's agent Colonel Tom Parker attended the same school for agents). I would skip home humming "Touralooraloora," stash the money in my dresser drawer behind the comic books, toy soldiers, and holy cards from school, and climb into bed, dreaming of Carnegie Hall. After a few wonderful weeks, I began thinking I was the luckiest and the richest kid in America as my earnings crossed the ten-dollar threshold and kept climbing.

It all ended one day after school when I came home to find my mother at the kitchen table, a look of tragedy on her face and a pile of coins in front of her. My coins. The jig was up. She froze me with a look.

"Michael. Son. What in God's name have you been up to?"

Uh-oh. Goodbye, Carnegie Hall. It wasn't hard to figure that my mother had been entertaining visions of her fair-haired boy involved in something too nefarious to consider. How else to explain that mound of silver—well over thirteen dollars—that added up to more than a week's pay for my father? What made matters worse—and I knew it—was the truth. If there was one thing my mother held in lower esteem than criminal behavior, it was the local tavern. Our family had paid far too dearly for my father's informal membership in that all-too-Irish club. She hated the place and all like it. The only thing worse was lying. That I couldn't do. It was time, literally, to face the music.

I took a deep breath and told the truth. "Ma, I've been singing at Rafferty's and they give me money."

The look on her face transformed from tragedy to consternation. To this day, I'm not sure if I didn't catch the slightest trace of a smile hidden beneath that stern visage.

"Rafferty's, is it? My own son? A nine-year-old boy in a saloon now? As if they won't be getting their hands on you soon enough as it is."

She shook her head in despair. It wasn't anger, but pain that darkened her face. It broke my heart to see her look that way. As much as I had loved every minute of my time at Rafferty's, I knew it was over.

Looking back now, I realize what a milestone in my life that night became for two important reasons. First, my mother was as happy as I was that people had actually paid to hear me sing. She took the time to let me know how terribly proud she was of my precocious accomplishment, and I knew she meant every word. Then, her voice took on a hard edge: "You've got to promise me, Michael, right here, right now. You will never, by God, never set foot in that place again."

I gave her my solemn word, and I kept it. My first foray into show business had been a smashing success—and hugely profitable—but it was over. I never visited Rafferty's again, or any other bar, saloon, tavern, gin mill, honky-tonk, or similar establishment unless it was through the stage door as a performing employee. That meant I had to swear off the sauce before I took my first sip. And I did. I have never had a drink in my life, and I think it's safe to say I never will. It's a little late to get started.

It's not a cause for me. I'm not a crusader against alcohol. Most of my friends enjoy a drink or two, the world of show business is awash in the stuff, and I have no advice to offer on the subject. I just don't drink myself and freedom from that Irish curse has been a blessing in my life. I know, I know. As Dean Martin would say, "That's too bad, because it means the best you'll feel all day is when you get up in the morning." Yeah, but Dino, when I get up in the morning, I feel great.

*

People still believe *The Mike Douglas Show* was a talk show, and I never correct them, but I don't think so. If you look at the reruns I think you might agree. It was really a music show, with a whole lot of talk and laughter in between numbers. A lot of talk shows didn't have music then, and most of them don't have it now. They could use it. The best thing that could happen to Jerry Springer or Sally Jessy Raphael would be to go to an all-music format. The sordid stories and unlistenable conversations they feature day after day would be transformed into comic operettas.

When it comes to music on television, I'm not going to blow my own horn. I don't have to. I had Louis Armstrong to do it for me. And Maynard Ferguson, Stan Getz, Doc Severinsen, Herb Alpert, and the Cleveland Orchestra. And I'm certainly not going to sing my own praises, not when the likes of Barbra Streisand, Robert Merrill, Aretha Franklin, Bing Crosby, Lena Horne, Sarah Vaughan, and Beverly Sills are waiting in the wings.

You get the picture, but you cannot truly imagine what it was like. The entire history of music in the mid–twentieth century, arguably the most exciting and diverse time music has ever known, was played out, live, on *The Mike Douglas Show.*

Some of you may know that years ago, before the Paul VI Audience Hall was completed, special concerts at the Vatican in Rome were held in St. Peter's Basilica. If the Pope himself was in attendance, he would sit in the exact acoustical center of this hallowed place, surrounded by heavenly art and international VIPs, listening to the music of a magnificent orchestra and the ninety-voice Sistine Chapel Choir. Far be it from me to compare myself to His Holiness, but I know how he feels.

For twenty years, I lived a musical fantasy, ensconced in the only ringside seat, serenaded by the best performers in every category, swing to soul, let-er-rip rock to laid-back jazz, big band to bossa nova, country bluegrass to cool blues, light opera to full orchestra. I could fill this chapter with just the names of quality musical talents who graced our stage and still not have room for half of them.

And they paid me for that. I'm sure someone had a better job, but I've never gotten his name.

*

Sometimes—about once a day—someone asks me who my all-time favorite guest was. If there's anyone else present, they'll often break in to help me out.

"Hey, don't ask him that. He had thousands of guests. He had everybody. It's not a fair question."

Maybe not, but I answer it the same way every time, without hesitation. We did have lots of guests. I valued the vast majority of them, was thrilled by hundreds, awestruck by several dozen. But the greatest of them all was Ray Charles.

Whenever he was booked, I was like a kid at Christmas. I could hardly wait because I knew what would happen. He would give a wonderful performance. He would say something that I would never forget. Like Santa Claus, he would bring gifts of vitality, generosity, and exhilaration, and dole them out like presents to the audience, the staff, and me. After a day with Ray, I always felt reinvigorated, proud to be part of the music business, glad to be alive.

Ray Charles is so talented, so unique a personality and such a joy to be around. Is there anyone who doesn't like Ray Charles? Anyone who doesn't appreciate his music? I don't think so. And that smile and infectious chuckle create a warmth that permeates everything and everyone. I know it's crazy, but Ray Charles makes being blind seem enviable.

The word "genius" is so bandied about nowadays, especially in the music business, that it hardly means anything anymore. Madonna is a genius. The guy they used to call "Prince" but he got so smart he doesn't have a name anymore is a genius. The Beastie Boys are geniuses. Every nineteen-year-old that writes a song with more than three chords is a genius. Record producers are geniuses. Promoters are geniuses. DJs are geniuses. You would think the entire music industry is an outreach program of Mensa. Please.

There was a time when the word "genius" was reserved for singularly brilliant, talented achievers. For many years, only two names came to mind when someone mentioned "genius": Albert Einstein and Ray Charles. It's impossible to compare the two, and I'm really not qualified

Mike with Ray Charles

because Einstein never made it on the show, but I'm pretty sure Albert couldn't sing worth a darn. I do know Ray Charles, and the man is a genius.

I loved rehearsing with Ray. He knew every note every instrument was to play in every bar of every song, and he never had the chance to see the charts. How could he do that? He had a sense of rhythm and tone that was incomprehensible, not just to regular folks, but to very good musicians as well. When Ray was working, everyone else was just a student in the class. But Professor Ray had a way of teaching without talking down to the pupils.

Over the course of dozens of appearances, Ray became more than a special guest. He was a special friend, and the comfort level was so high, we could talk on camera like old pals on a park bench. If there was a special quality to *The Mike Douglas Show,* that was it. When someone like Ray Charles bares his soul in conversation and then steps across the stage to deliver a song, the whole experience takes on a transcendent quality. His music brims with deeper meaning. In that context, the audience doesn't just listen to Ray, they embrace him.

Ray Charles lost his vision at seven, lost his parents at fourteen, suffered through years of drug addiction, faced numerous other unwarranted tragedies, and still emerged triumphant. How? Here are a few samples of the wisdom he shared with us:

"Before she died, my mother said to me, 'Honey, you're gonna be all right. You're blind, that's all, not stupid. You lost your sight, not your mind.'"

"Yeah, yeah. I did drugs. Nobody got me into it. I did that myself. Heh. I was seventeen, playing in a band, everybody was much older. During breaks, they'd do that stuff, smoke marijuana. I wanted to be like them. I had a yearning. They all tried to talk me out of it, 'Don't do it, Ray.' But it's an awful feeling to be left out of the group. I had enough of that . . . I was on drugs from 1948 to 1965. Yeah . . . It was my son . . . Any kid who loves his father that much. I said, 'Hey now, you got somebody who loves you so much, you don't want to make him suffer.' I didn't want some kid comin' up to him someday and saying, 'Your daddy's a jailbird.' So I quit. That's it."

"I started singing in a hillbilly band. Everybody, everybody was white. I didn't know. Maybe that was good . . . Kids don't know. If parents would leave kids alone, there would never be any prejudice."

"I don't have any problems to speak of . . . Maybe one. Insurance. Insurance companies think blind people are risky. That ain't right. Blind people are far more careful . . . don't take chances. You all try to run across the street to beat the traffic. Not me. Uh-uh. I don't do that."

"I can see. I truly see my children. I don't see them with my eyes, but I have a chance to see into the inner part . . . When I like someone, it's not because they're handsome or beautiful . . . [it's] because of what they really project. That's what I see. Lot of folks don't see that."

"I don't have to look at a lot of unnecessary things . . . If somebody said to me, 'Ray, in the morning you can see again,' I wouldn't get too excited about it."

Oh, if I could only see like Ray Charles.

*

There's something very special about blind musicians. Ray Charles, Stevie Wonder, José Feliciano, George Shearing, Tom Sullivan. The theory is that, without the gift of sight, their aural perception becomes preternatural. Their ears are finely tuned receivers, so far beyond those of us who rely on our eyes to confirm what we think we hear. Don't whisper in a room with Stevie Wonder. Don't sing an eighth note off key singing with Ray Charles. They hear everything.

One of the most rewarding shows we ever did was with the one and only Stevie Wonder. We had featured him early in his career, then several more times over the years. I loved the guy, I thought he was a magical human being, and I wanted him to go solo—the full ninety minutes. We could never work it out with his people until one day Stevie himself got on the phone with me. He said he would do it, but it had to be at his favorite place. "Sure, Stevie, anywhere you say."

That's how we ended up in our bathing suits in the hot tub at the Beverly Hills Tennis Club. I don't know if it was the relaxing environment or Stevie's personality or what, but it's one of the interviews I'm proudest of. I thought the questions were pretty good and every word from that man's mouth sounded so heartfelt and so meaningful—I can't imagine anyone turning the channel to see what else was on.

"Stevie, you've been sightless since birth. How—how do manage to incorporate so much visual concept in your music? How do you write something like 'You Are the Sunshine of My Life'?"

**With
Stevie Wonder**

"Oh, you can feel the warmth and brightness of the sun. I know it's got red, because red is the color of excitement. Just the word 'red' is exciting . . . and yellow, yellow is a happy color. Yellow wants to be happy . . . Blue is cool, very cool, like cool water or a cool breeze . . . I know colors, I keep colors in my heart."

Yes you do, Stevie, yes you do.

*

One of the greatest personal rewards of *The Mike Douglas Show* was that, for me, it was a twenty-year advanced course in the Art of Singing. It was a very advanced class and I was the only permanent student. I like to think I learned a little.

The structure of the show made it possible. We averaged one or two singers a day. Over a score of years, that meant about ten thousand vocalists visited the classroom, from the consensus all-time best to the brightest of the newcomers, many of whom would join that "all-time" group before long. And talk about front-row seats—even Bob Uecker had to take a distant second to my prized perch. Right there on the stage, a few feet away. I could hear things the microphones didn't pick up, see things the cameras missed. The slightest waver on a high note. A tiny bead of sweat trickling down the back of the neck. Believe me, it was a singular education in music unavailable at Juilliard.

I had been a professional singer for many years before the show started. I thought I knew a lot. I didn't know a thing. Let me tell you just a few of the things I learned.

Harmonics is the secret to sweet music. Everything in harmony. The singer with the music, the singer with the song, the audience with the singer. The obvious format is group harmony. We started with Singing Together 101 and went straight through to Advanced Theories in Harmonics. The Andrews Sisters begat the McGuire Sisters begat the Lennon Sisters begat Martha and the Vandellas, begat the Supremes. The Four Aces begat the Four Lads begat the Four Freshmen begat the Four Seasons begat Crosby, Stills & Nash. (Neil Young hadn't signed on yet. Music trivia footnote: who sang high tenor with Crosby, Stills & Nash in a precursor performance to CSN&Y? Mike Douglas. Thank you very much.)

*

The Mike Douglas Show is deeply indebted to one man for our ability to stay so far ahead of the pack when it came to music. Berry Gordy, Jr. We got into Motown a long time before it became the rage. Incredibly, black performers on television were still a rarity in the early 1960s. Berry was eager to showcase his remarkable assortment of young singers, but no one was listening. We did. And we quickly discovered they all had two things in common—contagious energy and amazing talent. We kept asking Berry for more and he kept sending over new ones. Dozens of them. It's a pretty good bet that someone is a superstar if they have worldwide, first-name recognition. Okay, how's this for a first-name lineup: Ray, Sammy, Aretha, Louie, Duke, Ella, Stevie, Diana, Count, Marvin, Michael, Tina, Otis, B.B., Eartha, Lionel, Chaka, Sly, and Janet? All legends, all black, and many came to us via Motown, directly or indirectly. (If you can't put a last name behind every one, there's a new gizmo out called a radio. You ought to pick one up, you're missing a lot.)

Many years into the show, I was backstage reviewing some material with co-host Diana Ross when Berry Gordy stopped by unexpectedly to visit Diana. He beamed at me and then proclaimed to all within earshot,

"There he is—the man who made Motown!" It was one of the most treasured compliments I have ever received. I didn't correct him then, but I will now. You had it all wrong, Berry. It should have been me saying, "There he is—the man who made *The Mike Douglas Show*!"

You want to talk about about star power? Voice power? Soul power? Aretha Franklin's first national television appearance was on *The Mike Douglas Show*. I had never heard her sing a note. She was pleasant and polite, grateful to be there. Good, I thought, another Motown tune. That'll bring some energy to the show.

Aretha Franklin

I introduced her and she started into "Respect." Oh my. Energy? She set the place on fire. For a moment, I thought something had happened to the sound system. I had never heard anything like that in my life. Aretha Franklin invented Sensurround Sound ten years before they gave it a name. I could almost see the sound waves of her voice, passing through the studio walls and beyond, across the continent and still going, finally waning somewhere in the outer reaches of the universe.

The only voice that I could compare to Aretha's is Ella Fitzgerald's. A guest many times, she was a friend for life and the first one who comes to mind whenever I hear the phrase "sings like a bird." One day, sitting in the co-host chair, she started into one of her legendary scat riffs. No backup, not a drum beat, never even left her seat, just out there, all alone, singing like a happy bird. There is no instrument, nothing ever made by man that can match the incredible sounds that lady could create with her voice, making it up as she went along.

I've heard, up close and personal, just about every notable singer there is over the past fifty years or so, but these two ladies remind me of that old Ben Hogan quote about Jack Nicklaus: "They play a game with which I am not familiar." Their talent level is off the charts.

Now I'm in for it. You can't mention Aretha and Ella without a word about Lena Horne, Gladys Knight, or Pearl Bailey. This book is nothing but trouble.

*

Because of the eclectic mix of guests, the opportunity arose for un-precedented performance combinations. Whenever possible, if the guests were willing, we weren't about to pass that up. Where else could you see a teenage Liza Minnelli pair up with Pearl Bailey? How much would a ticket cost for the Supremes and the Temptations, together at last? How about Engelbert Humperdinck and Olivia Newton-John? Some unusual chemistry there, but nothing compared to Arlo Guthrie and Florence Henderson. Patti Page and Eubie Blake was a perfect fit. Little Richard and Liberace had disparate musical styles, but I think they used the same tailor. Sammy Davis, Jr., and Andrea McArdle was a strange but joyful pairing. (Afterward, Sammy noted how often we had featured Andrea and the cast of *Annie* on the show. He leaned over and whispered to me, "You son of a bitch, you own that show, don't you?" I tried to protest, but he wouldn't hear of it. "Don't lie to

With Pearl Bailey

With Little Richard and Liberace

me, Douglas. I know you. You own a piece. They're on here more than Totie Fields.")

Marvin Hamlisch and Isaac Hayes was a first—don't tell me you saw them together all the time. Gene Kelly and Fred Astaire was timeless. Robert Merrill and Beverly Sills was, of course, classical. John Lennon and Chuck Berry belongs in the Rock and Roll Hall of Fame. Neil Diamond and Petula Clark started a wave of hit songs pairing male-female superstars.

One of my fondest personal memories was Lena Horne and Mike Douglas. We were booked to do "Here's to My Lady" and a prolonged medley together on a *Kraft Music Hall Special*. I was so thrilled, I kept making mistakes in rehearsal just so we'd have to do it over again.

Some classic twosomes we didn't even have to work at, they just walked in the door. We asked Bette Midler to do an extended set on one show. She had already been a guest and the reaction had been over the top. Bette has been widely acclaimed for many years now as a multital-ented star—singer, actress, comedienne—but I still don't think she gets enough credit. You want to be a performer? Go study tapes of Bette Midler. Talent, energy, enthusiasm, humor—she's the whole package and then some. The only thing she requested when she returned to the show was that she could bring along her own pianist. Sure. Why not? A lanky young fellow, he was a bit shy and more than a bit nervous, but he had a wonderfully approachable style at the keyboard and played the perfect straight man to Bette. Sang some, too. Pleasant voice. I believe when Bette Midler introduced him, it was the first time his name had ever been mentioned on national television. Ladies and gentleman, Barry Manilow.

*

James Taylor has been a star for over a quarter of a century now, and I think he's still underrated. In an age of unbridled extravagance on stage, he brings his message with a quiet power, a serenity that magnetizes an audience and draws them to him. A big part of it is his lyrics. Almost all of them are his own, and the theme is a consistently poetic Everyman. But that's not what I'm talking about. The man has a voice. His pres-ence and his message are so unassuming, so modest, you tend to over-look how capable a vocalist he is, handling difficult and complex tunes with a casual ease.

Carly Simon visited our show when she and James Taylor were mar-ried. There's another voice worth talking about. Carly always reminded me of a bird in a cage. It's not easy to get her to sing—the stories of her stage fright are well known—but when she does, look out. I thought they were wonderful together because their voices were a perfect match. You can hear it in "Mockingbird." I hope they'll forgive me for saying so, but I think one of the shared emotions that comes through in their voices is fear. I never thought about it until I saw what anguish Carly went through before one of our shows. I saw fear: palpable, inescapable fear. I know, because I'm no stranger to that kind of fear myself. After years of success, hundreds of performances, standing ovations, an adoring audience—it doesn't matter. Sometimes it just sneaks into your psyche before you step on stage and grabs you in a chokehold so tight you have to gasp for every breath. Fear of failure? Fear of death? Fear of life? I don't know, I don't think anybody does, and I'm sure not going to pay some shrink $200 an hour to give me his professional but completely unqualified opinion—did you ever meet a psychiatrist who could sing? Shove him out on stage in front of a few million viewers and see if he can explain his theories without bursting into tears or passing out. For a lot of performers, stage fright just comes with the stage, and you have to wrestle that monster to the ground whenever he shows up or find yourself a new career. Carly Simon knows that. I can hear it in her voice. And it isn't a quality that diminishes her, it's enhancing, adding a bittersweet veneer of vulnerability. I can hear it on occasion with James Taylor as well, a melancholy quality that bonds him closer to his audience.

*

And of course there were the classic duets. Steve and Eydie, Marvin Gaye and Tammi Terrell, Kenny Rogers and Dolly Parton, Hope and Crosby, Sonny and Cher, Donny and Marie, Ferrante and Teicher. We had more perfect pairs come aboard than Noah. And the best? My favorite twosome performance ever? Easy. Barbra Streisand and Mike Douglas singing Nelson Eddy and Jeanette MacDonald's signature ode to each other, "Sweetheart, Sweetheart, Sweetheart." I'd like to say I carried her, but that's not quite right. I was just carried away.

*

Some singers can make a song work exclusively with their voices. Sounds too obvious, but it's not. You can probably count them on the fingers of one hand.

The human voice is the most exquisite instrument there is, capable of incredible range, variety, and subtle modulation. But singing a song is a performance, with the full assortment of performing arts coming into play. A singer is an actor, like it or not, and a dancer, a mime, a poet, and sometimes a magician. Some of the most successful vocalists couldn't carry a tune in a wheelbarrow but it doesn't matter. It doesn't

Jimmy Durante

Mick Jagger

mean their fans are fools either. It's just that they do other things so well, the song comes through.

Examples? Yes, I can think of a few.

Jimmy Durante had one of the greatest voices I have ever heard. You think I'm kidding? The next time you hear one of his songs—and they still play them on all kinds of stations—listen closely. A raspy-voiced old codger? No, a voice brimming with humanity; sensitive, loving, and wise. Jimmy caressed the lyrics of a song with such genuine reverence, you couldn't help but get caught in them.

Mick Jagger can't sing very well. I'm sorry, Stones fans, but I've been there, six feet away, when he was doing his best stuff, and I'm telling you he wouldn't make the Glee Club. Not only is his timing off, he doesn't know how to breathe, he garbles some words, and his range is limited. That's probably the last time I'll get invited over to Mick's house for fish and chips, but I'm not through yet. When it comes to dancing, Mick Jagger is no Fred Astaire. He moves like some maniacal marionette with the stuffing removed and most of the strings broken.

Don't take it the wrong way. Here's the punch line. He deserves every bit of the status he's enjoyed for so many years because he is truly one of the world's great performers. Exuberant. Mesmerizing. Unique. I don't think it would matter if he was in a rock 'n' roll band or played the tuba. He would knock 'em dead. He is simply that powerful on stage.

The Rolling Stones. Now, that was a day. They've been around a long time, almost as long as I have (except they look a lot older, don't they?), and they've earned their reputation as "the world's greatest rock 'n' roll band." They were already superstars in 1965 when they agreed to do one show only—our show—on a break in their U.S. tour that year. I admit, I was excited. We had plenty of huge acts on the show, but at that time, you just didn't get any bigger than the Rolling Stones. Any show would have killed to get them and they had gone out of their way to do ours. I was warned that we had better have some extra security and brace ourselves for some headaches from rabid fans, but that was a small price to pay.

On the day of the show, I arrived early in the morning to find the entire studio under siege. It seemed like every fourteen-year-old girl in Cleveland was there, squealing, screaming, banging on doors and windows. A little extra security? We should have called out the National Guard.

I finally fought my way inside, but it was almost as wild inside as out. The Stones, their entourage, the press, photographers, frenzied staff, curious visitors—it was a madhouse. I managed to slip into the men's room and close the door. It was the only quiet place in the building. A moment later, I was standing at the urinal when I heard what sounded very much like girlish giggling. It was somewhat unsettling. I'm not used to hearing giggles when I'm standing at the urinal.

I zipped up and peered around the room. Nothing. But a few seconds later, there it was again. Giggles. I distinctly heard giggles. I walked over, opened one of the stall doors, and there were four adolescent girls who had somehow penetrated the cordoned-off premises and were waiting to pounce on the Rolling Stones at the first opportunity. These teenage stalkers were shocked into silence at being discovered, but I still heard giggling. I moved to the next stall, opened it, and found three more girls. Behind the third door, there had to be eight more, wedged like sardines into the tiny stall.

I wasn't happy. Besides headaches for the show and an ambush in waiting for the Stones, all I needed was a reporter from the *National Enquirer* to walk in and find Mike Douglas in a men's room with over a dozen teen girls and my career was over.

"I'm sorry, girls, but if you're waiting for Mick Jagger, you're out of luck. The Stones have their own setup—dressing room, bathroom, everything—stairway on your left, first door on your right."

That's all it took. I held the men's room door while they ran out squealing. There must have been more hiding God knows where because it reminded me of all the clowns getting out of the Volkswagen at the circus. Had to be two dozen. Fortunately, we didn't have any more problems with them because my directions took them right back outside to the loading dock.

*

Sonny Bono was one of my favorite all-time guests. He had a great sense of humor, an uncanny sense of what worked, he cared about people, and he was amazingly candid at all times. He was also the least vocally talented singing star I have ever heard. That's not a knock, it's a compliment.

He didn't sell so many millions of records because people felt sorry for him. A lot of the songs he composed and recorded, both with Cher and solo, are modern standards. Why? Sonny had guts. He tapped into something universal by demanding to be heard. Singing is not reserved for the best voices or restricted to the lucky ones with perfect pitch. Like laughter, it belongs to all of us. Sonny was saying, in effect, "I wrote this song, and I want to sing it for you, so listen." And we did.

Sonny wasn't the only one who could grab you with a song even if he didn't sound like Pavarotti. Burt Bacharach was one of many fine com-

With Sonny & Cher and Chastity Bono

posers we featured on the show over the years. One time, I said, "Why don't you sing it yourself, Burt?" He didn't laugh it off or go shy on me, just nodded reflectively. I think he'd been waiting for someone to suggest just that for a long time.

"You think so?"

"Sure. It's your song. Why not?"

So he did. Accompanying himself on the piano, barely reaching the high notes, struggling with the tempo, whispering through the lows with a scratchy, hesitant sotto voce, he sounded great—warm, human, vulnerable, and real. The audience swooned.

Lots of ways to skin a song.

*

Marvin Hamlisch was another of the great composers we managed to talk into singing a few tunes. It took a while because Marvin thought he might embarrass himself, but he didn't have to worry about that. His mother did it for him.

The week we featured Marvin as a co-host, we invited his mom to join us. This is what we called a "courtesy guest," and we rarely intended these nonprofessionals as more than an appreciative nod to the co-host, but Mrs. Hamlisch was an enjoyable exception. A sweet little lady with a fun-loving personality, she was as fearless on camera as a seasoned pro and had no qualms about speaking her mind. I knew the audience was going to get a kick out of her when I opened up with the easiest question of all.

"Mrs. Hamlisch, who's your favorite composer?"

"Gershwin," she said, without missing a beat, while her son stared at her in disbelief and the audience roared.

*

Like I said, it doesn't matter if you can sing, but then there's Barbra Streisand. There's a book called *The Perfect Storm* that details how every meteorological condition has to coincide just right for the fiercest of storms to occur in the North Atlantic—hundred-foot waves, 120 mph winds, roiling seas that can sink supertankers—a storm that only occurs once in a century.

Barbra Streisand has the Perfect Voice. I have no idea what human conditions had to come together just right, but I believe that this, too, only happens about once a century, and in the twentieth century, it happened in Barbra Streisand.

In our never-ending search for fresh talent, we had a loosely defined network of hundreds of talent scouts and agents constantly on the prowl for singers, actors, musicians, comedians. One of them was an astute young agent in New York, Marty Erlichman. In the fall of 1963, I called him after seeing his newest client sing a few bars on a local show in New York. He sent over some of those little 45 rpm records marked "Streisand." Nobody even listened to them for weeks. One day, Woody walked into my office and tossed the discs on my desk.

"This is Marty's new girl singer, Mike. You ought to listen when you get a chance."

Sometime in the next day or two, I popped one onto the player. They were not top quality recordings and the record player was a piece of junk, but the voice that came through the hissing and scratching was pure as snow. "Happy Days Are Here Again" never sounded like this before. I only had to hear it once. I ran to Woody.

"I want this girl, Woody. Call Marty. We've got to get her on the show."

"You want me to tell Marty we'll book her for sure? Sight unseen?"

"You can tell him we'll book her for a week. I don't care. Just get her."

Woody made the call and Marty was elated at the chance of getting this ingenue on *The Mike Douglas Show* for a week, but there was a problem. The next day, Marty called me and explained.

"Look, Mike, she'd love to do it, but you gotta help me out. I know you guys pay scale, and I don't have a problem with that, but this little girl's so broke, if she goes to Cleveland for a week and doesn't come back with a couple grand, she won't have an apartment anymore."

"What do you want me to do, Marty?"

"I hate to ask, but can you get her a gig while she's there? Something, anything—if she could do the show during the day and pick up a few bucks at night, she'll be okay."

"Marty, I'd love to help you out, but I'm not an agent. I don't do that stuff. I wouldn't even know who to call."

He pleaded with me to try something—anything—but if he couldn't promise her she'd make enough to pay the rent when she got back home, there was no way.

"And Mike," he said, "what you heard on the tape is nothing. Believe me, this girl is going to be a star, bigger than Lesley Gore."

That big, eh? Okay. I told him I'd try, but no promises. We had the staff make some calls to local nightclubs. None had any interest in an unknown teenage girl from New York. Finally, the owner of a tiny club in Lakewood, a sleepy suburb of Cleveland, told one of the staffers he would consider it if he could talk with me personally. After the show that day, I drove over to his place, ten miles from downtown. It was like a movie scene. A would-be supper club with a mini-stage and a few dozen tables. There was a man in a checkered suit puffing a huge cigar, sitting alone at the bar. He waved me over.

"You Mike Douglas?"

"That's me."

He looked me over, not quite sure if I was the same person he had seen on television or not. After a minute, he seemed satisfied I was no impostor.

"I don't watch much TV myself, but my wife thinks you're the greatest."

"Tell her thanks."

"So, you want I should hire this dame for a week, that right?"

"I'd appreciate it if you did."

"And you gonna mention my joint every day on your show?"

"Sure. Be happy to."

With Barbra Streisand

"Right out loud to the whole country—'the Chateau in Lakewood'—every show?"

"The Chateau in Lakewood—every single day."

"You gimme your word on that?"

"I give you my word."

"And this chick sings like Florence Nightingale?"

"This girl can sing with the angels."

"How much is this angel gonna cost me?"

I had no idea what the going rate was for a week in a place like this. I didn't want to wreck the deal by asking for an excessive amount, but I was mindful of what Marty had said about Barbra's needs. I shrugged like I knew what I was talking about and did this kind of deal every day. It was my first and only.

"Twenty-five hundred should do it."

"Sounds fair. You got a deal."

It sounded like a fortune to me, especially for a place the size of a pizza parlor that no one had ever heard of. But I wasn't about to ask any questions. We shook hands.

"Okay. Here's a number. Ask for Tony. And one more thing—"

"Yes?"

"You better be Mike Douglas or somebody's gonna get their legs broken."

Boy. This agent business was tougher than I thought. But it worked out fine. I *was* Mike Douglas, I *did* mention the Chateau in Lakewood every day, and Barbra Streisand performed every night in a storefront club that couldn't seat more than seventy people. A handful of lucky Clevelanders paid seven dollars apiece to see one of the great performers of this century put on an electrifying, one-woman show. The price may seem incredible now, but remember, it included dinner and a drink.

They weren't as lucky as I was. I spent a week on the air with a baby Barbra Streisand. It was like being on the set of a documentary version of *A Star Is Born*. Marty was right, she did turn out to be bigger than Lesley Gore.

*

One thing I learned is that the true superstars—not the overnight sensations but the unique performers who endure, the ones whose popularity seems to be renewed with succeeding generations—all share a common bond of integrity. They don't run scared, change with the weather, catching the wave of every new fad. They may adapt and expand their repertoire, but the core remains constant. They know who they are and it shines through. Sinatra, Durante, Duke Ellington, Ella, Barbra, Ray Charles. Unique. Inimitable. Permanent.

*

Talk about being comfortable with who you are. We did an entire show at Bing Crosby's magnificent home at Burlingame in Northern California. My first idol, Bing Crosby. If there was a singer, a performer, and a man I aspired to be like, it was Bing Crosby. In my youth, it was the mellifluous tones of his voice that came over the radio, beckoning me to sing along. In my navy days in World War II, I remember walking the streets of Calcutta, India, on shore leave one lonely night, so far from my home and my new bride, Gen. I needed something to lift my spirits. As I passed a Hindu man sitting at a street corner, I heard something strikingly familiar. I turned to see the man cranking one of those ancient Victrolas, like the one on the RCA logo with the horn-shaped speaker, and I heard Bing Crosby singing "Accentuate the Positive." I stopped

With Bing and Kathryn Crosby

and smiled in appreciative recognition. The Hindu man nodded and smiled back. The whole world knew and loved Bing Crosby.

I was as nervous as a tenement kid at a debutante ball. It's no secret that Bing was almost as accomplished an investor as he was a performer. Estimates of his wealth started in the stratosphere and moved up from there. He sang, told stories, treated us like we were next-door neighbors over for a little visit. I'll tell you how unassuming Bing Crosby was. Bing was a sweater guy, remember? Between the golf and his casual, comfortable attitude, he had gone through a herd of alpacas in his time. He wore a sweater for the show. A few minutes before we started taping, I looked over and noticed this one had a gaping hole in the elbow. I leaned close and whispered, "Bing, that sweater has a hole in it." How laid-back was Bing? He looked at me and shrugged. "They'll get over it."

*

I've got to spend a little time talking about Vic Damone. He's a fine singer, mellow and memorable, and his stage presence makes him the classic nightclub singer. But I'm not going to talk about his singing. I don't have to. You know Vic Damone, you've heard him sing. You don't need me to tell you how good he is.

I have to mention something else entirely. When I was still pretty much

Vic Damone

a kid singer, back in the ranks of the struggling after some glory years with Kay Kyser, I was working Lake Tahoe at the Nevada Lodge. It was the tail end of the season and I was singing to waiters and white linen more often than not. Twenty people in the room was a decent crowd.

Vic Damone was headlining at the Cal-Neva, the number one stage in Tahoe, packing them in, and one night I look out at the alleged crowd for my latest show and Vic was sitting there. This was in 1961 and Vic was already a major star. It was a thrill for me because I had never met the man.

He came back after the show, greeted me warmly, and acted like he was the newly elected president of my fan club. At that particular time, he would also have been one of the only members.

"You're one of the best singers I've ever run into, kid," said Vic. "Why haven't I ever heard of you?"

I shrugged. "I figure by remaining obscure, my career will last a lot longer."

He laughed, slapped me on the back, and invited me to come over and see his show. Gen and I were there two nights later when Vic spotted us, made me stand, introduced me to his crowd, and—get this—told everyone in the place that ". . . you ought to go on over there and see this great singer, Mike Douglas—ladies and gentlemen, please, do yourselves a favor and go see him."

The next night, and for the rest of my run in Tahoe, the crowd picked up nicely. I've always thought fondly of Lake Tahoe since then, and I will always think fondly of Vic Damone. That was one of the classiest gestures I've ever seen. The music business is not just demanding, it is one of the most fiercely competitive professions there is, and Vic turned that on its ear by taking the time in the middle of his own show to send the customers to see a competitor. I'll never forget it. If anyone ever asks why Vic Damone has the reputation of being one of the classiest guys in the business, give 'em my phone number.

*

I tried for years to get Judy Garland on the show but her managers insisted it didn't work for her. She did an occasional, prime-time, one-woman special. She didn't do guest shots. She didn't do daytime.

But our talent coordinators were like Texas Rangers. They always got their man (or woman) and they never gave up. They dogged her manager, who finally broached the subject to Judy, and—surprise!—she said yes. She was a regular viewer and said she would love to do the show "just for the hell of it." We booked her for a few weeks later and promoted the show heavily as a major coup for daytime television.

The day of the show came. We were halfway through rehearsals and I hadn't seen Judy yet, although I was informed she had arrived some time ago. I went to her dressing room and as soon as I got in the door I thought, uh-oh, this is going to be a disaster. Judy Garland was a lovely, elegant, and ferociously talented woman, but it's no secret that she had wrestled with some drug and alcohol demons for years. They had taken their toll. By the late 1960s, she had good days and bad days, and this was looking very much like a bad day.

At first, I thought I better get a bumper act to stand by. I didn't think she could even go on. She looked so tired and frail and was barely able to respond to my tentative small talk. Her makeup wasn't right and her dress was disheveled. She couldn't possibly perform. I didn't want her to embarrass herself. But after speaking with her for a few minutes, she seemed to perk up slightly. I didn't know what else to do except ask

Judy Garland

straight out: "Judy, are you all right? You still want to do the show?"

She looked at me like I was nuts. She was fine, and of course she wanted to do the show. That's why she was here.

Okay. Fine. I told her I'd see her on stage. It was probably more than a little self-serving, I'll admit. There were several million viewers out there who had been promised the one and only Judy Garland, and I didn't want to let them down. Looking back, the prudent course would have been to call it off, walk out there and tell the audience that Judy had taken ill and we would reschedule her appearance as soon as possible. But Judy said she could handle it, so—let's go for it, I decided, although I had serious doubts.

Twenty minutes later, I gave one of my most flattering introductions, crossed my fingers, and looked to my right. And there she was—Judy Garland, America's sweetheart for over thirty years. What a transformation! She looked radiant. Beaming with confidence, moving so gracefully in that magnificent gown. Pure star power.

She took a seat next to me and we talked like old friends about everything from her early days at MGM to special anecdotes about daughters Liza and Lorna. She was as lucid, well spoken, and fascinating as any guest we ever had. The audience was enthralled. I was in love.

It was finally time for her to sing and things had been going so well, I decided to take the risk and break the only rule the staff had given me about her appearance: whatever you do, don't ask her to sing "Over the Rainbow." Any other song, any question, any subject is okay, but not "Over the Rainbow." That's off limits.

"Judy," I said, "you promised us a song."

The audience applauded in anticipation.

"I know if we polled the audience here in the studio, if we polled the entire audience out there watching, the song they'd love to hear has got to be 'Over the Rainbow.' Is it asking too much for you to sing it for us?"

She gave me a look like, "oh, you Irish rascal." But then she smiled, nodded, and took the microphone. Maybe it was just the moment, but it was the finest rendition of "Over the Rainbow" I have ever heard Judy Garland deliver, and she had been singing that tune since 1939. The studio audience joined me in a prolonged standing ovation.

Judy, Judy, Judy. She gave that trademark, sophisticated bow and she was gone. I never saw her again. A short time later, she was gone forever, found dead in her bed at forty-nine. For me, the loss was tempered by the memory of one of the most spectacular performances ever on *The Mike Douglas Show.*

*

Judy Garland wasn't the only singer who came on the show with restrictions that we would try our best to circumvent. At his peak, Bobby Darin was on the brink of becoming, as he himself proclaimed, "the next Sinatra." And, like Sinatra, he reinvented himself a few times before some bad luck and serious health problems brought an untimely end to his promising career. He started off as a rock singer in the early 1960s with hits like "Splish Splash," then made a run at the Sinatra sound with the classic "Mack the Knife," came round again with a country kick on "18 Yellow Roses," then crossed over to folk for "If I Were a Carpenter." Bobby was a full-service singer, all right, and I had followed his rise to stardom with real interest. This dog could hunt.

I couldn't have been more pleased when Woody told me he had landed him for a guest spot. I suggested we clear at least two segments to provide enough time for several Bobby Darin songs. And one thing I knew that most people didn't was that Bobby was a skillful blues singer along with all the other facets of his vocal accomplishments. I was looking forward to highlighting this rarely seen aspect of his talents.

Woody shook his head. No can do.

What's the problem?

The Woodman had fought long and hard with a very tough agent just to get Bobby Darin. Although it was hardly ever a factor even with the biggest of stars, the money had been a sore point all along. We paid scale. Everybody knew it. Whether it was a street juggler, Barbra

Streisand, or the Beatles, we paid scale. The program was never meant to be a direct moneymaker for the guests; its overwhelming value was in showcasing and promotion. With twenty to thirty guests a week, that's how it had to be. Nobody got a premium. It was scale, take it or leave it.

Bobby's agent didn't get it. "Oh no," he said, "Bob Darin doesn't do anything for scale." Well, we would love to have him, but he's got to do *The Mike Douglas Show* for scale or he's not doing it at all. We went round and round for months. I think it was Bobby himself who insisted on doing the show, so the agent finally relented. "Okay, he'll do it. But he ain't singing any songs. That's the deal."

I wasn't happy when I heard the news from Woody. Bobby Darin also happened to be a very intelligent guy with a quick, quirky wit, so I knew we'd have a nice on-air chat, but that didn't make it. Bobby Darin's coming on the show but he's not singing? Didn't work for me, wouldn't fly with our audience, and I thought it was a disservice to Bobby. Don't hamstring the talent. Woody said forget about it. Not going to happen. Off the table. Don't even ask.

The day arrived, Bobby came on, took a seat, and we started talking. It went well. He was in a good mood, plenty of energy. I was aching to have him do a number, but I knew how futile it was. Besides, the band wasn't even set up. And then, it just hit me. The deal was, he wouldn't sing a *song*. Okay, but that doesn't really close the door, does it?

Instead of asking Bobby the next question, I sang it to him, with a little blues lilt. He looked at me for a second, then sang an answer with the same bluesy beat. My pulse stepped up. Hey, I think we just might have something here. I sang another question, worked it into a rhyme, and he jumped back with a full-blown blues answer. The crowd loved it and so did I. Bobby was having a good time, too.

I sang every question, he sang every answer. It wasn't easy for me, but at least I knew the questions I wanted to ask and only had to worry about making musical sense out of them. But Bobby had the hard part. He was making up the words and the music, fitting them to my beat and rhyming my words off the top of his head. And he sounded good. Darn good. The studio audience was so into it they started clapping along. Our drummer was on break, but he picked up on what was happening, jumped in, and gave us a solid beat. We stayed in it for the rest of the segment, an impromptu blues interview. Now, I know television has come a long way, but how often do you hear that on Jerry Springer?

As soon as we broke for commercial, Bobby and I collapsed into an embrace. He was laughing, I was laughing, the audience was cheering— it was one of my favorite segments ever. Afterward, walking back to the dressing room, Woody came up and gave me a bear hug.

"You are something, Douglas."

*

Ten thousand songs. And I swear, if you give me the time and a few hints, I can remember them all, some for the unforgettable voice or music, others for innovative arrangement, still others for unique styling or presentation. Some for completely nonmusical reasons.

I told you about "The Mix." Old and new. Classic and cutting-edge. Opera singers and teen idols. Most days that attitude worked to perfection and kept a vastly diverse audience coming back for more. Sometimes, it was a headache. Literally.

We didn't shy away from the new acts, we sought them out. David Bowie, Talking Heads, Rare Earth, Kiss—if they were hot, why not?

Mike and Bobby Darin

Let's see what the kids are into. We booked a group called Vanilla Fudge for the show once. Only once. In the late 1960s, Vanilla Fudge was reputed to be far more musically talented than your usual flavor of the month on the rock circuit, and I made it a point to hear them close up during a final rehearsal just before the show. The audience was already in the studio and I grabbed a seat in the host chair just a few feet away from the group as they prepared to play their song. They plugged in their amplifiers, counted down, and—

I thought it was the end of the world. I don't know about the quality, but the noise level was unbearable. It was like standing inside the engine of a 747. The studio shook. Tiles began falling from the ceiling. I could feel cells disintegrating in my inner ear. It only lasted about ten seconds before they broke it off to start over—I guess they heard something that didn't sound quite right, but how could they tell?—and it seemed like an eternity of torture. In the sudden, welcome silence, I looked out and saw an elderly lady in the front row, her arms wrapped protectively around her head, doubled over in pain. I waved for the Vanilla Fudge sound terrorists to hold up for a minute and turned my attention to the lady in agony.

"Excuse me—ma'am? Can you hear them all right from there?"

*

The closest thing to that noise level was without instruments, without amplifiers, even without a microphone. Ethel Merman. Ethel wasn't painful at all to listen to, but don't stand too close. She'd break your glasses with a B flat above High C. She was a wonderful performer with a 50,000 watt voice.

*

One singing star changed the course of our show. Sammy Davis, Jr., may have been this century's best all-round performer, and he meant a lot to me, personally, for a number of reasons, not the least of which was his landmark appearance as the very first superstar we ever managed to land. This was all the way back when *The Mike Douglas Show* was still a local Cleveland phenomenon and years before the city's widely hailed renaissance. It was tough to get name talent to Cleveland in those days, impossible to get superstars.

Sammy was there on a fluke. He was doing a favor for an old friend by appearing in a one-man show at the city's biggest theater, a brief stopover between New York and Chicago, and it wasn't turning out very well. The publicity and ticket sales had been poorly handled and half the seats remained unsold when he arrived a day before the event. To make matters worse, it was midwinter and one of those fabled "lake effect" blizzards had swept in and settled over the area, paralyzing everything. Schools and stores were closed and the streets were barely passable. Sammy's string of sold-out concerts was in serious jeopardy.

Cagey showman that he was, Sammy had his people call around and find out what the top-rated local show was. Fortunately, we were, by a large margin. His manager called and asked if I would like to have Sammy Davis, Jr., make a brief appearance.

Would I?

The staff jumped into high gear, rearranging the following day's show to accommodate the mighty mite. When I received a copy of the revised schedule that provided twenty minutes for Sammy before moving on to lesser guests, I ran for Woody's office.

"Woody, we've got to change this again."

"What's the problem, Mike?"

"You gotta clear the decks. Cancel everyone else."

"What do you mean? We can't ask him to do that. It's supposed to be a cameo. We'll have to beg for two segments."

"You don't know Sammy Davis. If we get him going, he'll do our ninety minutes, go right through the news and into prime time."

Woody shook his head in disbelief, but cleaned the slate anyhow and penciled Sammy's name in every segment. He kept a comic and an author on standby, just in case. Oh, ye of little faith.

Sammy arrived for rehearsals with a couple sheets of music. He was all business. When our young associate producer, Larry Rosen, saw the music, he looked past Sammy's shoulder, searching in vain for an accompanist.

"Did you bring your piano player, Mr. Davis?"

Sammy gave him a nasty scowl and shoved the music at him.

"My guy gets ten grand, kid. You better find a way to make this work."

Larry balked, wide-eyed.

"Mr. Davis, I don't think—we only have about an hour before—"

"Well, let me know soon, because if you can't, I'm walking."

Larry couldn't find Woody and came running to me with the problem. At the time, Sammy Davis, Jr., would have been the biggest star we had ever featured on the show, by far, and we were about to screw it up. Instead of raising my voice, I lowered it to a whisper.

"Larry, listen to me. Give Ellie the music. If there's any problem, call the union and hire some help. If you have to, call the Cleveland Orchestra and have them send enough musicians over here so that Sammy can sing and be happy. And then go back out there and tell Sammy that you're sorry, and if there's anything he needs or wants—anything—your only job is to make sure he gets it."

There weren't any more problems. Sammy was happy. And so was I. He sang, he danced, he did impersonations, he played the drums, he joked about Frank and Dino, he took questions from the audience. As predicted, he did ninety minutes without taking a deep breath.

We also promoted the heck out of his show that night, and enough people braved the blizzard to make it a sellout, a feat that did not go unnoticed in New York and L.A. And Sammy helped spread the word—if you're anywhere near Cleveland, do *The Mike Douglas Show*. They'll

Sammy Davis, Jr.

With Richard Pryor and Sly Stone

treat you right and that Douglas guy's not bashful about pushing your gig. Shortly after that, the big names started rolling in.

*

Sly Stone did a week as co-host. Sly Stone and Mike Douglas. Two of a kind, eh? Busy week. Sly was as good-natured and affable as you can get, although I wouldn't go so far as to claim it was a strictly natural high he was on back in 1974. One day, Richard Pryor joined us, along with Arlo Guthrie. It's a good thing I got along so well with the local police or I could have been busted for aiding and abetting. I didn't dare even go backstage once the show started. The Green Room smelled like Woodstock. There must have been some fumes in the air or something because I honestly don't remember the entire week very well and I know Sly doesn't remember a thing. A friend of mine ran into Sly a few years afterward and mentioned he had seen him on *The Mike Douglas Show*. Sly looked up slowly.

"Who's Mike Douglas?"

*

I don't mean to make it sound like everything was roses when it came to performers. The great singers and musicians are wonderfully talented, but they can also be difficult, skittish, and unpredictable. Once in a while, when you least expect it, they'll give you a swift kick for no reason.

With June Carter and Johnny Cash

Johnny Cash. The man in black. Another one-of-a-kind. People don't confuse Johnny Cash with any other performer. There was a time, years ago, when Johnny was on a personal roller coaster, not an unfamiliar situation for too many performers. We had him on the show, loved him, and invited him back to co-host for a week.

Johnny looked a little wobbly that Monday, but he started off just great, doing one of his signature songs in the first segment. At the first break, he excused himself for a moment. No big deal. If you gotta go, the break's the time to do it.

Except, when Johnny Cash said "I gotta go," he really meant it. We came back from the break and I was all alone on camera. No Johnny Cash. I mumbled some excuse and stumbled through the segment. At the next break, we started a frantic search for Johnny. He wasn't near the set and wasn't backstage. It didn't take long to realize that Johnny Cash had left the building. I didn't know whether to call his agent, call his home, or call the police and put out a missing persons bulletin. All I knew was, we had another eighty minutes of live show to do and I would have to play to an empty chair.

The show must go on. That's what we did. I told the audience that

Johnny had to leave because he wasn't feeling well, nothing serious, and we hoped to have him back tomorrow when he was better.

I don't know how he was feeling by then, but he wasn't back the next day or the day after. No phone call, no note, no telegram from his agent. Johnny had simply disappeared. It was like *The Mike Douglas Show*'s version of *The Twilight Zone*.

I didn't hear from Johnny Cash for years after that. Never called to explain or apologize. Nothing. Finally, we had a forced face-to-face in the same Green Room when we were both scheduled to appear on a *Carol Burnett Show*. I was already there when he walked in, said a brief hello, and shook my hand. Then . . . silence. A few minutes later, when we were alone, he turned and looked me straight in the eye.

"Mike, I want to apologize to you. I know I screwed you up a while back. I'm sorry. I . . . I was a mess. I didn't know what time it was, I didn't know what day it was. I'm past all that now, but I owe you a show. I haven't forgotten."

It was as sincere and manly an apology as I've ever heard and I admired him for it. I told him he didn't owe me a show, he didn't owe me a thing.

Johnny Cash doesn't forget. A short time later, he returned to *The Mike Douglas Show*. He brought June, all the Cashes and Carters, the whole band, and put on the whole dog. He adamantly refused to accept a dime, picked up the whole tab himself, and insisted we donate the guest fees to a charity in Nashville.

Johnny Cash has this reputation as a man's man. A lot of things in this business are pure hype. Johnny Cash is the real McCoy.

*

Roger Miller did the same thing to us about three years later, but it was the comic version. He was in Dallas, scheduled for *Mike Douglas* the next day. He didn't forget, but he got up the next morning, had a few short ones, a few more at the airport, then got on the plane for Philadelphia. Around noon, I got a phone call. They said he insisted on talking to me personally.

A funny thing happened on the way to Philadelphia. Roger got off the plane, walked out to the curb, climbed in a cab, and told the driver to take him to the Mike Douglas Studio. The driver said he could do that, but it would cost him two thousand bucks. The cabbie let Roger vent for a while about cabbies and ripoffs, then quietly informed him that he was in Sacramento and two thousand for the ride to Philly was a bargain. Wrong plane.

*

There was one musical innovation our show brought to television that I am proudest of. Not the debuts of some of the brightest names in music, not breaking many of the headline groups, not even throwing the doors open wide to Motown. We had the luxury of time on our show and that afforded the opportunity for a little payback.

All my life, I owed a debt that I could never pay. I sang and people paid me. It was me on stage or in the studio, it was my voice all right, but it wasn't my music or my words. I had access to this treasure chest of music. Open it up and this marvelous array of precious gems glittered with promise, there for the singing.

The creators of our songs have never received the recognition they deserve. Sure, their names are on the sheet music and they get paid (some-

With Roger Miller

times), but except for Sinatra and a few others who always had the courtesy to credit the composer when introducing a song, they are rarely mentioned and seldom seen. It's not right, and I think we took a few small steps to correct that by inviting every living composer and lyricist of note that we could think of over the course of the show. I just wish we had started the show a little earlier so I would have had a chance to talk with Cole Porter and George Gershwin.

We did manage to reach back far enough to include a few of their contemporaries. Eubie Blake was writing songs just past the turn of the century. He was one of the co-founders of ASCAP, a Hall of Fame composer and a memorable guest.

Most of them were unaccustomed to the limelight and few were performance-oriented enough to make a big impression. That didn't matter to me. Sitting with Johnny Mercer at the piano in his antebellum home in Savannah, singing his songs, accompanied by the master himself—how many singers get that close to heaven?

I watched Henry Mancini tinker at the piano, listened to Hoagy Carmichael describe how he created "Stardust," witnessed Paul Williams come up with a good new tune right before our eyes. I've seen Anthony Newley use his marvelous hand gestures to build blocks of melody in the air, listened to Chuck Berry recount writing songs in prison that became the foundation of rock 'n' roll, heard Paul Simon explain why he wanted to fit a song around Joe DiMaggio.

A few shows were lucky enough to have Elton John, still one of the most amazing performers and easily among the most prolific composers. But I don't know of any that welcomed both Elton and his gifted lyricist, Bernie Taupin. That was a seminar in songwriting.

Sammy Cahn, Jimmy Webb, Neil Sedaka, Jimmy Van Heusen—they were visiting royalty to me, and their words on the show, like their wonderful music, meant so much. I doubt if anyone who heard John Kander talk about *Cabaret* didn't have a much deeper appreciation of that show. I know I listened to "Evergreen" from a different perspective after the insight provided by Paul Williams. Anyone who listened to John Lennon knew a lot more about what made the Beatles so spectacular. I watched Michel Legrand mesmerized by Ray Charles singing one of his songs. And who wouldn't be moved by hearing Harry Warren talk about the girl who inspired him to write "I Only Have Eyes for You"?

Our show didn't make it on the air in time to have Michelangelo and

With
Eubie Blake

Leonardo da Vinci (although some of you might think so), but we did feature more artists whose works would live forever than any show in TV history—the songmakers, the composers and lyricists who put down the soundtrack to the twentieth century.

Just for a moment, try to imagine what life would be like without them and the gifts they gave us. No music? Don't tell me your life wouldn't be immeasurably diminished. And me? Well, I guess I'd be working for the railroad in Chicago.

3

A Thousand Clowns

With Your Host, Mike Douglas

Ace Trucking Company * Don Adams * Joey Adams * Morey Amsterdam * Dan Aykroyd * Lucille Ball * John Belushi * Jack Benny Milton Berle * Joey Bishop * David Brenner * Mel Brooks * Carol Burnett * George Burns * Ruth Buzzi * Sid Caesar * John Candy George Carlin * Judy Carne * Art Carney * Tim Conway * Irwin Corey * Bill Cosby * Billy Crystal * Jane Curtin * Bill Dana * Rodney Dangerfield * Jimmy Dean * Dom DeLuise * Phyllis Diller * Jimmy Durante * Totie Fields * Redd Foxx * Henry Gibson * Jackie Gleason * George Gobel * Frank Gorshin * Shecky Greene Goldie Hawn * Sherman Hemsley * Buck Henry * Bob Hope * Artie Johnson * Danny Kaye * Emmett Kelly * Alan King * George Kirby * Robert Klein * London Lee * Jay Leno * Jackie Leonard Jerry Lester * David Letterman * Jerry Lewis * Rich Little * Little Rascals * Paul Lynde * Moms Mabley * Bill Maher * Howie Mandel * Marcel Marceau * Rose Marie * Dean Martin * Steve Martin Groucho Marx * Jackie Mason * Donny Most * Zero Mostel * Muppets * Bill Murray * Jan Murray * Bob Newhart * Louis Nye

Pat Paulsen * Minnie Pearl * Penn & Teller * Tom Poston * Freddie Prinze * Richard Pryor * Gilda Radner * Tony Randall * Carl Reiner * Don Rickles * Joan Rivers * Mickey Rooney * Rowan & Martin * Nipsy Russell * Soupy Sales * Second City * Dick Shawn Allan Sherman * Phil Silvers * Red Skelton * Smothers Brothers Stiller & Meara * Three Stooges * Danny Thomas * Marlo Thomas Lily Tomlin * Fred Travalena * Vivian Vance * Dick Van Dyke * Jackie Vernon * Slappy White * Flip Wilson * Henry Winkler Jonathan Winters * Jo Anne Worley * Henny Youngman

D ID we ever have any comedians on the show? Funny you should ask.

What's your favorite brand of comedy? Solo stand-up? One-liners? Straight man and clown? Impersonations? Character bits? Pantomime? Improvisation? Vaudeville shtick? Irish anecdotes? Jewish monologues? British deadpan? Zany madcap? You name it, we had it. Performed by the best of the best.

Who's your favorite comic? Bob Hope? Jack Benny? Bill Cosby? Lucille Ball? Dick Van Dyke? Billy Crystal? Richard Pryor? Steve Martin? Jimmy Durante? Phyllis Diller? Jackie Gleason? Red Skelton? Jerry Lewis? Emmett Kelly? Jonathan Winters? Lily Tomlin? All of the above? Well, come on in and have a seat. You're going to enjoy this.

*

People have asked me if I have any lingering injuries from the thousands of stunts we did on the show. I kind of wish I did because it's like of badge of honor among the truly great physical comedians. Buster Keaton, Dick Van Dyke, Jerry Lewis, Chevy Chase—they all have chronic bad backs, necks, or knees from one too many head-over-heels or half gainers off banana peels. In spite of all the wrestling bears, parachute jumps, ostrich races, practical jokes, and pratfalls, I was never seriously injured. A few nicks and bruises, but nothing to speak of, in spite of the fact that it was obvious after a few years that Woody Fraser was trying to kill me. But I do have one chronic physical defect brought on by *The Mike Douglas Show*. My ribs are permanently dislodged from laughing so much.

On most TV shows with a live audience there was a big LAUGH sign to let the folks in the studio know when something amusing had happened. We never had one. I think one of the Westinghouse execs suggested it one time. I just looked at him for a moment and said, "What for?"

Writing this book has been a joy in many ways. The mention of a name or the reminder of a particular show brings back a flood of fond memories. But this chapter has been particularly hard on me. You would think it might be enjoyable to reminisce about the funniest moments and people on the show, and it is, but you try to condense all the brilliant comedy and comedians of three different decades into a handful of pages in the book and see if you don't wake up in the middle of the night screaming things like, "Oh no, we forgot Jackie Mason and the pastry chef!" or "We've gotta find the tape of Redd Foxx and the rabbi!"

When I asked my researchers to cull through the guest lists and print out only "the very best comedians," they gave me a list of 185 names. The editors heard about it and sent me a fax with a stern warning: "This cannot be a twelve-volume book." After weeks of wrangling, we pared the list down to ninety. I can't mention more than a few dozen and still have room for the other chapters, but I've looked over the "final" list several times and cannot find one name to cut. I guess the only thing to do is start at the top of the comedy mountain and not stop writing until they take the pen out of my hand.

*

"Comic Legend." It's a term that's been bandied about ever since the first Neanderthal stepped closer to the fire and said, "A funny thing happened on the way to the cave tonight . . ." I don't use the term lightly myself, but I have had the honor of working with more than a few people whose talent for amusement was impossible to describe without slipping the word "legend" into the conversation.

How many Jackie Gleasons are there? How many comedians have a repertoire of characters more famous than most real stars? Reginald Van Gleason. The Poor Soul. The immortal Ralph Kramden. One of the greatest honors ever bestowed on our show was when Jackie included me in a special episode of *The Honeymooners*. I believe it was the first "crossover" show on television, with Ralph and Norton and their wives following an unlikely sequence of events to end up appearing on a fantasy version of *The Mike Douglas Show*. And working with the Great One, Art Carney, and Sheila MacRae was a fantasy come true for me.

Jackie and I became fast friends, partly because we were both avid golfers, and I wish I had had a video camera with me every time we took to the links together. That "larger than life" personality that he projected on TV was no act. His golf cart cost more than a Rolls-Royce (if you include the bar inventory, more than a Learjet), and there was more pomp and circumstance to his golf routine than most coronations. He loved the game and loved the competition. The only thing he didn't care for was losing, and it took me several outings to find that out. Every time he won, whether it was $2 or $2,000, he would march into the clubhouse triumphant, regaling everyone with grossly exaggerated highlights of his round, buying drinks and holding court for hours. But the match I remember most had Jackie and his favorite partner, Jack Philbin, paired up against Bob Newhart and myself. Now, Bob is a wonderful guy, but he carried what we often referred to as a "celebrity handicap"—an impressive number about 8 strokes less than it should have been. Everyone knew it. People would send limos to pick him up for golf matches. Anticipating the worst, I slipped several extra bills into my wallet that morning before heading for the first tee.

As luck would have it, Bob Newhart played the round of his life that day. Not only was he hitting the ball well, but he caught some very fortunate bounces and made some seeing-eye putts. In spite of my shock, I played quite well myself, almost parring the course. Jackie and his partner kept pressing, certain things would turn around. They never did. Bob and I walked off the eighteenth green big winners.

I couldn't wait to get into the clubhouse and see what Gleason would do after a rare loss. I never got the chance. As soon as Bob and I tipped our caddies and turned around, Jackie was gone. A glum Jack Philbin handed us a sealed envelope. Inside were our winnings, to the penny. Jackie's stretch Lincoln was already heading down the driveway.

He was a comic genius all right, but some things just weren't funny. We didn't play golf again for a year. When we finally did, he met me on the first tee, looked around and said, "You didn't bring that sandbagger Newhart again, did you?"

With Jackie Gleason

Red Skelton was comparable to Jackie in the public's mind. So many wonderful characters, so much humor that didn't require any dialogue, and such a warm, creative edge to his performances.

But Red was one of kind, too. Jackie was an entertaining emperor. Red was the common man's comedian. In rehearsals, he spent all his downtime with the crew, entertaining them with his stories. Before the show, he would wander through the audience, chat with the ladies, do tricks for kids.

He was unique in more ways than one. Red got started in the old vaudeville days and he had some bizarre habits that carried over. Money was scarce back then and it wasn't uncommon for comics to get stiffed after shows by theater owners caught short on cash. In turn, they would often sneak out of hotels or bounce checks, leaving unpaid bills. That prompted severe treatment of vaudevillians by hotel and restaurant owners, who often demanded cash up front. As a result, Red carried large amounts of money and other readily negotiable valuables with him at all times. Old habits die hard. Many years later, vastly successful and instantly recognizable everywhere, he still did the same thing.

One day when he was co-hosting, we strolled outside and Red asked me to accompany him to his car to pick up some prop he had there. I watched as he popped the trunk and began rummaging through its contents. I noticed something sparkling in a velvet pouch, tied with a drawstring.

"What's in there, Red?"

He grabbed it and absently tossed it to me.

"A little insurance."

I loosened the string and peered inside. It looked like he had robbed Tiffany's—an assortment of oversized diamonds, rubies, and sapphires. I couldn't believe it. Untold thousands of dollars' worth of jewels.

"My God, Red—what are you doing with this?"

He waved me off.

"Oh, that's nothing," he said, grabbing a small satchel from deeper in the trunk. "Here, take a look at this."

I opened the satchel. Money, lots of it. Stacks of hundreds, five hun-

With Red Skelton:
freeloaders

dreds, and even thousand dollar bills. I don't think I had ever seen a thousand dollar bill before. Plus cashier's checks, all made out to "Mr. Red Skelton"—$10,000 each. I leaned against the car, trying to catch my breath, looking to see if anyone was watching. My best guess is he had a few hundred thousand dollars' worth of cash, checks, and baubles in the trunk of his car.

"Red, are you nuts?"

"You never know when you're going to get caught short, Mike."

He explained he just felt a lot more comfortable with a ton of money "real close by." Besides, it came in handy sometimes. My favorite true story of Red's propensity to act as his own traveling Skelton National Bank was the time he and his wife, Little Red, were driving through Bel Air a few years earlier. Little Red noticed a magnificent home. She told Red it was the loveliest home she had ever seen. Red pulled over, walked up, and knocked on the door. An elderly woman in a housecoat answered, ill at ease with these redheaded strangers (she didn't recognize Skelton). He asked if the home was for sale. Offended, she brushed him off. "Absolutely not."

Before she could slam the massive door in his face, Red produced a stack of thousands and flashed them in front of her eyes. He said he would consider paying as much as $200,000, right there on the spot.

The woman's eyes widened. She looked around to see if there were any Candid Cameras in the bushes, then beckoned to Red. "Please come in."

The Skeltons bought the house that day.

When Red was on the show, the writers came up with a skit with both of us made up as Freddie the Freeloader, one of Red's signature characterizations. I was hesitant. Red Skelton owned Freddie and America loved him. I thought it was asking a little too much to let me "borrow" him for a quick turn on *The Mike Douglas Show*. But Red absolutely insisted. He gave me tips on how to walk and how to flick the ashes from the cigar butt. I was touched, and worked hard to make it perfect. Afterward, he gave me a big, heartfelt hug and made me an "honorary Freddie." Some comics can be difficult in real life. Red Skelton was a saint.

*

Jerry Lewis may not be a saint, but he is a genius. And I'm not even French. Every time he was on, we would marvel at this man's range as a

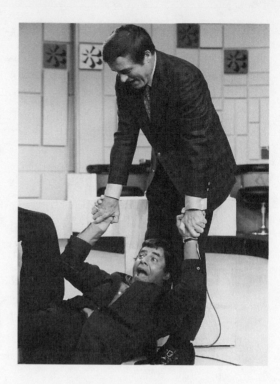

With
Jerry Lewis

performer. He could be as silly as a toddler and as serious as a brain surgeon two minutes later. (What you had to watch out for was when he was acting like a silly brain surgeon.) Jerry could choreograph a complicated dance number while he was doing it, play instruments, conduct an orchestra, then do a ten-foot pratfall off the stage. And that was all before the first commercial. Backstage, he was all business, but turn on the lights and wham—the one, the only—Jerry Lewis.

Once in a while, you hear that Jerry Lewis can be tough to work with. The rumor is true, and I'll give you a firsthand example.

Jerry's generosity was legendary. One day, I happened to notice the unusual watch he was wearing. Beautifully crafted in gold, it bore two faces, one for East Coast time, one West Coast. I thought it was elegant and attractive and I mentioned it to him. The following day, a package came from Jerry Lewis—an exact duplicate of the Watch with Two Faces, inscribed to me. I was floored. Jerry and I got along fine, but we weren't that close and this was obviously a very expensive gift. Gen and I went out that week and found a silver bracelet to send to Jerry as a heartfelt thank-you. It was the least I could do.

A week later, another package arrived—a *gold* bracelet from Jerry. I told Gen, who dutifully rushed out to find another appropriate return gift.

This went on for weeks. Every time I turned around, something else arrived and we would scramble to keep pace with his endless generosity. I finally had to call him up.

"Jerry, please—stop! You're killing me with kindness."

He laughed. "I'm just having fun, Mike. Listen, if I don't spend a grand before noon, it's a wasted day. But okay, I hear you."

The next morning a package arrived at our home. Gen opened it. An expensive antique vase from Jerry Lewis. The guy's a maniac. I'm just glad I never mentioned how much I admired his wife.

*

It doesn't happen often, but sometimes the biggest names in show business have the smallest egos. I'll never forget the day Jimmy Durante finally agreed to appear on the show. One of the most cherished stars in the world for half a century. I spent the morning making sure everything was perfect, fretting about what to ask and how to act with this show business giant. I grew up laughing at Jimmy's antics. It was hard to believe I was about to appear with him on national television. It was a fantasy fulfillment. As a kid, I imagined myself up there on that huge screen, laughing and joking with Jimmy Durante. Now it was going to happen just that way. It scared me to death.

He came on about midway through the show, after a break. I hadn't even had a chance to meet him yet. The curtain parted and there he was at the piano. He did one of his patented numbers, tipping his trademark hat with a few humble bows. The lights went down, we went to a commercial and I stepped over to greet him and walk him back to the chairs for the next segment. You have no idea how I felt when I reached the piano and Jimmy Durante wasn't there. Gone! My jaw dropped. One of the crew said he grabbed his coat and headed out the back way. I looked at the clock—about a minute and we'd be back on the air. I didn't care. I raced after him.

About a hundred feet down the hallway I caught up to him just as he was about to leave the building.

"Jimmy!"

He turned and smiled at me.

"Hiya, Mike! Tanks. Tanks a lot for lettin' me do da show."

"But—but Jimmy! It's not over! You've got to come back!"

"But I was only s'pose ta do one number."

"Right, but Jimmy, you've got to come back and talk."

He shook his head and rolled his eyes.

"Oh no. I'm no good at dat kinda chitchat. You don't want me to do dat."

"Jimmy, you've got to! Just for a minute. Please."

I was only a few seconds away from getting down on my knees. He didn't say anything. The only sound was the applause beyond the studio door. I took that as cue.

"Jimmy—listen to that! They love you! You can't leave them like that."

He stopped and scratched his head.

"Okay, Mike," he said, flashing that angelic Durante smile. "Maybe it'll help my career."

We just made it to the chairs before the red light came on. No offense to him, but Jimmy Durante didn't know what he was talking about when he said he wouldn't be any good at "dat chitchat." We talked for twenty minutes. His stories were wonderful. His anecdotes were hilarious. The audience fell in love with him. So did I.

*

Mel Brooks is either a comic genius or he's crazy. And really, what difference does it make? Lots of performers have a set routine, and they don't like to change the tiniest detail. Mel Brooks is just the opposite. For him, scripts and setups just get in the way. He prefers to work freestyle. At his best, no one can touch him for spur-of-the-moment one-liners.

Mel is fearless when it comes to comedy. He knows his instincts will carry the day, no matter what the situation. There were times when he would dare me to try to stump him on the air. Once, we were about to close a show that he was co-hosting. He was really cooking, so I thought I'd toss him a hard curve just to see if he could do something—anything—with it.

"Mel, we don't have much time—say something profound."

Mel looked at me for a minute, expressionless, then turned to the camera with a duly profound look on his face.

"Cotton."

*

Danny Thomas? Not just your run-of-the-mill comic genius. Danny had become a comic institution years before. By the time he came on our show, he had transcended comedy to the status of all-around genius. I mean, if we had Dr. Christiaan Barnard on the show, he and Danny would get into a very technical discussion about heart transplants. He could talk about rocket propulsion with Wernher Von Braun and comparative literature with Gore Vidal. He had already won every possible award for comedy performance and humanitarianism, I'm just surprised he never won the Nobel Prize in physics.

As interesting and informative as he was, I couldn't help but nudge him back to the Danny Thomas that I loved—the comedy storyteller. Sometimes, he'd be expounding about new discoveries in quantum mechanics or something and I would break in:

"... And Professor Walters at Stanford tells me that—"

"Danny, wasn't there a character named Walter in one of your stories?"

With Burt Reynolds, Mel Brooks, and Engelbert Humperdinck

With Danny Thomas and Connie Stevens

"I'm sorry?"

"Walter. Wasn't Walter the guy with the apple pie and coffee?"

"Oh, you mean the 'immigrant at the diner' story."

"That's the one! Oh, you've got to tell that!"

"Well, it's a true story. Walter was an immigrant from central Europe—this is in the 1930s—his cousin gets him a job hauling gravel, and

With
Lily Tomlin

every day they go to the same diner for lunch. He doesn't speak a word of English, but his cousin teaches him how to say 'Apple-Pie-And-Coffee,' so every day he walks in, sits down, and when the waitress speaks to him, he says 'abblebie-n-coofee.' Now this goes on for a month. All the poor guy ever gets to eat is apple pie and coffee. He never wants to see another piece of pie, so his cousin teaches him to say 'hot dog.' He's so happy. He goes to the diner the next day, the waitress comes over, he says, 'hot dog.' She says, 'You want mustard, ketchup, relish, onion, cheese dog, chili dog, the works, or what?' He stares at her, paralyzed. She waits. He says, 'abblebie-n-coofee.'"

I confess, I would trick Danny into telling his great stories that way all the time. One day, it must have been too obvious. After the show, he burst into my dressing room and grabbed me by the lapels, blowing cigar smoke in my face.

"You no good Irishman! You made me do my old act!"

Danny wasn't the only clever member of the Thomas family we had on the show. It was a natural to have Marlo Thomas as a guest when her father was co-hosting. Danny's daughter was starring as *That Girl* on TV, and this is my chance to thank her for providing *The Mike Douglas Show* with one of our best on-air news scoops.

Marlo was a star performer herself and very comfortable on the show, sitting next to her proud father. This was just about the time that rumors had begun swirling, linking Marlo to the hot new kid on daytime television, Phil Donahue. Neither Marlo nor Phil had uttered a word about it in public until Marlo, intentionally or not, blurted out a line that made the papers the next day: "Mike, you know I love you—why, you're my second favorite talk show host in the whole world!"

The next time I saw Danny, he said Marlo had been grounded for a week for that.

*

Like many other trades, comedy used to be a man's world. It was the late 1960s before Marlo helped break some barriers by starring in her own "single girl" comedy series. I like to think we did our part for the women's movement by opening the doors to a flock of female funnypersons, including the lovable Totie Fields, marvelous Moms Mabley, fabulous Phyllis Diller, and many others, but one of the most brilliant minds in comedy, male or female, had to be Lily Tomlin. She could transform herself into all these fascinating characters—Ernestine, the snorting tele-phone operator, the gossipy little girl in the giant rocking chair, the hip guy—after a while, we didn't even ask what she was up to, just give her ten minutes and let her loose.

One of my favorites was the self-confessed "rubber addict" who started in high school by chewing on pencil erasers. It was a tragic case. Within a few years, she had worked her way up to those huge tires on diesel trucks. This young lady's mind worked in strange and wondrous ways.

*

Some of you might think John Byner is an unusual nominee for comic legend. Just ask around. John is one of the most inventive talents in the business. It's impossible to describe on paper, but his Donald Duck voice leaves me helpless. It doesn't matter what he says. How does he make that sound?

He was wonderful with Woody, collaborating on skits and visuals that brought down the house. My favorite will always be the "World's Smallest President" sketch. It was John's idea. Woody loved it and had the crew whip up the oversized-scale podium, with the White House seal on the front. John walked out, very dignified in his presidential blue suit, took his place at the podium, and began speaking earnestly about the great issues of the day. But, with the top of his head two feet below the microphone stand, his serious words were lost in hoots and howls. He looked a perfect three feet tall. Only John kept a straight face, and never told one joke during this bit. Didn't have to.

And Now, for the First Time Anywhere . . .

At first, it wasn't easy to get big name stars. Even later, it was often diffi-cult to make arrangements on superstar schedules for Cleveland or Philadelphia, so we learned to keep an eye out for talent. It turns out we had 20-20 vision.

Among the newcomers we took a chance on were a few that might cost a little more than the paltry guest fee we paid if you tried to book them now. One of them was a brand-new stand-up named Michael Keaton. He was good, but not great, and I had my doubts that he would make it on the comedy circuit. I was right. He didn't. But he does get about ten million dollars a movie now.

When he was in the chair, he flattered me by saying, "Do you know I had to change my name because of you? My real name is Mike Douglas."

Years later, after our show had gone off the air, I saw Michael Keaton on TV again. This time he was on *The Tonight Show* to promote a new movie, chatting with the substitute host, actor Michael Douglas. Keaton turned to Douglas and said, "Did you know I had to change my name because of you?"

I had to laugh. That's show biz.

*

In 1970, many of the stations that carried our show in syndication were NBC affiliates. They asked us to do them a favor and we gladly obliged. They had just started limited broadcast of an experimental weekend show and wanted to showcase the unknown cast of youngsters. Sure, bring 'em on.

For the record, that was the first time the *Saturday Night Live* Not Ready for Prime Time Players appeared on national television.

Saturday Night Live was still in so few markets that Gilda Radner was thrilled to get a chance to say hello to her folks. She asked, "Will they get us in Detroit?" I think it was John Belushi who chimed in before I could give her the good news: "Oh, they'll see us in Detroit, Gilda, but they won't get us in Detroit."

I don't know how much credit we can take, but *SNL* did pretty well after that.

Dan Aykroyd, John Belushi, Gilda Radner, Garrett Morris, Jane Curtin, producer Lorne Michaels—just about the whole gang was there, except Chevy Chase. He was scheduled, but didn't make it to the taping. I never found out what happened to him that day.

In a bizarre coincidence, many years later, Chevy was booked to do our show to promote one of his *National Lampoon Vacation* flicks. I liked Chevy and his off-the-wall humor. Since we had missed connections the first time around, I was glad to hear we were finally going to get a chance to correct that omission. Would you believe he didn't show up again, and never called before or after to apologize or explain? Of over thirty thousand guests booked for *The Mike Douglas Show*, we only had a handful of last-minute cancellations or missed connections, but the only guest that ever outright stiffed us was Chevy Chase. Twice.

**With the
All in the
Family** *cast*

I never figured that out and I wouldn't mention it now except I hope Chevy runs into Jerry Lewis some day and admires his watch.

*

We showcased casts from a few other shows over the years. Ozzie and Harriet brought Ricky and David over for a week in the 1960s. In the early 1970s, we booked Gabe Kaplan and his *Welcome Back, Kotter* kids, including a teen heartthrob named John Travolta. A year later, Ronnie Howard, Henry "Fonzie" Winkler, and the *Happy Days* gang checked in. *All in the Family, The Dick Van Dyke Show, Room 222, Three's Company, Gunsmoke, Mary Tyler Moore*—we took regular trips through the TV looking glass for extended visits with the most popular casts on the air. Our audience loved it.

*

My favorite cast-oriented week included a wild bunch from a midsummer replacement show on NBC. A few months before, we had featured a veteran comic stand-up team that had worked for years in Vegas and on the club circuit, but hadn't done that much TV. Producer George Schlatter signed them to a TV deal a short time later and tossed in a bunch of relatively unknown comics and fresh-faced kids looking for work. Now what did they call that? Oh, yeah. That's it. *Laugh-In. Rowan & Martin's Laugh-In.*

What a week that was. Rowan & Martin. Goldie Hawn. Arte Johnson. Ruth Buzzi. Henry Gibson. Alan Sues. Gary Owens. Jo Anne Worley. Judy Carne. I'm not sure what day we completely lost control of the show, but I think it might have been Tuesday. After that, it was *Rowan & Martin's Laugh-In with Mike Douglas Hanging on for Dear Life*.

They were already into that raucous rhythm that made their show a TV landmark. Nonstop jokes, topping each other, full speed ahead, no holds barred laughathon. Schlatter had these kids molded into a well-oiled comedy machine. At the time, summer replacement shows were just that. Temporary fill-ins. Eight weeks and gone. I said, on the air, "This will be the number one show in the nation." With the talent they had on that show, it was kind of like predicting the Yankees would win another pennant someday.

The *Laugh-In* guys were great but the *Laugh-In* gals were spectacular. Three of the greatest female laughs in show business belonged to Jo Anne Worley, Ruth Buzzi, and Goldie Hawn.

The teenage Goldie was my favorite. She played that airhead giggler to perfection, but there was so much more to Goldie. I asked her if she had any plans beyond *Laugh-In*. Those giant blue eyes opened extra wide. "Oh, yes. I'd like to do this for a couple years, but I'd love to have a show of my own, then get into features. And then I'd like to direct movies, you know, maybe even produce." Sounded funny at the time.

Goldie Hawn

*

The beauty of comedy is that it works in all directions. The *Laugh-In* lunatics were completely unpredictable. David Brenner is a good example of the counterpoint. He was as unpredictable as a clock. Absolutely methodical and professional. Every line, every take in his act was programmed to perfection like a new computer. He had a list of ad-libs for any occasion, memorized, loaded, and ready. David was very serious about his comedy. He worked at his craft and his material had staying power. I still remember many of his stories.

One of the best was his subway story that he insisted was absolutely true. One day, riding on the subway in New York, he was sitting on a newspaper when a stranger sat down next to him.

The man gestured at the paper and asked, "Are you reading that?"

"Yes I am," David replied. He stood up, turned the page, sat back down and continued "reading."

*

Jerry Stiller & Anne Meara made a rare combination: a Jewish-Irish, husband-wife act. I thought they were the best since Mike Nichols and Elaine May. A few years later they gave up stand-up for bigger things. Jerry's a comic actor in great demand in film and on TV. He was wonderful on *Seinfeld*. Anne's a top-flight TV director-producer. Now there's another star in the family—their son, Ben, is emerging as a great talent in his own right, star of one hit movie after another. Ben looks so young, you may be surprised to know that he has been in this business over a quarter of a century. He made his national television debut on our show in 1972, with his parents and sister, Amy. I don't know what he gets for a picture. We got him for a candy bar.

*

Steve Martin, Flip Wilson, Bill Maher, David Steinberg, Gallagher, Minnie Pearl, Frank Gorshin, Fred Travalena, Sherman Hemsley, J. J. Walker, Joan Rivers, Al Franken, Howie Mandel, a former weatherman named David Letterman, a lantern-jawed stand-up, Jay Leno, an oversized character comedian named John Candy, a couple of wild-eyed kids who called themselves something like the Asparagus Valley Cultural Society (later simplified to "Penn & Teller")—a parade of talent crossed our stage on the way to standout careers.

And some of them didn't make it. Remember London Lee, the "Poor Little Rich Kid"? He's got to be in the top twenty-five for appearances on *The Mike Douglas Show*. He had some good material, a nice presence, and a memorable, oddball laugh (Heh-heh-heh-heh-heh-heh-heh). But for whatever reason, the gods of comedy didn't smile on London. After a few years, it was back to the mansion.

And don't tell me you've forgotten Monti Rock III? I never will. Monti would probably classify himself as a singer, but I have him firmly on the comedy side of the ledger. I'm not sure how much was a put-on, but there's no denying he could be very funny, in a most unusual, Brooklyn-hairdresser-lost-soul kind of way. And then one day he just seemed to disappear from the face of the earth, or at least the face of television.

What amazes me is that they were the exceptions. Success was the rule.

The most tragic case was Freddie Prinze. He wasn't much older than Ben Stiller when he first appeared with us. What a talent. I've never seen a kid so young take charge of an audience with such ease. Backstage, he was just as easy to like, intelligent and personable. Within months, he was signed to star in a TV series, *Chico and the Man*. He couldn't vote yet and he was on top of the world. A few years later, he was gone, a shocking suicide. To this day, it saddens me that drugs drove him to take his own life with nothing but greatness in his future. Freddie should still be here, making people laugh, still in the prime of an outstanding career. Lots of things are funny. Not drugs.

*

We ran into a few other talented young comedians over the course of twenty-three years. One kid we signed for an appearance was fresh out of Temple University and still living at his parents' house in Philadelphia. Tall, good-looking, and athletic, he had gotten nice reviews for his stand-up takes on growing up in the inner city. We gave him a shot and the audience reaction was enough to tell us to bring him back again. In a later appearance, we learned that he had been quite a track star. That led to another Woody Fraser inspiration. We set up a high hurdles track and dared him to race against one of our staff members. He confidently accepted the challenge. He didn't know until the last minute that we had altered the rules slightly. Instead of a staffer, Woody imported Bob Beamon, the all-time greatest high hurdle star in sports history. To his credit, the youngster didn't back down. A real competitor and a great sport, he ran his best, finishing a respectable second to the world champion.

In retrospect, it was a very rare moment. The next thirty years proved that this young man didn't lose very often at anything. We didn't know

With Bill Cosby

it then, but we had two world champions on the show that day, in sports and comedy. Bob Beamon was one. The other was Bill Cosby.

*

In the 1970s, we often used another kid named Bill as a bumper act. Whenever we ran into those inevitable last-minute problems—a scheduled guest missed a plane or caught a cold—we could give little Bill a call. A baby stand-up and impersonator, Bill was so grateful for the national exposure, he'd show up on an hour's notice and fill the slot, usually with no time to do anything but wing it. The biggest joke was on him. The kid was such a natural, we would have begged him to come on if he hadn't been so darn willing. Not only could he do drop-dead takes on Muhammad Ali and Howard Cosell, he came up with fabulous lines out of nowhere. Most of the mimics, even the best of them, can't compete with the straight comedians when it comes to ad-libbing. Billy could run with anybody.

We did our best to give Billy's career a boost. He saved us enough times, we owed him that. Fact is, he went on to a pretty decent career. You might have caught his act once or twice. He made a splash on the stand-up circuit, did some other TV, hosted some specials, even a few roles in the movies. Billy Crystal?

**With
Billy Crystal**

The Troopers

When it comes to show business dedication, comics are the best of the best. The show must go on. Put on a happy face. Break a leg. I suppose it dates back to the grind of vaudeville, but there is no harder-working, more loyal bunch. When you need them, they'll be there. When it's showtime, they will turn it on.

Phyllis Diller and I have been fast friends since she first appeared on our show in 1963. Not exactly an ingenue, Phyllis had just started making noise on the small-club circuit as this wacky housewife with a husband named Fang whose self-deprecating shtick was getting big laughs. Even then, we were taking chances. When Woody told me he was going to book a middle-aged housewife as a stand-up act, I just shrugged. Filling seven and a half hours of live national television from a tiny Cleveland studio every week was tough. Sometimes, you had to reach.

What a pleasant surprise Phyllis was! You could see in the first five minutes how great she was with an audience. A late bloomer, Phyllis Diller's leap into stand-up comedy brought her real personality shining through. Not only did she have some great routines, but she was quick and light on her comic feet. Comfortable with any guest or in any harebrained skit we might dream up, she always delivered. And the joke was usually on herself.

And talk about pros. Phyllis was one of the precious few stars we could always count on when we really had our backs against the wall. I would

*Mike and
Phyllis Diller*

hate to count the times we called her the night before a show with one or
two whole segments suddenly wide open because of an unexpected problem or cancellation. My spirits always rose when I would see her walk in,
that big crazy smile on her face, a half hour before airtime.

I called her from Miami once. The show was on the road, broadcasting on location for the entire week. My leadoff guest singer had just
been scratched with a sore throat. Phyllis's agent tracked her down in
Montreal. For once, it looked impossible. She was headlining at a top
club there, booked solid for the week. They said it couldn't be done, but
they didn't know Phyllis. She flew down on a red-eye, opened our show,
knocked 'em dead, jumped back on a return flight, and walked out on
stage for the Montreal dinner show, fresh as a Diller daisy. What a
dame.

*

Another one-of-a-kind veteran I could always count on was Shecky
Greene. Most of you don't really know what a terrific performer Shecky
Greene is. We tried our best to showcase Shecky's talent for a TV audience, as did Johnny Carson, Merv Griffin, and others, but something
about Shecky's electrifying Vegas performances was lost on the small
screen. Even with that handicap, he was very good on our show, always
funny and surprising.

He could do so many things. Dead-on impersonations, weird characters, wonderful stories, perfect zingers. Shecky could sing. He could dance. Shecky did his own stunts.

But the Shecky Greene moment I remember most tells you something about the man. I've met a lot of people you could call "tough" in this business, and many of the greatest pro fighters ever, who were often guests on the show. I even spent some time in the ring myself back in the fearless and foolish days of my youth. But whenever I hear the phrase "tough guy," only two words come to mind. Shecky Greene.

Shecky was raised on the meanest streets in Chicago. He learned to use his fists long before he started making a living with his wits. When Las Vegas discovered him and he discovered Vegas in the late 1950s, it was the perfect match of a tough young entertainment town with a tough young entertainer. He became one of the Strip's most talked about citizens, both for his talent and his late night exploits.

He often amused our audience with rueful stories of his memorable adventures. One night, he drove his convertible right into the central pillar of the fountain at Caesars Palace, calmly stepped out into the knee-deep pool, and asked the first officer to arrive on the scene for "the works with a wax job, please." Another time he broke up a street robbery, overcame two thugs, and made citizen's arrests on both, holding them for the authorities. When police arrived, he turned them over, then announced he was making a third citizen's arrest—himself, for public intoxication.

There was one incident that he never mentioned on the air, but it was legendary in show business circles. It involved the biggest name of them all, Frank Sinatra. One night at the Desert Inn, Frank became infuriated when Shecky's opening act ran forty-five minutes long (he was really rolling). The Chairman of the Board sent five heavies out after the show to find Shecky and teach him a lesson.

They did. Shecky took a beating that night. But not before two of his assailants were laid out cold and the other three had paid dearly for the privilege of laying hands on old Sheck. This man could dish it out, and he could take it.

It's a good thing he could, too, because we really put him to the test on our show. I cringe every time I think about it. (But not as much as Shecky, I'm sure.)

Shecky was co-hosting for a week in November of 1975. It was only moments before the day's show was scheduled to start. Shecky was following our first guest (young folksinger Emmylou Harris) onto the set. Unaware, Emmylou let a backstage door swing shut as Shecky reached out to push. The door clipped his index finger against the jamb, severing the tip. Poor Shecky buckled over in pain and surprise, blood spurting on the walls. Some of the crew were almost in shock when Shecky calmly asked them to help him find the rest of his finger. Ouch. This should be in Stephen King's next book, not mine.

Did Shecky go to a hospital? Sue the show? Hit me with his good hand? None of the above. Believe it or not, he refused any help, wrapped up his finger with a couple of a Band-Aids and a wet towel, and went on with the show. It wasn't one of my best performances because I spent the whole ninety minutes thinking what anguish Shecky must have been in. He was his usual hilarious self.

After the show, he let us rush him to a hospital and they tended to his wound (although they were not able to reattach his fingertip and the scar endures as a badge of courage for the only recipient of the *The Mike Douglas Show* Purple Heart medal).

Shecky was the only one we permanently damaged, but there were so many other troupers in the comic ranks who deserve medals for service above and beyond the call of duty.

*

You want to talk about old pros? The Three Stooges were stars before I was born (and I hate to tell you how long ago that was). They had already been entertaining generations of kids around the world when Moe Howard agreed to do a guest shot in 1973. (I would say the "inimitable Moe Howard," except he and his fellow Stooges have been universally imitated since I was a kid). I remember smiling whenever a Three Stooges short started flickering across the screen from my first days as a moviegoer back in Chicago. Having Moe talk about the Stooges' wonderful antics was going to be special for me. I left early for the studio, looking forward to the day.

It was a little before 8:00 A.M. when I arrived. And who do you think was the only one there, sitting patiently in the lobby, waiting for someone to open the studio doors? Moe Howard. He had good ideas for some bits and wanted to make sure there was enough time to review and rehearse them. In his seventies, the core of a world-famous comedy stage and screen act since the 1920s, he was as eager and as dedicated as a kid breaking into the business. The audience adored him, of course, and he returned again and again, always the first one there in the morning.

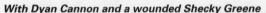

*

Alan King wasn't just a fine stage and screen star and a decorated veteran of the comedy trenches, but a real student of the game. The first time he was on the show in the late 1960s, I wasn't sure if we were going to hit it off or not. I visited him in his dressing room and found him pensive and concerned. What did I want him to do after the monologue? What were we going to fill the time with when we were just sitting there? He wasn't used to working this way and was worried that it wouldn't come off very well. I gave him my standard "just relax and have fun" speech, but it didn't seem to have any effect. On a hunch, I changed the subject entirely. I asked Alan if he had ever seen an old comic named Jackie Miles. Long forgotten by most, he had once been the king of vaudeville and I was lucky enough to have seen him long ago in Chicago. Alan's face lit up. Sure he had! He worked with him once. I mentioned another old stand-up named Lou Holtz (not the Notre Dame

With Dyan Cannon and a wounded Shecky Greene

coach, although he can be pretty funny, too)—an opening act in the Kay Kyser days. Alan knew him well. He fired off a few obscure names of his own, name comics who had come and gone long before TV made instant stars out of kids with a flash of wit. For the next half hour, we traded stories about the old guard. Alan King could teach a course in the history of comedy and he relished the chance to expound on it.

An hour later, we continued the conversation on the air. Professor Alan King returned several times, taking us from Comedy 101 to Advanced Comedy Theory. I think he enjoyed it. I know others did. Over the next several years, I can't tell you how many new comedians—many of whom you know well today—would tell me during a break that the "fresh" stuff they just used to kill the audience was lifted from one of Alan King's discourses on our show. A lot of people are environmentally sensitive today, but comedians were miles ahead of that curve. They've been recycling for years.

*

Bob Newhart was Old Faithful.

Humor is a fragile commodity and comedians are notoriously volatile. On one day, off the next. With more than a few, you just never know until they step before the camera. I could never count the great laughs—the bits and skits, monologues and one-liners that scored a 10—that I witnessed on *The Mike Douglas Show*. But over twenty-three years, you can bet that enough comics died in front of the red light in Studio No. 2 to fill a good-sized cemetery.

Not Bob Newhart. He never had a bad day. The place, the audience, the weather, his horoscope—it didn't matter. He was always funny. I think our show was the first to give him the time to do the full-length version of his wonderful phone monologues. The mythical seventeenth-century Englishman listening to Sir Walter Raleigh explaining his New World discovery—cigarettes—was a classic.

"What do you call it, Walt—tobacco?

". . . Yeah, Walt, I see—it's a plant. Uh-huh . . .

". . . And what do you do—eat it?

". . . I see. Well how about tea? Can you maybe make some tea with . . .

". . . Uh-huh . . . Okay.

"Now, let me get this straight, Walt . . . you take this tobacco stuff,

*Bob
Newhart*

you roll it up in little pieces of paper, and then you stick it in your mouth? . . . Yeah. Then what?

". . . You set it on fire?

"Yeah, Walt. Sounds like a winner all right . . ."

Newhart knew if he wanted to lay me out, he could always fall back on the "symphony in a box" routine. Bob would take one of those old-fashioned matchboxes out of his pocket and hold it up for the audience to see.

"What have you got there, Bob?"

"Oh, this? I got this overseas. There's a tiny symphony orchestra inside this box."

"An orchestra?"

"Symphony orchestra."

"Bob, you can't have a—"

"Shhh. Just listen for a second . . ."

He'd open the box oh so carefully and a seventy-piece version of Beethoven's Fifth would fill the room (producer Roger Ailes at the audio dial). I always knew it was coming, but it never helped. I always lost it.

*

The funniest line ever delivered on the *The Mike Douglas Show*? I couldn't begin to tell you, but there is one that stands out in my mind as the most meaningful. Totie Fields was another of our proud discoveries and a regular, riotously funny guest. You want to talk about troupers? We had Totie booked one time, two months in advance. In the interim, she fought a critical bout with diabetes. Hospitalized in grave condition, she agreed to let her doctors amputate her left leg to prolong her life. Incredibly, she showed up for her scheduled appearance only weeks later. Do you know what she said when I asked her how she was doing?

"It's great to be back on my foot again."

The Wild Ones

Some of the funniest performers believe that humor and discipline are mortal enemies and, as far as they're concerned, never the twain shall meet. There are some inherent hazards with a philosophy like that, but some comics were so enormously talented that they emerged as stars in spite of themselves. For others, it cost them dearly in their careers.

I'm not sure where Professor Irwin Corey fits in that equation. I'm not sure where he fits in any equation, but I do know he was a very funny man. I don't know what university gave him his degree, but I'm sure he majored in comedy. *Cum laude.*

I know he never made any sense, but it seemed so logical and so hilarious at the same time, he couldn't just be talking gibberish. The only problem was, he never knew when to stop. I swear, if our show had been nine hours long instead of ninety minutes, it would have made absolutely no difference to the Professor. He would keep right on talking.

Over the years, fans have mentioned special shows to me, the moments that stick in their minds. They have often reminded me of the time two crew members walked on stage, hoisted Irwin Corey on their shoulders, and walked off stage with him still rambling on about the ". . . imperfect structure of our society, and, in essence, the universe itself, composed of both yin and yang, Yoko and Ono, in direct opposition yet harmonious, but who plays the harmonica anymore? Nevertheless . . ."

Everyone thinks it was a clever bit we rehearsed. It wasn't. We were

With Prof. Irwin Corey and Liberace

just frustrated. Time was up and there was no other way to get rid of the little guy. For all I know, he hasn't stopped talking yet.

*

Paul Lynde could deliver one-liners that stopped the whole show in its tracks. Paul seemed so harmlessly pleasant, he could get away with anything, and often did. I remember when Rocky Graziano was on the show, talking about his boxing career and looking tough enough to step back into the ring at the sound of the next bell. Paul was the co-host. He sat there listening for a while, hands crossed in his lap, while Rocky described a particularly brutal bout. At the end, he reached over and tapped Rocky playfully on the shoulder, gave him that crocodile grin and sassy wriggle. "Touched you last."

For a moment, I didn't know if Rocky was going to laugh or break him in two. Thank goodness everybody else was already rolling in the aisles. Including me.

One day Paul came on the show with a mammoth book in his hands, well worn, with ribbons marking numerous pages. I assumed it was a Bible, which kind of surprised me because he had never mentioned reli-

Paul Lynde

gion in the course of many appearances. I had no idea where he was going. All I could do was ask.

"Is that a Bible, Paul?"

"No. These are my fears."

*

Richard Pryor was the cutting-edge bad boy of stand-up, the comic symbol of a rebellious era. I thought he was brilliant, and our show was the only one to book him repeatedly when he was virtually blacklisted by the networks. There was a time when Richard was considered too brash, too hard to handle, and—let's face it—too black for network television. All I knew was that, at his best, Richard was one of the funniest, most inventive comics I had ever seen perform. He was always welcome on our show, always devastatingly funny. I love Richard, and I wish I could say there were never any problems either, but I don't think it will shock you if I admit that wasn't quite the case. Adrenaline always ran high when Richard Pryor was around.

I never cared for it when some comics would use profanities and obscenities. Things have changed about that, for better or for worse, but in the mid-1960s it was often just a literally vain attempt to put energy into a sagging act. Except for Richard. He didn't say it for effect, he was born that way. Cameras on or off, sooner or later he was talking a blue streak. It's a good thing we had gone from total live to tape delay by then or it would have been the end of *The Mike Douglas Show.*

As it was, Richard cost a fortune in videotape. Sometimes, we would go months without an interruption. A straight ninety minutes, every show, week in, week out. Then Richard would show up and we would be forced to use more footage in a week than James Cameron did on *Titanic.*

But if laughter is good for you, Richard Pryor added years to my life. He could have me doubled over, completely at his mercy, when he was rolling with one of his great character monologues, from the old ghetto street people to white suburbanites.

There was a scary day when Richard was scheduled with Martha Mitchell, wife of the U.S. Attorney General, and the wives of three leading U.S. senators, Mrs. George McGovern, Mrs. Jacob Javits, and Mrs. John Dellenback. Remember "The Mix"? Well, this was like nitro and glycerin. I begged Richard not to misbehave. We didn't need to be investigated by the Justice Department and the Senate.

They weren't on camera together for two minutes before Richard started. One of the ladies mentioned that "We live, eat, sleep, and breathe politics." Martha gave Richard the opening he wanted.

MARTHA: Together?
RICHARD: (trying to help) She thought you were talking about an orgy.

With Martha Mitchell and Chubby Checker

MARTHA: Thank you, Richard.

RICHARD: Sure . . . You know, we've met before, on the first Amtrak train to Chicago.

MARTHA: I remember that. I christened that train. You were on that train?

RICHARD: Yaz, ma'am. I was the porter.

Uh-oh. Here we go. But a funny thing happened on the way to the disaster. Martha had a wonderful wit herself, and she took no offense. In fact, she loved Richard.

MARTHA: How nice. Did you carry my bags?

RICHARD: Oh yes'm.

MIKE: Did she give you a tip? (Don't ask why I joined in. Richard makes people crazy.)

RICHARD: Uh-huh. Blue Boy in the fifth.

They carried on like that for the entire segment. Everyone was in stitches. The timing and the rapid-fire punch lines were so perfect, you would have thought they were a team. Richard Pryor and Martha Mitchell. I would pay money to see that.

Richard's most electrifying moment on the show wasn't a comedy routine. It wasn't even funny. Milton Berle was a guest one day when Richard was co-host, and the two of them got into it. It was an uncomfortable but telling exchange, tensions flashing before a national audience. Still, it was fascinating to watch—a confrontation between comedy generations.

Uncle Miltie, remember, had pretty impressive credentials of his own, and no shortage of self-confidence when it came to teaching young comedians a lesson. He had been successful at the game a long, long time. After all, he was the master of ceremonies at the signing of the Declaration of Independence.

Richard had the attitude that goes with youth and pure, raw talent, and he wasn't known for respecting his elders.

Milton's autobiography had just been published. He was well into his spiel about the book, with a hefty dose of juicy stories about the many and varied women in his life. Milton wanted to let the audience in on his rakish reputation as a ladies' man. For some mischievous reason, this tickled Richard, who had been listening serenely until then. He chuckled over the wrong line. You could see Milton bristle.

MILTON: . . . I say Linda Smith and I'd better keep saying Linda Smith because I hope I don't slip one of these days and say who it really is.

RICHARD: Eleanor Roosevelt?

MILTON: Maybe I'd better tell the story another time.

RICHARD: I'm sorry, Milton, I was out of line. (Then, to himself) Shut up, now. The man's trying to tell a story, so shut up.

MILTON: Let me tell you something, baby. I told you this nine years ago and I'm going to tell you right on the air in front of millions of people—pick your spots, baby.

RICHARD: All right, sweetheart . . . I'm sorry, Milton, honest, I'm just crazy.

MILTON: No, you're not crazy.

RICHARD: . . . I wasn't laughing at you. I was enjoying it with you. I've seen you in dresses, so watch it.

MILTON: I want to know why you laughed.

RICHARD: I laughed because it's funny, man. Funny to me. It ain't got nothin' to do with you.

MILTON: Because it didn't happen to you?

RICHARD: No, it's just the insanity of all this that's funny. You understand? And I laugh, and so I'm crazy. I apologize because I don't want to hurt your feelings because I respect what you do—but I don't want to kiss your ass.

By this time, you could see the steam coming out of Milton's ears. He had had more than enough of Richard. He turned to me.

MILTON: . . . If you want to cut here, it's okay with me . . . It would be better because this is a serious situation and I'd rather not discuss it anymore.

We didn't cut and we didn't delete the exchange from the tape. It wasn't so bad to let the audience see, for once, that comedians were human, with fiercely competitive streaks and dark sides to their happy personas. The segment was the talk of the comic circuit for a while. The old veterans thought Uncle Miltie had put the upstart Pryor in his place. The younger comics thought Richard had KO'd Milton. Me? I didn't even mark my scorecard. As far as I was concerned, it was six solid minutes of airtime in the can. Everyone else can spend time analyzing what happened yesterday. I've got another show to do.

*

George Carlin was on our show back in the days when he was still doing the "Hippy-Dippy Weatherman" routine. The audience enjoyed it, but I can remember George being unsatisfied. Backstage, he kept talking about a "new level" of comedy. Frankly, I didn't know what he meant. But I found out one night in Detroit.

George was performing at the Rooster Tail, one of Detroit's top clubs.

George Carlin

I was scheduled for a run of shows there and dropped in a day early to finalize some details and catch George's act. His first set drew only a mediocre response. It was that night, between shows, that the transformation of George Carlin took place. Frustrated with the audience and himself, he returned to the stage with a vengeance. It was like Dr. Jekyll and Mr. Hyde. Disdaining his standard material, George launched into a monologue about the "seven forbidden words." For the time, it was unbelievably bold. I'm still surprised the Detroit police didn't stop the show à la Lenny Bruce. But George not only got away with it, he brought the house down. It was shocking, but shockingly funny as well. A new George Carlin emerged that night. No more suits, no more old-fashioned sketches. After twenty years in the business, George became an overnight sensation, comic crusader for freedom of speech, the freedom to talk dirty on stage.

I look back on that now and wonder. George won that battle, but did he lose the war? Today, he's one of the least vulgar comedians on the scene. He doesn't need to shock, his material scores on a more cerebral level. And he's funnier than ever. Now, he's a Hall of Famer, still out there playing his position, rapping hits every day. I wonder if he's pleased or disturbed by the new herd of comics that stampeded through the door he opened, so steeped in vulgarity, you need a shovel to dig through to the punch lines. Some of these kids use more references to obscure body parts than they do in anatomy class. Seven dirty words? More than a few of them can do a whole set without using seven that aren't. Is George proud of that or does he think he created a monster? I don't know, you'll have to ask George.

*

We had so many funny folks do killer stuff on the show, but there was one comedian who really almost killed me. And I'm not kidding.

I'm not going to mention his name, but he was a regular on the TV-movie-Vegas circuit who had what the Irish call "a wee temper." We had him on several times and never had any problem. One morning before his scheduled appearance, we were rehearsing a skit written especially for him. My guess is that he had been out fairly late the previous night, as he was known to be on occasion, and wasn't feeling his best. But for some reason, he decided he didn't like the skit. I mean, he really didn't like the skit.

Before I knew what was happening, this comic had whipped out a revolver and was pointing it at Woody. My friend and producer just stood there staring, a deer in the headlights. Our guest was complaining loudly about something in the skit, but I don't remember what he said, I was too focused on the gun. I couldn't just stand there and let him shoot Woody (although I've been tempted myself a few times). I looked him in the eye, gently pushed the pistol aside and said very calmly, "Hey buddy, put the gun away. It's too early in the morning to shoot someone."

I wasn't sure that it was a real gun until I felt the cold steel against my hand. I had thought that maybe it was a strange revision to the skit that no one had mentioned to me. No such luck.

Obviously, he didn't shoot me. Otherwise, you would have read a headline about twenty years ago that said, "COMEDIAN SHOOTS MIKE DOUGLAS IN SKIT FEUD" with a sub-headline like "Tells Cops 'Jokes Were Awful': Will Plead Justifiable Homicide." With a good lawyer and some of our worst skits stacked up as evidence, who knows?

The good news is, after I stepped in, the frazzled comic slipped the gun back into his pocket and we went on with the rehearsal as if nothing had happened. We used the skit on the show that day, and it played pretty well, with no changes and no gunplay. There were no apologies afterward. The armed and dangerous guest meekly left the studio with no words said. He never returned as a guest, but not because of any grudge. It's just that there are too many ways to get killed in show business without running the risk of assassination-by-guest.

*

I never tried to top a comic or steal a scene. It worked for me, and seemed to work for the show, just to let myself be putty in their hands. Silly putty. If they needed a straight man, I was there. ("I was in Washington last week." "You were in Washington?") If one of their lines called for a look or a raised eyebrow, I tried to provide it. If a chuckle was called for, I was usually good for one, but I never faked a laugh in twenty-three years. Never had to. I like to think I scored a few times myself, but that was just to keep the momentum going. When you've got the funniest comics in the world sitting next to you, you don't have to worry if anything amusing is going to happen.

Our format lent itself to a range of comic performance inconceivable today. When a performer (especially a comic) knows he only has four minutes to make his mark—well, that's a lot of pressure. We had ninety minutes a day. For a co-host, that meant seven and a half hours of opportunity. Time enough to take an amusing thought and take it as far as it could go. I look at some of the tapes of Billy Crystal and Jerry Lewis, Don Rickles and Shecky Greene, Bill Cosby and Danny Thomas, Bob Newhart and Sid Caesar—amazing, one-of-a-kind performances that would bring them to their feet on Broadway's finest stage.

I was not shy about laughing, but I didn't lose it very often on the show. The circus can't go on if the ringmaster is doubled up in the corner, paralyzed with guffaws, so I knew I had to stay in control. But I have to admit there were a special few who had my number.

I loved all kinds of humor, but for some reason, I could hardly look at Dom DeLuise without falling apart. He knew it, too, and instead of taking pity on me, Dom tortured me every time we tried to get through a skit together. He'd lead me on for half a minute or so, then flash one of those big, round, dimpled grins and I was finished. I couldn't talk. I could hardly breathe. People think he's such a warm, wonderful, cuddly fellow. I swear he was a lot like Woody. He was trying to kill me. Instead of with stunts, he was going to make me laugh myself to death.

*

Jonathan Winters was another one. Automatic hysteria. And when I confess that I couldn't contain myself when Jonathan was around, I know I'm not alone. You could start a Jonathan Winters Anonymous organization and there would be chapters all over the country. I hope you saw the show when we just let him loose on a stageful of random props. It may have been the most uproarious twenty minutes of television ever broadcast.

And I have to tell you a story you didn't get to see. It's no secret that Jonathan Winters was so far out there, his imagination so boundless,

With Dom DeLuise, Dr. Teeth, and Jim Henson

With Jonathan Winters and Dyan Cannon

that he occasionally needed help to maintain a proper perspective between fantasy and reality. Several times, burdened with exhaustion and his own incomparable conceptual genius, Jonathan Winters has checked in to a mental health institution to regroup and recharge his creative batteries.

Gen and I were guests at a party at the home of singer Peggy King that Jonathan was due to attend. It was only days after his discharge from what he himself called "the funny farm." Peggy was a dear friend of Jonathan's and she spent a good deal of time prior to his arrival counseling the other guests. "Whatever you do," Peggy reminded us, "don't say anything about—you know. Not a word." By the time he arrived, everyone was well aware of the subject to avoid. Jonathan walked in, looking happy and refreshed. Before any of the guests could say a word, hostess Peggy, trying to be helpful, welcomed him with a hug and offered a bowl of cashews.

"Nuts?" she said innocently.

Jonathan's face turned to a melodramatic scowl.

"What are you trying to say?"

Silence. Then that Winters giggle—only kidding.

*

With Don Rickles

Don Rickles could do me in, too. I can't explain why I found it so enjoyable to have a little bald man hurl a string of insults at me on my own show, but I sure did. And unlike Dom DeLuise, Rickles was truly heartless. When he had me down on the floor, struggling with spasms of laughter, he would kick me with a few more one-liners.

But there is a side to Don Rickles that I have to tell you about. I'm not trying to ruin his career, but that comic viper you know so well is a big act. Years ago, Don invited Gen and me to a party to celebrate his twenty-fifth anniversary in show business. It was a lavish affair, with people in formal wear, banquets of food, a full orchestra. We were there for about half an hour before it struck me. I leaned over and whispered to Gen, "There aren't any other show people here." I couldn't understand it. A complete mystery. One of the biggest comedy stars in the nation celebrating his career, he could have had hundreds of name performers. Where were they? Finally, I had to ask. Don smiled and put his arm around me. "Mike," he said, "this is a very special night for me, and these are very special people. Everyone here is someone that helped

**With
Groucho Marx**

me when I needed it, someone that made my life better. We can do the show biz thing anytime. Tonight's different. These are people that I love."

I had to walk away. I didn't want Rickles to see me with tears in my eyes.

The Kings of Comedy

Just about everyone I've mentioned is famous for being funny, and if you described several of them as legends, no one would correct you. But there are a few comedians so world-renown for so long that they have become icons. Above all, from the show's first days, those were the guests we wanted. It took a while, sometimes, but we got them. Every one.

All I have to do is wriggle my eyebrows or flick an imaginary cigar or walk like a duck and you know who I'm talking about. Groucho Marx. Is there anyone you would want more than Groucho as a TV guest?

For years, we didn't even try for him. He hardly ever did TV anymore, we had heard he wasn't well, and there was a persistent rumor that, like W.C. Fields, he didn't care for Philadelphia. I finally told the staff we had to try. The worst that he could do was turn us down. As it happened, he jumped at the chance, booked a date on the first phone call. I didn't meet him until show time, and he quickly dispelled the Philly rumor. I asked him straight out.

MIKE: Is it true you don't like Philadelphia?
GROUCHO: Certainly not. I love Philadelphia. It's you I don't like.

We were off to a great start. There are a lot of ways to be funny, and it's a good thing, because if being quick-witted was the only way, everyone else might as well pack up and go home after Groucho. In his seventies, he was still a world-class sprinter as far as wits were concerned. He came on once right after a serious discussion about discrimination. There was no subject he couldn't turn into fodder for laughs, and he jumped on that one. Groucho started off by saying he knew a little about discrimination firsthand. When he first moved to Los Angeles, already a star, his daughter had come home crying from a ritzy country club. They wouldn't let her swim in the pool because she was Jewish.

"So, I wrote them a letter. I explained that I was a Jew but her mother was a Christian. I said, 'Since she's only half Jewish, is it all right if she just goes in up to her waist?'"

*

If you want to talk comic legends, you have to talk about Bob Hope. He started off a song-shtick-and-dance man and ended up a national institution.

Like Garrett Morris used to say on *Saturday Night Live,* "Show business been berry, berry good to Mikey." There's an awful lot I have to be grateful for over the past sixty years, but one of the highest honors of my career is that it gave me a chance to be a friend of Bob Hope.

Did you know he is the most decorated civilian on earth, recipient of more humanitarian awards than anyone else in the world—ever? No one ever did more to elevate comedy to the status of honorable profession and no performer ever contributed more in service to his country and his fellow man.

Did you know that he's also a very nice guy?

The first time I dared to ask Bob Hope to do our show, I could hardly breathe. I was talking to Bob Hope! You know what he said? "Sure, kid, when do you want me?"

He appeared on the show dozens of times and never told the same

With Arnold Palmer, Bob Hope, and Gerald Ford

joke twice. It is said that he has offered his personal catalogue of jokes to the Smithsonian but they had to turn him down. They didn't have room for it.

Being Bob's friend meant a lot more than having him on the show. It meant you could expect a call anytime, day or night, from anywhere in the world. I remember picking up the phone once and hearing that unmistakable voice.

"Hey Mike, how ya doin'?"

"Good, Bob."

"Listen, I'm doing a little charity gig for the flood victims in Baltimore this Friday. Lotta good people. Lotta fun. I need an MC. You doing anything Friday?"

I already knew I was going to be there, but I couldn't help but ask: "Aren't you going to be master of ceremonies?"

"Oh, I'm gonna do my act, but this show's gonna go about three hours and the MC's gonna have to wing it the whole way. I can't do that. That's a special talent. I need you."

What could I say to that?

"When do you want me, Bob?"

There's not much I need to add to all you know about the Comedy Champion of the Century, but I hope you don't mind if I mention one thing. Some younger people might not have seen much of Bob Hope except for his last few variety specials on television. Surprising as it is that he could still do those patented double takes and deadpan smirks in his nineties, the champ had admittedly lost a step since his days as Packy East, fighting for the Cleveland amateur title in World War I days. But I wish you could have seen him at his peak, which lasted over sixty years. His timing was as smooth as Fred Astaire's, and his material, like his credit rating, was always A-1. No one could get more laughs by moving fewer muscles, with the possible exception of Jack Benny.

*

And that brings me to my favorite story about comedians in all the years *of The Mike Douglas Show.*

As you can see by now, we had them all. There wasn't a name comic in the world that hadn't passed before the cameras on our show. Except one. One of the all-time greats. Jack Benny.

Don't think I didn't try. One thing I had to be proud of was that we were like the Mounties. We always got our man. Once we circled a name on a list, we would do what it took, come hell or high water, to put that name on the guest list. We succeeded over ten

Jack Benny

thousand times. But I just couldn't get Jack Benny. He was always courteous, always took my call. It was a kick to just talk to him on the phone. But he always turned me down. "Too busy out west." "Going overseas." "Too much on the schedule." "Maybe sometime when I'm in Philadelphia." "Let me see what I can do a few months from now."

He finally did a few days in New Jersey, just across the water, a short stint in a special performance, and I was not going to be denied. I called him in his dressing room and insisted that he come on the show while he was so close by. He begged off—the schedule was so tight and he had been tired since he arrived. I wasn't about to let him slip through my fingers this time. There had to be something, some hook that would lure him on the show.

"Jack," I said, stalling for time, "you've got to do this because, uh—because our guys put together a bit that will be one of the funniest things you have ever done in your entire career." There was a long, Bennyesque pause on the other end, then Jack responded in the dry monotone that he owned. "I'll be the judge of that."

An opening. One shot to get the great Jack Benny. And reader, I swear to God, I made it up right then and there.

"Okay, Jack, here it is. I'm standing out on Walnut Street in front of the theater at the beginning of the show, pumping up the audience about how excited I am . . . 'one of the biggest guest stars we've ever had is going to be on the show. His limo will be arriving any second and I wanted to be out here to greet him myself . . .'" I finished the pitch in less than a minute. Another long pause.

"I'll be there."

And so it came to pass that Jack Benny made his spectacular debut on *The Mike Douglas Show.*

There I was the next day, opening the show on the sidewalk in front of the main entrance to the studio, looking up the street for that shiny black limo.

"Ladies and gentlemen, one of the most beloved performers in the world will be joining us as a surprise guest today . . . He should be here any moment . . . I think that might be his limousine down the block . . ."

As I looked off in the distance expectantly, a well-worn Philadelphia city bus pulled up and Jack Benny stepped out, counting his change. I stared in surprise, holding the take, while a belly laugh echoed across America.

And you wonder why I loved that show so much.

*

In my next book, I'm going to tell you about George Burns's scrambled eggs, Louis Nye's exchange with Yoko Ono, how the Smothers Brothers used me to blast CBS, Tom Poston's slow double take, Carol Burnett's

Q&A session with my audience, Robert Klein's leg, Moms Mabley and Ralph Nader, two Geraldines with Flip Wilson, Jackie Vernon's rant on waiters, and David Letterman's blooper.

There's so much more. But the men in the white coats are here now and pens aren't allowed beyond the security gate. I've got to stop or I won't get pudding with my dinner.

*

Let me just finish by saying that the fondest memories I have of the show are not of presidents or kings, Oscar winners or music superstars, honored as we were to have them all. In my mind, the very best moments were all punctuated with laughs—uproarious, uncontrollable laughs. We didn't do brain surgery or solve any great problems or find a cure for cancer, but we could put a little dash of humor into homes across the nation, and I think we did. I know we did. I've got the lines on my face to prove it. If laughter is the best medicine, then we were the Mike Douglas Medical Center.

I think back about these wonderfully funny people all the time, and I'm reminded of a saying I took to heart long ago. "What you are is God's gift to you, what you make of yourself is your gift to God." A sense of humor is a gift. You can't learn it. You can't buy it. You can't work out in a comedy gym until your funny muscles shape up. It's a gift.

If God has a sense of humor, and I firmly believe he does, he has some very generous people on this planet. And I've been lucky enough to share laughs with the best of them.

4

Inside Hollywood

With Your Host, Mike Douglas

Ann-Margret * Fred Astaire * Lauren Bacall * Jacqueline Bisset
Marlon Brando * James Cagney * Michael Caine * Dyan Cannon
Frank Capra * John Cassavetes * Carol Channing * Paddy
Chayevsky * Joan Collins * Jackie Cooper * Francis Ford Coppola
Joan Crawford * Bing Crosby * Jamie Lee Curtis * Tony Curtis
Bette Davis * Robert De Niro * Bo Derek * Angie Dickinson *
Marlene Dietrich * Kirk Douglas * Michael Douglas * Richard Drey-
fuss * Faye Dunaway * Robert Duvall * Clint Eastwood * Linda
Evans * Peter Falk * Mia Farrow * Farrah Fawcett * Rhonda
Fleming * Henry Fonda * Jane Fonda * Joan Fontaine * Jodie
Foster * Harrison Ford * Judy Garland * Greer Garson * Jeff
Goldblum * Linda Gray * Pam Grier * Gene Hackman * Margaret
Hamilton * Richard Harris * Laurence Harvey * Goldie Hawn *
Sterling Hayden * Helen Hayes * Margaux Hemingway * Charlton
Heston * Dustin Hoffman * William Holden * Anthony Hopkins
Rock Hudson * John Huston * Lauren Hutton * Anne Jackson
Glenda Jackson * Ben Johnson * Van Johnson * James Earl Jones

Diane Keaton ✳ Gene Kelly ✳ Grace Kelly ✳ Deborah Kerr ✳ Stanley Kramer ✳ Cheryl Ladd ✳ Hedy Lamarr ✳ Dorothy Lamour ✳ Burt Lancaster ✳ Martin Landau ✳ Jessica Lange ✳ Lassie ✳ Peter Lawford ✳ Janet Leigh ✳ Jack Lemmon ✳ Joseph E. Levine ✳ Jerry Lewis ✳ Virna Lisi ✳ Sondra Locke ✳ Gina Lollabrigida ✳ Sophia Loren ✳ Karl Malden ✳ Jayne Mansfield ✳ Andrea Marcovicci ✳ Walter Matthau ✳ Melina Mercouri ✳ Robert Mitchum ✳ Paul Newman ✳ Jack Nicholson ✳ David Niven ✳ Nick Nolte ✳ Jennifer O'Neill ✳ Jack Palance ✳ Gordon Parks ✳ Walter Pidgeon ✳ Sidney Poitier ✳ Otto Preminger ✳ Priscilla Presley ✳ Robert Preston ✳ Vincent Price ✳ Anthony Quinn ✳ Vanessa Redgrave ✳ Rob Reiner ✳ Burt Reynolds ✳ Debbie Reynolds ✳ Ginger Rogers ✳ Cesar Romero ✳ Mickey Rooney ✳ Jane Russell ✳ Eva Marie Saint ✳ Susan Sarandon ✳ Roy Scheider ✳ Maximilian Schell ✳ Arnold Schwarzenegger ✳ George C. Scott ✳ Lizabeth Scott ✳ Peter Sellers Omar Sharif ✳ Martin Sheen ✳ Cybill Shepherd ✳ Brooke Shields Jean Simmons ✳ Elke Sommer ✳ Sylvester Stallone ✳ Blaze Starr Rod Steiger ✳ Jimmy Stewart ✳ Ben Stiller ✳ Jill St. John ✳ Gloria Swanson ✳ Robert Taylor ✳ Gene Tierney ✳ John Travolta ✳ Lana Turner ✳ Liv Ullman ✳ Peter Ustinov ✳ Jon Voight ✳ Max Von Sydow ✳ Robert Wagner ✳ Eli Wallach ✳ Jack Warden ✳ Lesley Anne Warren ✳ John Wayne ✳ Raquel Welch ✳ Esther Williams Shelley Winters ✳ Natalie Wood ✳ James Woods ✳ Joanne Woodward ✳ Jane Wyman ✳ Susannah York ✳ Robert Young

IN my mind, one of the most telling analogies is that between actors and horses. Some people in Hollywood might resent that, and some people in Kentucky might resent it even more, but I don't think either group should be offended.

We're all actors of sorts. No matter what age or station in life, we spend a fair amount of time role-playing, reciting lines, and appearing in scenes of our own making. But the great actors are a breed apart, most like thoroughbreds. They are magnificent creatures, impossibly talented and captivating to watch, but they can be skittish and temperamental, not to mention expensive to keep in oats or caviar, as the case may be.

The volatile nature of many famous actors is not so hard to figure. Over the years, the line between the memorable characters they've played on screen and their personal lives becomes blurred. The perception of who they are is clouded by the impression of who they pretend to be. It can make for a disconcerting private life, if they have much of a private life at all. No wonder that they are hesitant to appear as themselves, wary of any forum that provides no concealing mask, strips them of what they do best and still asks them to perform.

The Mike Douglas Show afforded little comfort to these performers. No director to guide them, no writer to furnish witty lines of dialogue, only a bare stage, a chair, a microphone, and me. Some of those who had delivered bravura performances on Broadway or starred in movies seen by millions welcomed the chance to star as themselves for twenty minutes on national television. Others recoiled at the thought.

As far as the talent level, I think you'll find *The Mike Douglas Show* was hard to beat when it came to the credentials of the actors and actresses we featured. I don't know the final tally, but when we tried to add them up once, around 1980, we figured the performers appearing on our show had won over two thousand Academy Awards, Emmys, and Tonys. Among them, they had portrayed virtually every famous fictional character imaginable. The trick was to get them to play the most difficult role of all. Themselves.

*

Some could jump right in, absolutely fearless. Right after his career performance as General George Patton, George C. Scott paid us a visit. It was that time in his life when the world was paying due homage to his formidable talents and the vast accomplishments of his career. He had been showered with awards and testimonials from all sides for many months, including the Oscar for Best Actor, and we felt it would be a little redundant to simply continue the parade of accolades, so we reversed that. It was a concept that worked well on the show many times over— if the unanimous direction is one way, go the other.

We asked George if he would mind having some fun with his impeccable image as America's finest dramatic actor. What do they say nowdays?—George got game.

We told the audience that George C. Scott would do a dramatic reading on the show that day and they were thrilled. In the setup, I explained that George was a fan of some of the great contemporary composers, and that he had found deep meaning in some of the modern songs. He had opted to lend his talents to a reading of selected lyrics by acclaimed composer Burt Bacharach.

The lights dimmed, drums rolled, and there was George C. Scott, reading "Raindrops Keep Fallin' on My Head." His voice and his presence are so powerful, the audience didn't get the joke for a while. Right through the first stanza, they were on the edge of their seats, listening with deep respect as the great thespian intoned:

Raindrops keep fallin' on my head . . .
Crying's not for me . . .

It wasn't until the rain started that we heard a few guffaws. We set up a little sprinkler over George. As he proceeded, the occasional drops turned to a shower, then a driving rain, and finally a drenching downpour. By the end of the reading, he was soaked. George never blinked, never wavered, and finished the reading without cracking a smile. With apologies to Patton fans everywhere, it was, for me, his finest performance.

George C. Scott

Some of the legendary performers didn't appreciate our antics with as much aplomb as George C. Scott. In the early years of his career, Dustin Hoffman joined us for a day. It was already obvious from *The Graduate* and *Little Big Man* that he was not only a superb actor, but he had a wonderful sense of humor as well. We ran with that. Dustin was given a script we borrowed from a CBS soap opera and set up to play the romantic lead in a series of brief scenes that featured women from our audience. It was a hoot. The "leading ladies" ranged from giggly to

*With
Dustin
Hoffman*

surprisingly good, and the bit worked like magic. Dustin played his part well and came off like a great sport and a very funny young man. In my mind, it was a win-win. We got a great show out of it and Dustin Hoffman looked good doing it.

I guess Dustin didn't see it that way. When we contacted his agent to have him back a year later, we got a curt no. Six months later, the same thing. Another year, another rejection, and I finally inquired—"was it something I said?" The answer came back, as a matter of fact, yes. Dustin Hoffman was deeply offended by the embarrassing stunt we pulled, hated the setup, felt it was demeaning to his stature as an actor, and had no interest in appearing on the show ever again. Wow. Little did I know. And this was the guy who went on to win acclaim for wearing a dress and falsies in *Tootsie,* a soap opera movie. We didn't even ask him to change out of his street clothes.

Oh, well. I'm sorry he was offended. In the meantime, it didn't deter us one bit from putting actors in stranger scenes than anything Shakespeare ever created.

*

One of the greatest actors of all time and supposedly one of the most difficult was Marlon Brando. After enough years, enough thousands of shows, there were few names on the guest list that really got my adrenaline flowing. Marlon Brando. There's one. Getting a chance to meet the man I considered perhaps the finest actor of our time, and then have him come on the show for a rare interview—if I wasn't the host, I guarantee you I'd be watching that day.

Marlon was hardly a regular guest on television. Every show on the air had tried and failed to lure him into an appearance. He even passed up accepting his Oscar for *The Godfather,* sending a Native American surrogate to accept for him while he went out to dinner.

How did we manage to get him? Easy. He called us. Another one of those phone calls.

"Mr. Douglas, Marlon Brando's on the phone . . . I think it's really him."

"Lynn, everyone does Brando. How would you know?"

"He's not doing the Godfather. He's just doing . . . Brando."

It was the real Marlon Brando all right. He said he liked our show and he wanted to appear on it. He would like to be on the air for exactly twenty-eight minutes. (Okay, Marlon, I'll bring a stopwatch.) We set a date right there on the phone.

I spent many hours preparing Marlon Brando questions. I researched his career, talked to some old friends and co-stars, even rehearsed some questions with Gen (who doesn't look a bit like Marlon, but can do a passable Godfather imitation). I never spent that much time and effort preparing an interview—I never had time—but there was so much I wanted to ask this man, I wasn't about to let the opportunity slip through my fingers.

When we contacted him the week before the scheduled show, complications set in. He had made a commitment to appear, he would appear, but he only wanted to discuss the plight of the American Indians. Nothing else.

Ouch. So much for my research. No career stuff? No *Godfather?* No *On the Waterfront?* No *Streetcar Named Desire?* Concern for Native Americans was a worthy subject and we welcomed his thoughts, but this was Brando, not Russell Means. What I wanted to hear about, what the nation wanted to hear about, was his acting and Marlon himself.

Marlon, can we talk?

No.

That's when our staff went to work. I asked if we could possibly book Francis Ford Coppola as a guest on the same show. They did, just like that, which gave me the reason I needed to call Francis and explain my plight. Could he talk to his good friend Marlon?

No.

Francis sympathized with me, but he knew Brando well and assured me that wasn't the way. If he tried to intercede, it would only make him more intransigent. Francis had a better idea.

"Just ask me the questions."

"What?"

"Just ask me the questions you want to ask him."

I wasn't sure where he was going with that, since they could only be answered by Marlon himself, but I had faith in Francis. I hoped he knew what he was talking about because Marlon's people cautioned me again the morning of the show—he's here to talk about (always the same exact words) "the plight of Native Americans"—and nothing else. If you ask him other questions, he'll walk.

After the perfunctory introductions and the anticipated ovation, we got down to business. At first, Marlon was about as talkative as Marcel Marceau. I went right to Francis for the rescue. After some talk about *The Godfather,* I headed down the Brando path. Focused on Francis, I asked him about some of the actors he had worked with. Francis responded, always citing "one actor" as an example. We worked our way to specifics. One caught Marlon's attention.

"Is it true, Francis, that one actor even put on a lot of weight to give a more realistic portrayal in one of your most successful films?"

Francis started to answer, but—surprise!—Marlon suddenly jumped in. No, that's not right—he insisted he didn't mean to do it, it was Coppola's fault.

MARLON: Francis is a wonderful cook, you know. He made me the pig I am.

The audience laughed. Brando smiled. The ice was broken. From then on, Francis was no longer needed as intermediary. I was one-on-one with Marlon Brando.

MIKE: Marlon, the story is that you wanted to play the role of the Godfather so much, you auditioned it for it. Did you have a sense this would be one of the immortal screen characters?

With Marlon Brando

MARLON: No, no, no. I had no frame of reference for playing a sixty-five-year-old Italian.

MIKE: Why did you take the part?

MARLON: I hadn't worked in a year and a half and I needed the money.

On his acting method, he finally explained his famous habit of neglecting to memorize his lines, forcing directors to have them written on the walls, the floor, the furniture, anywhere on the set not visible to the camera.

"You don't know what you're going to say next in real life. You have to think about it. You don't know anything about what's coming next in real life . . . I'm like the audience. I want to be surprised."

He was expansive about his career, his co-stars, Tahiti. He was good. So honest. One hundred percent Brando. We took a break, then spent one full segment on "the plight of Native Americans." He was and is a compassionate spokesman for that cause.

But here's the point, and it's *the* point of a show like ours—I believe people listened more closely to his message because they were more sympathetic, because they had gotten to know Marlon Brando a little bit. After fifteen minutes, they were thinking, "This Marlon Brando's all right, now let's hear what he has to say about Indians." It worked out better for all of us.

*

Marlon Brando appeared for exactly twenty-eight minutes. He appeared for nine minutes in the movie *Superman*. The producers paid him ten million dollars. We paid him four hundred and eighty-five dollars. Excuse me for that interruption, but there are some fun facts about *The Mike Douglas Show* that I get a kick out of.

*

Some of the great ones aren't difficult or uncooperative, they're just not very comfortable in front of a camera in their own skin. That's my theory of the "uneasy actor syndrome." Instead of just being themselves, they try to play themselves and fumble for the next line of dialogue.

I remember when we scored a real coup, a finesse that worked exactly as we had hoped, then backfired in our faces. We booked Diahnne Abbott for the show. She was a talented stage actress but not well known beyond theatrical circles. She was also the wife of Robert De Niro and that had more than a little to do with the booking. We hoped our ploy would endear the show to De Niro, one of the few stars never, ever seen on television, and maybe, down the road, who knows? Better yet, we hoped De Niro might accompany his bride to the taping and we could snag him for an impromptu guest shot right then and there.

I didn't know until I walked out on stage how clever we had been. One of the amazing things about De Niro is the contrast between his powerful screen presence and his real-life appearance. It's an anomaly I can't explain. All the other great ones I can think of are the opposite. Brando is overpowering on screen and just as overpowering off—an unmistakable presence. Far from any stage, when Frank Sinatra walks in a room, the temperature goes up, all eyes turn and hearts flutter. Cary Grant, Paul Newman, Clint Eastwood, Stallone, Pacino, Schwarzenegger—whether they're at the Academy Awards or stopping at the corner deli for a ham sandwich, the electricity never turns off. That larger-than-life charisma is always with them.

Not De Niro. He has this ability to flick the switch. In a crowded room, he's almost invisible.

I started my opening monologue and noticed a man in the second row who looked a little like De Niro. Strange coincidence, I thought, but it couldn't be him. Someone would have said something to me. I glanced over a few minutes later. Hey, wait a minute—that's Robert De Niro. Couldn't be. Even the people sitting right next to him had no clue. I edged a little closer and risked a stare. Robert De Niro, all right. We had caught the big fish just like we hoped and didn't even know he was in the boat.

At the first break, I told Ernie DiMassa, one of the show's producers, "DeNiro's sitting in the second row!" We huddled briefly and decided to go for it cold. During the next segment, I announced that a very special guest was in the audience. Ladies and gentlemen, Mr. Robert De Niro!

There was no chance for escape. The cameras turned. He stood, a little awkward, and acknowledged the applause. With the hook firmly set, I reeled him in. Robert, please—come on up and join us for a minute.

I could see he'd rather be at the dentist getting a root canal. He shrugged and edged toward the stage with a self-conscious grin.

Here it was at last, a rare chance to interview the elusive Robert De Niro. And how did it go, you ask?

Terrible. One of my worst interviews. Not that I didn't try, nor was Robert unresponsive. I gave it my best and so did he, I think, but it just didn't happen. It was as if I was talking to a friend of Robert De Niro who knew him, but not that well. There was no insight, no depth. After a few minutes, I simply gave up. The interview wasn't going anywhere,

With Robert De Niro

why prolong the agony? I came away disappointed, but my respect for Robert De Niro was undiminished. He is a peerless actor, but he has no desire and maybe no ability to dissect his craftsmanship in public. It isn't ego or conceit, only the reality that his acting artistry speaks for itself. Others can talk about it all they want, but he has nothing more to say on the subject. Any comment would be redundant.

It reminded me of the cryptic line he delivered to John Cazale in *The Deer Hunter* while holding a bullet up in front of his face: "This is this!"

End of discussion.

*

Robert De Niro wasn't my only failure when it came to interviewing actors. Richard Dreyfuss was quick and self-deprecating, but nervous as a cat and I couldn't get him to loosen up.

Vanessa Redgrave was wary of me, cautious with every word. I felt that if I could find the right key, she would expound on a wide range of subjects she cared about deeply. I couldn't find it.

James Woods was too enthusiastic. It happens. There's a balance between being accessible and being too eager to please. The audience doesn't want an actor to be a comedian or a comedian to be a political analyst.

Brigitte Bardot was sweet and beautiful, but painfully shy, and had one insurmountable problem. She really couldn't speak English. You remember her speaking adequate English with a strong French accent, but that was in the movies, lines she memorized. In conversation, her English is hardly recognizable and she can't comprehend questions in English very well. There's nothing wrong with that, but I don't speak French.

Harrison Ford speaks perfect English but he really doesn't care for interviews, he suffers through them.

Brigitte Bardot

With
Harrison Ford

It's part of his job and he fulfills the obligation, but he doesn't like it. You can tell. His chin goes down to his chest and he talks just above a whisper. According to the box office tally, he's the most successful movie actor in history, and there's so much people want to hear from him, but it's not going to happen. Off screen, he's a very down-to-earth and very private man and he doesn't like talking about himself on TV. The only time I got him to perk up and laugh was when I mentioned the rumor that he absolutely hated to do television interviews.

Rod Steiger is also a shy and private man, but he takes the opposite approach. He doesn't enjoy TV interviews either, but instead of whispering, he shouts. He has that projecting theater voice and he summons it for interviews as well. You open with, "How are you, Rod?" and he says, "Fine, thank you very much!" and it reverberates off the walls of the studio.

Warren Beatty is another one. He's hardly shy but he is never going to let his guard down on television. I liked Warren from the first time I met him. He's a pleasant and articulate gentleman. We always got along well, but I never got a great interview out of him. He laughed when I told him that and said, "You never will." I kind of admire him for that. He knows what the audience wants to hear about and the answer is no.

But the all-time worst actor interview I ever suffered through was Jack Palance. He's kind of a scary guy to begin with and I had my doubts that he would be the gregarious sort in a casual interview. It didn't take more than a minute for it to become very clear he would not.

To each of my first seven questions he responded with one-word answers. Yes. No. No. No. Yes. No. No.

He didn't smile, didn't frown, just sat there with the same iceberg expression on his face while I envisioned the entire show sinking like the *Titanic*. There were eighty-seven minutes left and I was dead in the water. Nice to have you with us, Jack, and will somebody please throw me a life preserver?

There was a long, uncomfortable silence after his last monosyllable. I gave up. I finally turned to him and said, "Are you putting me on?"

His eyes lit up, he burst into that throaty, he-man laugh and said, "Yes!"

That darn Woody had rigged the whole bit, conspired with Jack to leave me twisting in the wind. Add that to the laundry list of paybacks I owe my sadistic producer. But I have to admit, the relief at realizing it was a joke and we could move on with a show that wasn't DOA was exquisite. In fact, Jack Palance proved to be a funny and charming guest and we had him back for many encores. He showed a playful side that belied his granite-like countenance and joined the ranks of our Most Pleasant Surprises. Years later, he made my day when he told me that he believed his out-of-character appearances on our show opened the door to his being cast in his Academy Award–winning role in the hit comedy *City Slickers*.

*

Richard Harris was another happy surprise. I was warned he could be rowdy and troublesome. Nothing but a gentleman, and nothing but the best storyteller, always Irish, always allegedly true, always with himself playing the fool.

He told us of the time he had rented a car in Ireland, but it was a model he was unfamiliar with and a stick shift that he never quite mastered. He was stopped at a light one time and couldn't get the thing back in gear. The light changed several times while he struggled with it. Finally, an Irishman climbed out of the car behind him, sauntered up, and stuck his head in the window.

"Excuse me for askin', but was it a particular shade of green you were waitin' for?"

With Richard's talent for dialect, his anecdotes were irresistible, and he had hundreds of them. Richard also took full advantage of our standard offer to co-hosts to add their own choices to the guest list. He often turned the show into an excuse for his drinking companions to join him, first on the air, then in the nearest Philadelphia pub.

*

The Men of Hollywood were great, but the Women of Hollywood. Oh. Sometimes I really did have to sit back for a moment and say to myself, "What a great job this is."

I hope it doesn't shock you to learn that we intentionally sought out beautiful women. It wasn't me, but the Television Rule Book mandates that entertainment shows must average no fewer than one beautiful woman every 17.5 minutes or risk being expelled from the airwaves. We tried our best to maintain the standards.

*

Sometimes beauty is only skin deep and sometimes it runs right through to the bone. Let's start with an easy one. Princess Grace of Monaco.

Already hailed as one of most alluring of women in her Hollywood days, Grace Kelly didn't just marry into royalty when she became Princess of Monaco, she assumed the throne as the world's most enviable beauty. She had it all—what a face, what class, what presence, what a castle! You would think that she would be unapproachable. It's got to be difficult to let your hair down when people bow every time you walk into a room. Well, she did with us, and we didn't start it, she did.

We did a week with the royal family in Monaco, but we never expected the royal treatment we received. The first night, Princess Grace stopped by for a visit. No entourage, just Grace. She just wanted to talk. The conversation soon turned to the kids, and she was surprisingly candid. Princess Stephanie wasn't even a teen yet and Grace was concerned about her moving too fast into the blue blood, European fast lane. Gen mentioned that she was worried about our little Kelly getting too much attention in Philadelphia because of the high-profile TV show. That opened the gates. It was something to see, Princess Grace of Monaco and my Gen, talking like neighbors over the back fence.

Even on the air, it wasn't hard to penetrate that royal shield. We had been told that she did not talk about her Hollywood days and we shouldn't start. I got the feeling it was a sensitive subject with Prince Rainier. But it came up anyhow, accidentally on purpose, when we were

With Princess Grace

discussing her children. I asked an obvious question. "Don't your children see your films on late night television?"

Yes, they did! And they asked a million questions about her co-stars, locations, and making movies. That led to Hitchcock, Cary Grant, Gary Cooper, and all the rest. That's what our audience wanted to hear and she was happy to oblige. What a fairy-tale life and a real princess of a lady.

*

In my book, Sophia Loren is royalty, too. A delightful woman. She wore her beauty like a comfortable old dress, something she just threw on and gave no thought to. I liked her story of her agent's absolute insistence that she never wear her glasses in public. It was totally contrary to her image and she must never, never do it.

"I always wear them," she said. "I never knew how much I couldn't see! I love them. I wouldn't go anywhere without them. My agent? He's a man. He talks, I don't listen."

One of my fondest memories is sitting in the kitchen of my own home in Beverly Hills, watching Sophia Loren at work over a hot stove. I felt like Marcello Mastroianni. We invited her over and she insisted on making dinner. She cooked Italian style, of course—a little of this, a dash of that, take a taste, add a pinch of this. She was so at home and so appealing, we filmed the whole thing and used it on the show. And the dinner? Magnifico!

*

I'm making this sound too easy. Not every beauty was such a joy to have on the show. Sometimes it's impossible to scratch that perfect veneer and get beneath the surface. And sometimes, Beauty comes with the Beast.

Bo Derek came on the show shortly after her splash as the perfect "10." The claims to perfection were not exaggerated. I can't think of anything that needed improvement. If 10 was the highest possible number, they could probably have called the movie "11." That wasn't the problem. The other side of the Derek coin was her husband, John.

John Derek was a good-looking guy who had been a successful actor but seemed to have transformed himself into some sort of Svengali for gorgeous women. I don't know what his job description was exactly, but if you put it in the want ads, you could have filled Yankee Stadium with hopeful respondents. His last three wives, in quick succession, were Ursula Andress, Linda Evans, and Bo Derek. Ursula, Linda, and Bo . . . oh, my.

Bo was very young, very sweet, and very innocent, and was the

*With
Sophia Loren*

hottest young beauty in the business. So, my only question was, what the heck was John Derek so crabby about?

He agreed to come on the show with Bo just as they were releasing her *Tarzan the Ape Man* movie. I guess John was in control of the picture and that may have been what put him in such a mood. It's hard to believe you could make an unwatchable film starring Bo Derek, but *Tarzan* came close. It was obvious that they had come to the conclusion that the only way to sell tickets was to play up the steamy side, Tarzan and Bo romping in the jungle. To that end, John had brought along a film clip for our audience's viewing pleasure. We previewed it before the show. It was the early 1980s and television had come a long way, but not that far. John Derek had a film clip that would make Larry Flynt blush. I was embarrassed to watch it with Bo in the room. There was no way to show it. If we edited the objectionable parts, there would be nothing left.

John Derek was furious. He insisted we show the clip. I told him it was impossible. He demanded to know who he could call at Westinghouse to get me overruled. This was John Derek, after all, he didn't have to put up with this. Someone explained that it was *The Mike Douglas Show*. Westinghouse could help him with electricity or lighting prob-

With Bo Derek

lems, but there wasn't anyone there with veto power over the show. He threatened to take a walk. Okay, see you later. He threatened to walk and take Bo with him. Not as easy a goodbye, but goodbye just the same. When he realized we wouldn't budge, he backed down and the show went on. Bo and John appeared as scheduled. The program went without a hitch, but we didn't show one frame of *Tarzan the Ape Man*.

Afterward, John let us know he would never do the show again. But that decision had already been made. On that particular program, Me Tarzan.

*

Bo Derek wasn't our only beautiful problem. When we took the show to London, we went out of our way to book Joan Collins. The actress had made a big splash on the big screen when she was still barely out of her teens, appearing opposite such stars as Gregory Peck and Bette Davis. That had been some twenty years earlier, however, and most recently her film career had stalled somewhat. Still, she was a ravishingly beautiful woman, and was reputed to be lively and outspoken. The hook for her appearance was a British-made film called *The Stud*, based on the novel by Joan's best-selling sister, Jackie Collins. Joan's appearance in some of the movie's steamy scenes had propelled the modestly budgeted feature to big box office in Europe and had launched a career comeback for Joan. The film sounded like a hot topic, and we figured she would be an exciting guest. The staff went to a good deal of effort to locate her in Europe. She readily agreed to do the show and never mentioned any restrictions on what she would talk about—until she arrived. It was only then that she insisted she would not discuss *The Stud*.

"Wait a second, Joan," I said. "Isn't this your hit movie? Haven't you been promoting it all over Europe for the past year?" What's wrong with this picture, I thought.

The problem was, she didn't want talk of *The Stud* to "discolor her American image." The movie had not been released in the States. If it ever was, the plan was to reduce it to a much tamer version. The plan reminded me of the old days in pictures when certain films would have a "U.S. cut" and a "European cut," as though movies were beef to be divvied up into hamburger and filet mignon, depending on the neighborhood in which it was to be marketed.

I wouldn't buy it, and I told Joan I *had* to ask about the film. She finally conceded the issue, and I have to give her credit—once she came around, she didn't hold anything back. Joan proved to be a great guest, a very entertaining lady, and so very lovely. Her enticing talk about *The Stud* provoked quite a response. Soon thereafter distributors closed a deal to release the movie in the U.S., and Joan made the rounds of other shows to promote it. Charming her way back into the American public eye, she was suddenly in great demand again, and soon after, she emerged a major TV star as lovable, despicable Alexis Carrington, the classic vixen on *Dynasty,* playing opposite "good girl" Linda Evans. I'm just surprised John Derek never married Joan as well.

Joan Collins

*

Sometimes, beauty wraps a surprise package. Andrea Marcovicci was emerging in movies and on television when we first met her. We planned to talk about her acting but she asked if we would let her sing. We did, and she had a wonderful voice. We invited her back just to sing, never mind the movie talk. Her second career blossomed. Today, Andrea is a fine actress in far greater demand as a show-stopping vocalist.

*

Sometimes beauty is hardly wrapped at all. In the 1960s and early 1970s, there were new ideas about fashion. Only a few years before, no woman would be caught with her slip showing. In the Age of Aquarius, it was nothing to go on TV wearing just a slip. Oh, the times they were a-changin'.

As the 1960s marched into the 1970s, the dress code for women seemed to evaporate along with a large portion of their wardrobes. Skirts turned into minis, then micros. Blouses went from cotton to sheer to see-through. One day, we had Paula Prentiss and actor-husband Richard Benjamin on the show. Paula was a fun guest with a refreshingly casual attitude that included a carefree dress style. That day, she was wearing one of those thin, cotton T-shirts that were in vogue. You could read a map right through it and her personal topography was quite evident, but I shrugged it off. I didn't control ladies' fashion and I didn't tell guests what to wear.

The day after the show aired, I got a call from Jackie Gleason. He was beside himself. How could I allow a woman to dress like that on my show? Why don't I go get a purple suit and a high-finned Cadillac and open for business on the side? Little kids are watching after school and I'm giving them a lesson in pandering. He huffed and puffed and hung up the phone.

I was a little confused at first. We were on tape delay then, and the shows were on the air about two weeks after completion. Gleason kept talking about "that woman" and "yesterday" and we had just finished taping with Betty White as co-host. She's an attractive lady, but I couldn't imagine anything she had worn that would raise Jackie's ire. Her sexiest outfit was a blue blazer with a turtleneck sweater.

I finally figured out what the Great One was talking about. He may have been overreacting—he did that sometimes—but his point hit home. We were a very popular family show, and some responsibility came along with that. Never mind the fads of the day, it was our job to deliver a show that didn't violate the trust that people placed in us. If we couldn't get ratings with interesting guests, good talk, and creative entertainment, we didn't belong on the air. For the duration of the show, we maintained an informal code of good conduct. On very rare occasions, we let certain guests know: we don't do that, we don't say that, we don't wear that. It may not have helped the ratings, but it didn't hurt. We stayed number one for another ten years. Plus, there was one added bonus. When I get up in the mornings, I can still look at myself in the mirror.

*

Don't get me wrong. There's no getting around the fact that television is a visual medium and one of the most joyful sights in the world is a beautiful woman. If I had a nickel for every beauty we had on the show, I'd be richer than Bill Gates. In fact, there was such a plethora of beauty available to us that we decided to really go with it one time and dedicated an entire week to nothing but gorgeous women. Some people think I had it easy, but that week was a rough one. One after another after another. Elke Sommer, Cybill Shepherd, Linda Evans, Lauren Hutton, the Golddiggers, Jayne Kennedy, Miss Americas, Miss Universes, Virna Lisi, Angie Dickinson, Pam Grier, Susan Sarandon, Charlie's Angels—what am I complaining about? Try it sometime. That kind of guest lineup makes it hard to think. And how many times in one week can you say "Wow!" Oh, the things I had to go through.

*

There was only one topic that several of the most famous and loveliest women we had on the show absolutely refused to discuss on the air. I never kept an exact count, but as I go over the lists, I know of at least ten female guests who raised the issue in preshow discussions, and all said almost the same exact words.

"Please don't mention Frank Sinatra."

"Mike, please don't ask about Frank."

"You're not going to ask me anything about Sinatra, are you?"

"Let's not talk about Frank."

"For God's sake, don't say anything about Sinatra."

I'm not Mr. Blackwell, so I'm not going to give you the list, but I will tell you one of them was Mia Farrow. She was so delightful. She couldn't have been twenty when we had her on and looked about fourteen. She was already a star herself in both TV and films and we had lots of subject matter without getting into Old Blue Eyes, but it was right at the time when their romance was the hottest twosome topic since Burton and Taylor and I knew what people wanted more than anything else was some firsthand Frank stories from his new love.

I'm going to let you down here again, reader. Barbara Walters, Geraldo Rivera, and a platoon of other hosts would have put it right to her and probably gotten some good stuff on Frank. I didn't do that. I admit that the "nice" label cost us sometimes, reducing some shows from outstanding to good, but that was the price we paid. Mia Farrow's innocence wasn't an act. She had this vulnerable quality about her and if talking about Frank was going to hurt her feelings, I wouldn't do it. Let somebody else get the skinny on Frank. I wasn't about to make Mia Farrow cry.

*

Among my favorite guests were the ladies who knew everything there was to know about Tinseltown and had seen most of it firsthand. Bette Davis, Joan Crawford, Hedy Lamarr, Gene Tierney, Dorothy Lamour, Olivia de Havilland, Gloria Swanson, Joan Fontaine, Rhonda Fleming— the *grand dames* of the Golden Age of Hollywood, and they shared an abundance of something sorely lacking in postmodern show business: class. So gracious, so elegant, so comfortable with who they were, they

With Bette Davis

rarely came to pitch or promote, just talk, reminisce with the nation about the best of days gone by. For me, that was Hollywood.

Joan Crawford was an ideal guest. A lovely lady with fascinating stories. After several appearances, she was comfortable enough to bring along her daughter, Christina, an aspiring actress. It was another good show, with lots of happy family talk. Years later, that prompted me to give a guest a pretty rough time for one of the very few times in my entire career when Christina Crawford was scheduled to promote her tell-all book about her mother. *Mommie Dearest* was not just a major best-seller, it was an unpleasant breakthrough in publishing, precipitating an avalanche of sordid family exposés. I only knew Joan Crawford from the movies and her appearances on the show, but I didn't like the book. I'm old school enough to still believe in family loyalty and the value of discretion when it comes to dirty laundry. (I hope you're listening to this, kids.)

I remembered Christina's appearance ten years before, when her mother tried to give her career a boost. Now, she was back with a vengeance and the horror story of a mother from hell.

Still, I had no intention of grilling Christina. I told you what I felt about a host's role. I was confident the audience would make its own judgments about *Mommie Dearest*. But something happened just before the show that changed all that. One of our staff handed me a letter from

Joan Crawford

Christina's sister. It began by explaining that she had just learned Christina was booked for the show. She was mortified that her mother would be disparaged before a huge audience without rebuttal. She said it wasn't fair. She added a list of errors, distortions, and exaggerations in the book, page by page, and begged me to present them to Christina on the air. I wavered, but it seemed fair enough to raise questions of fact from the only other person who knew the story firsthand. I finally decided to use some of the letter.

After introducing Christina and getting an overview of the book, I took out the letter, told her what it was about, and asked if she would mind if we discussed some of the points her sister raised. To Christina's credit, she took a deep breath and braced herself for the storm.

You could hear the rustling as the studio audience shifted, listening close. Christina could dish it out. Now we were going to find out if she could take it. I read verbatim from the letter.

It was tense. She took some hits, but I have to say Christina acquitted herself fairly well in the face of heavy fire. Regardless, I didn't feel good about it afterward. It may have been fair enough considering the tone of her tattletale book, but I had a bad taste in my mouth. This was *The Mike Douglas Show*, not *60 Minutes*. That was the last time I ever put a guest under the hammer.

*

There was one aspect of old Hollywood that is an endangered species today, but it was perfect for TV. The musicals. The musical stars were triple-threat performers, stars who could sing and dance as well as talk. There is no better guest.

Hollywood's best song-and-dance man ever? Has to be either Fred Astaire or Gene Kelly. Fred Astaire was effortlessly elegant, graceful as a cat, while Gene had that wonderful exuberance and athleticism. We managed to book them together for a week as double co-hosts.

Fred Astaire looked like he just strolled out and tripped into those spectacular routines, but we learned in rehearsals that they were anything but spontaneous. He was a methodical perfectionist with every single step: over and over, every gesture studiously executed. Remember, this was 1976, and that's how old Fred was then—seventy-six—and he worked for hours every day, sometimes just on eight or ten steps. What an honor to watch him work.

That week was one of the great memories, but it wasn't without traumatic moments. One of our co-stars took a walk on Tuesday and wasn't coming back.

Fred Astaire and Gene Kelly. Together at last. What a great idea. Except we never thought of the egos put in play when you create that kind of dynamic on television. Fred and Gene were friends, and they had great respect for each other. Both also had a lot of pride in their work and reputation. A couple steps into the first show, I started to realize this could turn into a kind of song-and-dance man's Battle of the Bands, and we really didn't intend for that to happen.

After what I thought was a great show Tuesday, with both of them dazzling the audience with steps and stories, Fred's agent quietly asked me to spend a few minutes with the great star in his dressing room. I knew it was trouble because the messenger was an agent. If it's good news, a star will always call you one-on-one. Bad news—here comes the agent. I hurried down the hall. Fred Astaire was sagged on the couch, half dressed, looking frail.

"I don't think I can do the rest of the week, Mike."

I didn't say a word.

"I certainly don't want to be an inconvenience, but I'm sure Gene can carry it for you . . ."

I realized he wasn't sick or physically tired. The man was in wonderful shape, even in his mid-seventies. Fit, trim, sharp. That wasn't it. He was miffed that Gene Kelly was slightly ahead on airtime in the first two shows. He never said that, never said a bad word about Gene, but that's what he was trying to tell me. I got the message.

I told him I understood, I hoped he could continue but we were glad

With Fred Astaire and Gene Kelly

to have had him for two days. But instead of shaking hands and walking out, I sat down on the couch with him like I wasn't planning to go anywhere else for a while. And we talked.

We talked about the old circuit theaters and the different kinds of stages and the great old hoofers that were never on TV and no one knew their names anymore. We talked about some of his best movie numbers and how he did them, the fabulous firecracker routine and the mystifying dance up the walls and across the ceiling.

Then I started getting upset. What was the matter with my staff? Why hadn't they gotten more background from him? We were missing the boat, spending way too much time on "Singin' in the Rain."

I asked him to do one more day to cover some of those highlights, but we would be lucky if we got to half of it. What a shame. Here was America's chance to learn the stories behind the greatest dance sequences ever and we had dropped the ball.

Fred to agree to hang on through Wednesday. He stayed right through until Friday. We spent lots of time revisiting his great routines and he enjoyed himself immensely. I think he would have gone another week if I had asked.

*

Ann-Margret was another one who had avoided television for most of her career. Not that she was above it, but she was one of many who was uneasy with the small screen. Movies, nightclubs, stage shows—she loved performing and wasn't fazed at all by huge live crowds or sound-stages, but there was something about that little red light that made her blood run cold. She believed the few brief appearances she had made on television had gone badly, overtaxed her nerves, and didn't help her career at all.

In 1977, she had no choice. She was booked for a major network special based on her spectacular Las Vegas show. A full-blown extravaganza, it included a full orchestra, special choreographed numbers with motorcycles, battalions of dancers, light shows—the whole megillah. The brass at CBS insisted she make the talk show rounds to promote it.

Ann-Margret took a deep breath and agreed, with one qualifier—she had to do *The Mike Douglas Show* first. When her manager told me, I was flattered but puzzled. I had never met Ann-Margret. He said she had been a fan for years and just had faith that I would be nice to her.

Let me tell you, it's not hard to be nice to Ann-Margret.

She came on the show and was great fun, in spite of her nerves. We were rolling along when we went to a commercial. This happened to be just a few days after I had gotten a prominent mention in the papers for acting as MC at a regional event for Alcoholics Anonymous. Ann-Margret turned to me and started a conversation that had the crew doubled over.

"Mike, can I ask you something?"

"Sure."

"You're an alcoholic, aren't you?"

"No, no I'm not."

"Really?"

"Really. In fact, I've never had a drink."

"Oh."

I knew she felt embarrassed, and I didn't want to leave it that way.

We were going back on the air in twenty seconds.

"But if you like, I'll be happy to start right after the show."

We went back with a laugh.

*

Maybe I didn't drink, but we knew enough to have a few bottles of spirits backstage for any who might desire a wee nip or two before throwing themselves into the lion's den of live national television. I never kept a tally, but over the years I noticed a clear distinction among groups of personalities. Amateurs almost always had a drink or two to steady their nerves (which is an old wives' tale, by the way: booze may loosen the tongue, but I've noticed it really doesn't decrease the anxiety level one bit). My guess would have been that musicians would imbibe the most. Not true. Most singers didn't touch the stuff. Politicians, on the other hand, were not averse to a drink before the show, but almost always just one and almost always vodka. But the hardest drinkers of all were actors and actresses. There was something about going out there without a script that lent itself to a good stiff drink.

Even the great John Wayne was not immune. He was a magnificent guest to have and just as you would expect—on film, on camera, or backstage, he was John Wayne. There just wasn't anything else. No dark side, no hidden personality quirks, nothing but pure John Wayne. One reason that he was such a fine actor is because he was so comfortable with himself. Still, when I joined him in his dressing room just before the show and asked if he needed anything, he replied in two words.

"Yeah. Scotch."

We raced to get him some and he threw down two quick ones, exactly the same way he did it in the movies. Two hefty shots, no ice, no soda, no water, nothing. Scotch in a short glass, straight up and straight down. He put the glass down, wiped his mouth with the back of his hand, and sauntered out toward the stage with that classic John Wayne walk like he was heading out to the street for a gunfight. Three more words were all he said.

"Let's do it."

*

As far as drinking before the show, I'm not going to get into telling tales out of school here, but I have to mention the all-time champion. That

With John Wayne

lovable old character actor Pat O'Brien came over to my house in
Philadelphia the night before a show. He drank an entire bottle of scotch
by himself while amusing us all with his wit. How he managed to show
up the next morning, I'll never know. The most amazing fact is that it
didn't faze him a bit. He laughed and joked and told his well-crafted
Irish stories like he had polished off a bottle of Evian water. I was in
worse shape than he was. After every question, I couldn't help thinking,
"This poor man is going to keel over any second!" Never happened. He
never slurred a word.

*

My most rewarding experience with an actor was Sylvester Stallone.
When *Rocky* hit, we were doing the show in Philadelphia. The movie
was set there, Sly was from there, and it was a natural for us to have
him for a week.

I loved the film. I also assumed that Sly Stallone was pretty close to
Rocky in real life, a tough and tough-talking Philly street kid with a lot

With Pat O'Brien

of heart but not all that much in the brains department. I mean, that body was no makeup job. He looked like he had been punching sides of beef most of his life. And those fight scenes were the most realistic I had ever seen on film. He had to be a boxer. Nobody learns how to fight like that for a movie.

How wrong I was. This was no flash-in-the-pan pug turned actor. Sylvester Stallone proved to be a thoughtful and thought-provoking guest, a reflective man with an admirably detached point of view about stardom, Hollywood, and life. I was amazed at the scope of his interests and the depth of his conversation. I had badly underestimated this man and told him so. He laughed it off. "With this face and this voice? I'm lucky they let me in the theater."

*

The best Hollywood guest? That's just about impossible to say. Maybe I could narrow it down to a top ten, but even that is agonizing because of the final cuts I don't want to make. Just a few remarks about a few very special guests.

Jimmy Cagney had been such a huge star for so long, then took a noble retirement, unseen for many years until his return for a screen encore in *Ragtime*. He agreed to do the show and that was enough for me. I don't remember a thing I asked. I just wanted to sit there and admire him. He looked so grand, a lion in winter.

Jack Lemmon and Walter Matthau fell into their Odd Couple routine, Jack sputtering and stuttering while Walter slouched in the chair, dozing off for a few minutes, then tossing in a laconic quip.

Jack Nicholson talking about *One Flew Over the Cuckoo's Nest*. "I don't try to see the big picture. I just do my lines and go to lunch. I hope everybody else knows what they're doing."

Sterling Hayden was an accomplished actor and also a fine writer and

With Sylvester Stallone

novelist. He told the story of sailing his own ship around the world while he wrote his first novel. It took him a year. The night he finished the last of eight hundred and some pages, he had some drinks to celebrate. His mood changed, he became morose, went down to his cabin, seized his novel, and tossed it overboard. Not a single page had been copied. It was gone forever. I'll never forget that story.

Jimmy Stewart was so much fun—he told great, lengthy anecdotes—but because of all the impressionists, I couldn't get it out of my head while listening to him—"he does such a perfect Jimmy Stewart."

Jodie Foster, Brooke Shields, and Tatum O'Neal, all little girls when we had them on, all precocious, all sparkling with talent. One big difference: Brooke had her mother hovering backstage, Tatum had three agents hovering backstage, Jodie was her own girl. No one was telling her how to act or what to say. It was like they dropped her off for a national TV spot and asked what time they should pick her up.

Eli Wallach and Anne Jackson, one of the great acting couples, would do anything. Skits, songs, pie in the face—anything. We did one entire week in 1974 with Masters and Johnson, the authors of the best-selling studies of sexual behavior. At the time, it was a huge step for daytime television. Masters and Johnson were respected experts and the conversations were anything but titillating, but the subject was sex, the vocabulary was specific, and the discussions were frank. It was one of our most provocative weeks, with lots of mail praising us for the effort and lots of critical comments, too.

Personally, I think it worked, although it would have been greatly diminished without Eli Wallach and Anne Jackson. Masters and Johnson were clinical experts, but, sooner or later, you've got to humanize any discussion about sex to allow people to identify with the message. Eli and Anne had no qualms about doing just that. On the show with the sex experts, they jumped right in, using their own experience as reference. I sat there in amazement. Eli Wallach and Anne Jackson talking about their sex lives in front of the nation. They were excellent, but I couldn't do that if you put a gun to my head. It was hard enough for me to be using words like "penis" on the air, these two were revealing what happened in the bedroom last night to make a point. They are something else.

*

With Anthony Quinn

But the most fascinating Hollywood guest, time after time, had to be Anthony Quinn. One of the greatest actors we have ever had and one of the greatest off-screen characters as well, he was completely at home with us. He could expound on any subject and pretty much let the world see him for what he was—a man. The ladies loved him, the men admired him. He had an old-world attitude about a lot of things and he didn't mind letting you know about it. And he had no problem making fun of himself.

One of his best stories was about *Requiem for a Heavyweight,* with Anthony starring as the beleaguered fighter opposite Jackie Gleason's streetwise manager. There was one scene where Anthony had to appear exhausted after a bout. He ran around the block several times before shooting began and returned to see Gleason relaxing in a chair, reading the paper, smoking a cigarette. Gleason looked up.

"Where ya been?"

Anthony was panting, dripping sweat.

"Running . . . getting into it . . . you know . . ."

He saw Gleason wasn't impressed and asked him about his own methods.

"You don't ever do anything to get ready for a scene?"

The Great One shrugged and flicked his ashes.

"That's why they call it acting, kid."

5

Wide World of Sports

With Your Host, Mike Douglas

Hank Aaron ✻ Kareem Abdul-Jabbar ✻ Muhammad Ali ✻ Sparky Anderson ✻ Mario Andretti ✻ Eddie Arcaro ✻ Arthur Ashe ✻ Ernie Banks ✻ Rick Barry ✻ Johnny Bench ✻ Patty Berg ✻ Yogi Berra George Blanda ✻ Vida Blue ✻ Terry Bradshaw ✻ Lou Brock ✻ Jim Brown ✻ Dick Butkus ✻ Suzi Chaffee ✻ Wilt Chamberlain ✻ Ezzard Charles ✻ Roberto Clemente ✻ Jimmy Connors ✻ Howard Cosell Larry Csonka ✻ Jack Dempsey ✻ Donna DeVarona ✻ Marcel Dionne Tony Dorsett ✻ Leo Durocher ✻ Lee Elder ✻ Carl Eller ✻ Julius Erving ✻ Chris Evert ✻ Peggy Fleming ✻ Flying Wallendas ✻ Whitey Ford ✻ George Foreman ✻ Joe Frazier ✻ Joe Garagiola ✻ Kid Gavilan ✻ Althea Gibson ✻ Frank Gifford ✻ Pancho Gonzalez ✻ Rocky Graziano ✻ Hal Greer ✻ Jimmy the Greek ✻ Roosevelt Grier ✻ Dorothy Hamill ✻ Harlem Globetrotters ✻ Franco Harris ✻ Bob Hayes ✻ Gordie Howe ✻ Sam Huff ✻ Reggie Jackson ✻ Carol Jenkins ✻ Magic Johnson ✻ Jean-Claude Killy ✻ Billie Jean King ✻ Don King ✻ Evel Knievel ✻ Olga Korbut ✻ Tommy Lasorda ✻ Meadowlark Lemon ✻ Nancy Lopez ✻ Joe Louis ✻ Jerry Lucas ✻ Larry

Mahan * Carol Mann * Mickey Mantle * Rocky Marciano * Willy Mays * Rick Mears * Don Meredith * Lenny Moore * Nat Moore Joe Morgan * Stan Musial * Joe Namath * Martina Navratilova Jack Nicklaus * Jesse Owens * Arnold Palmer * Jim Palmer * Ara Parseghian * Floyd Patterson * Pele * Cathy Rigby * Bobby Riggs Brooks Robinson * Jackie Robinson * Sugar Ray Robinson * Pete Rose * Kyle Rote * Wilma Rudolph * Bill Russell * Nolan Ryan Mike Schmidt * Arnold Schwarzenegger * Bob Seagren * Tom Seaver * Hurricane Smith * Mark Spitz * Jo Jo Starbuck * Willie Stargell * Roger Staubach * Jan Stephenson * Lee Trevino * Bob Uecker * Bobby Unser * Bill Walton * Chuck Wepner * Tiger Woods

I told you, I'm a fan, and that has always included being a sports fan. Baseball, football, basketball, track and field, golf—doesn't matter. I grew up in the shadows of Soldier Field with the ivy-covered walls of Wrigley not far away. So you can imagine, when a kid from the stickball streets of Chicago gets his own TV show with lots of time to fill, why not ask a few athletes to stop by? And while you're at it, why not start with the all-time heroes and work your way up from there?

My first love was boxing. In the old days, Chicago was filled with sparring gyms and would-be Jack Dempseys. When my father wasn't working at the Canadian Pacific, he was managing amateur fighters on the side, so it was no surprise that my brother, Bob, and I received personal instruction in the sweet science from an early age. Growing up in a tough neighborhood, we were called on to use what we had learned more times than I care to remember, and Dad was even more serious about his boys defending themselves than we were. Once, on the way home from school, I passed a group of Italian kids on a street corner and one of them gave me a shove hard enough to knock my armload of books all over the sidewalk. It was no big deal and the odds weren't great, so I shrugged it off, retrieved my books, and continued on my way. I dodged that fight, but when I got home, my father walloped me. Unknown to me, he had witnessed the incident from the doorway of a nearby tavern and was not a happy Irishman.

"Don't you ever take nothin' from those I-talian kids! I taught ya how to use your dukes, so do it!"

After that, I did. I wasn't big, but I was quick, and I paid attention when Dad taught us how to throw combinations. It was enough to earn me some ring time on the Chicago amateur circuit. I never lost a decision. At least, not until a few years later when I was working in Oklahoma City.

Any thoughts I had of a pugilistic career were rudely knocked into next week by a young fellow named Smith. Once I settled in as the "house singer" at WKY, I found a local gym for workouts and was doing time on the heavy bag, minding my own business, when this Smith fellow asked if I'd like to be his sparring partner for the day. No problem. I climbed in the ring, intent on showing Smitty that Chicago boys know a thing or two about the fight game.

I could see he was pretty good, but I was undefeated myself, so I thought I'd flash a few of my chops. I got cute with him in a clinch, slipping a left hook around to tag him on the temple. A moment later, he responded in kind, with a one-two volley I never saw coming and didn't remember after. The next thing I knew, I was sitting on the canvas with a broken rib and a dislocated jaw. Too late, I learned that this was not just any Smith, but Dicky Smith, Oklahoma State Champion and the son of famed heavyweight Gunboat Smith.

That was not just the end of my boxing career, it was almost the end of my radio career. I staggered back to the radio station with a renewed dedication to show business. It was a tough profession, I knew, but there wasn't nearly as much chance of getting killed on the job. I didn't dare tell the manager I couldn't take a deep breath or open my mouth wide enough to whistle for a good while. You wonder how the boy tenor managed to sing with all that mangled interior hardware? Softly, very softly, for several weeks.

I quietly retired from the circle in the square, but remained an intense fan. That's one reason my favorite sports guests were boxers. If you look at the list of names at the beginning of this chapter, you'll notice that virtually all of them are in their respective sport's Hall of Fame. We didn't go for the Player of the Week; we sought out the Players of the

Century in every field, arena, diamond, and ring. But my bias was for boxers, and we had them all.

The great boxing champions were all great characters as well. There are no teams in boxing. It's always a man alone, as alone as you can get, stripped down to nothing but a pair of shorts and a pair of gloves, facing an opponent whose goal is to knock you senseless while the rest of the world watches. And good luck, kid.

Boxing, like the Marines, builds men.

In 1970, I fulfilled one dream by bringing Jack Dempsey himself on the show. The Manassa Mauler was the first real superstar of the ring when I was a youth, and here he was in the flesh, still looking fit enough to step back between the ropes. The producers wanted to feature a skit with the two of us in the ring sparring a little. No thanks. I learned my lesson from Mr. Smith.

*

One of our best sports shows featured three legends of the ring that may not have been familiar to younger viewers, but their parents and grandparents had to be in awe at seeing these three champions together for the first time. Joe Louis, Ezzard Charles, and Jersey Joe Walcott. From the 1930s to the early 1950s, these were the three finest heavy-duty fighting machines in the world.

One thing I remember about that show was that all three gave exactly the same answer to one question. In your entire career, who hit you the hardest? These were three of the toughest competitors who ever stepped between the ropes. Among them, they had over 150 knockouts. And yet, all three had the same far-away look in their eyes when they responded: "Rocky Marciano."

Ezzard Charles, a mild-mannered gentleman revered for his ability to take a punch, said that Marciano had hit him so hard in the left bicep, he could not lift his arm for three rounds. Can you imagine what a punch like that would do to your head?

You don't have to imagine. You can see it in the famous *Life* magazine photo of Rocky knocking the previously undefeated and most celebrated of champions, Joe Louis, right through the ropes with a cannon shot to the head. The flesh on Joe's face was a good half inch off his skull. I asked Joe—"Do you remember that punch?" He answer brought a sympathetic laugh from the audience: "Yes and no."

And Jersey Joe, the reigning champ overthrown by Marciano for the title, ducked at the mention of Rocky's name. He had led all the way in their title bout, right up until Rocky laid him out in the thirteenth round. "I would have won if it had been a twelve-round fight," he said. And it might as well have been. He couldn't remember anything after the bell rang to start the thirteenth.

Rocky Marciano remains one of our most revered guests. There was something very honorable about this man. He was so genuine. I like to think we had something to do with one of the most intriguing events in Rocky's life. It still saddens me to say it was also one of the last.

Rocky Marciano

We had Rocky on in early 1969. It was many years after he had retired, at the peak of his unblemished career, as the only undefeated heavyweight champion in the history of the fight game, a record still unmatched today.

We talked about the great champions who had followed him to the throne. He agreed, as most do, that the best of them was Muhammad Ali, also undefeated at the time. I asked Rocky if he would have liked to have had the chance to step in the ring against Ali. His eyes lit up. It wasn't hard to tell Rocky had spent more than a few idle moments speculating on a bout against the "Greatest." He even mentioned some of the strategy he would use to get inside Ali's lethal jab and "do some body work." It was a dream match-up, but it could never be. Rocky was thirteen years and forty pounds away from his last bout.

Murray Woroner was one of the viewers who saw that show. Murray was an independent producer-promoter who had already gotten some mileage out of a "Fights of the Century" film concept that used old fight footage, added a computer analysis, and produced "fantasy bouts" between some of the century's most famous fighters who had never actually faced each other. Jack Johnson vs. Jack Dempsey, Gene Tunney vs. Floyd Patterson—it was a clever gimmick. Seeing Rocky inspired him to concoct his most ambitious project. He contacted Rocky and Muhammad and asked if they would "stage" a fight that he could film. He would then feed the footage to his computer and render a decision on a winner. Rocky was up for it and Muhammad had the time—he was still in limbo, banned from the ring, while the appeal of his draft-dodging conviction wound through the courts (he was unanimously exonerated by the Supreme Court and returned the following year).

It meant that Rocky Marciano and Muhammad Ali would put on the gloves and face each other in the ring. Instead of real fighters, they had to be stunt men, going through all the motions of a genuine fight without actually blasting away. They fought seventy rounds over ten days before the cameras.

The greatest thing about it, and it certainly enhanced the authenticity, was Rocky's enthusiasm. He wanted this fight. He got down to his old fighting weight, worked out for weeks, and showed up looking like the Rocky of 1954. He even had a perfect hairpiece made as the crown jewel of his rejuvenation.

Rocky came back and visited after it was complete but before the footage was edited, computerized, and released. It was wonderful to see him. He was in the best shape he'd been in since ring days and so pleased with what they had done. He had also gotten to know Muhammad in the course of the project and had come to like and respect him, as both a fighter and a man. Off the air, he was honest enough to say he didn't really know who would have won if the two had met when both were in their prime. "He's got the body of a heavyweight and the moves of a lightweight—I never saw hands that fast."

Rocky never got to see the finished product. Just a short time later, in August of that year, he was killed in a light plane crash. He never learned how the computer called the fight. Rocky Marciano by a knockout.

*

We featured all the greats, sooner or later, including the modern titans. Joe Frazier was a natural for the show because he was born and raised in Philadelphia and still made his home there. At his peak, Smokin' Joe was everything they said about him and more. Up close, he reminded me of a small boulder with arms and legs. Solid.

Joe was a guest on one show that also featured Richard Pryor and Sly Stone, both in their wackiest heydays. Backstage in the Green Room,

Richard and Sly had been up to no good most of the day. They had gone to lunch together and returned wild-eyed and mischief-minded. I guess it was too much coffee. They were laughing, giggling, and bouncing off the walls when Joe arrived. He silenced them with a look, then announced to everyone else present: "You've seen how two [expletive deleted] act. Now you're gonna see how a black man acts."

Richard and Sly didn't take anything from anybody, but they didn't say a word to Joe and behaved themselves for the rest of the day.

The most fascinating boxing show had to be the feature bout with Smokin' Joe and his nemesis. Joe Frazier was a magnificent fighter. If not for one man, he may well have been remembered as the greatest champion of modern times. That man was Muhammad Ali, the self-proclaimed Greatest of All Time. I know the fight game, I know fighters, and I'm here to tell you, he was all that. I was fascinated by Ali as a fighter and a man. Over the years, we became friends. As remarkable as he was in the ring, he was even more amazing outside of it. There is no other guest who electrified audiences so much with his presence. No other athlete as quick-witted and entertaining. No other human being who displayed such genuine affection for people, all people. Acknowledged at the time as the most famous person in the entire world, Muhammad Ali was as accessible as a cop on a street corner. Little kids idolized him. Adults were in awe of him. Entertainers and other sports stars clamored to be on the show when he was booked.

We had Joe Frazier many times. We had Ali many times. But we were hesitant to book them together. The rumor was the bad blood between them was not an act, it was real, and if we ever had them on together and something started—well, who was going to pull them apart? We only had thirty-some people on staff.

Finally, it happened. The promoters of the second of their classic three-fight series in the early 1970s wanted the publicity, both fighters agreed, so the match was made. It was nothing like we expected. Although the banter and the prefight taunting was hot and heavy, it was clear there was an underlying mutual admiration between these two champions. Grudgingly or not, they both knew they were the two best fighters in the world, two of the best ever, and that made them fellow members in a very exclusive club.

We almost made it. The one-liners were flying as fast and furious as Ali jabs until Joe seemed to take legitimate offense at one of Ali's barbs

With Muhammad Ali

and leapt to his feet, fists raised. Ali jumped up, too, ready for the challenge. He threw a few shadow punches at Joe with some more teasing remarks tossed in and Joe started firing back. The audience thought it was great fun, a real put-on, but I was close enough to see the fire in Frazier's eyes and thought I better do something before the face-off turned real. I stepped in like a reluctant referee, waving them both back to their corners. Just as I managed to get between them, Joe flicked a jab past my upraised hand. It missed my chin by an inch but it did catch my watch, just barely, but enough to send it spiraling around my wrist like a tiny satellite in orbit.

Joe thought he had clipped me, and stepped back. The situation was defused. After the show, Woody approached me with a very serious look.

"Mike, are you nuts? Stepping between those two guys? Don't ever do anything like that again. You'll get yourself killed pulling a stunt like that."

This from the same producer who had me wrestling bears and fighting bulls every chance he got just for a lark. Between Woody, Ali, and Joe, I'm lucky this book isn't being written posthumously.

*

Muhammad Ali appeared on our show many times after that, and I could tell you a memorable anecdote about each one, but the greatest story about the Greatest didn't happen on the show. It was a private moment and it involved the two most famous human beings on the face of the earth.

We spent a week with Ali at his training camp in Pennsylvania. He was tuning up for his landmark "Rumble in the Jungle" against George Foreman, when he would recapture the heavyweight title in a stunning upset.

Doing roadwork with Muhammad was a special pleasure. All week, we would run together in the morning, then spend a private hour or so together. My staff and his left us alone. I used the excuse that we needed the time to prep for the show each day, but the truth is he didn't need two minutes' rehearsal. Life was one big show for Muhammad and he was always ready, always on. Most of the time I spent listening to him tell stories with that velvet voice and kibitzing with him about the great old fighters. It always amazed me that he knew the styles and records of the ring legends like a sports historian.

One day, one of his people appeared with a phone. Muhammad didn't usually take calls during our private sessions, but he took this one, chatted for a moment, then handed me the phone. "He wants to talk to you." I took the receiver, not knowing who it was.

"Hello."

"Hello, Mr. Douglas. Uh . . . listen, I, uh, I never miss your show."

"Thanks . . . Who is this?"

"Elvis."

"Elvis Presley!"

"Yessir."

"Well, it's nice to talk to you, Elvis."

"My pleasure, Mr. Douglas . . . And I just wanted to tell you I'm sorry."

"Please. Call me 'Mike,' Elvis."

"Well, awright, Mike."

"What are you sorry about, Elvis?"

"Well. Ah don't know if you heard, but it was your show that was on when I shot up that TV." (It had made the national news when Elvis shot his television set to smithereens.)

"That's okay, Elvis."

"Ah just didn't want you to think it was you. Uh, I mean, I've always loved your show. Ah just got fed up with that Robert Goulet." (I didn't find out what that was all about until years later. When Elvis was in the army, one of his girlfriends spent some time touring with Bob Goulet as a backup singer. Bob sent Elvis a courteous note assuring him he was "taking care of her." Elvis took that remark the wrong way and carried a grudge against Bob forever after.)

"Forget it, Elvis. No problem."

"'Preciate it, Mike."

I wasn't about to let a chance like this go by.

"Say, Elvis . . ."

"Yessir?"

". . . If you like the show so much, why don't you come on. How about next week?"

"Aw, I couldn't do that."

"Sure you could, Elvis. Just drop in for a few minutes."

"I'd love to. I—I—I just couldn't."

"I promise you, Elvis, we'd have a great time. C'mon, just say yes."

"I'm sorry, Mr. Douglas. Mike. I can't. Honest to God. I just can't."

"Elvis, why not? You don't even have to sing if you don't want to. Just come on and talk to me for a few minutes."

"That's just it. I could sing, all right. But I'd be scared to death sittin' there talkin'. I wouldn't . . . I mean, I don't know how y'all can do that. Just sit there and talk like nobody's watchin'. I just . . . I just can't. But thanks for askin'. Y'all take care."

I talked to Elvis a few more times over the years, but he never changed his mind, never did the show. It was small consolation that he never appeared on any other TV talk show. In Vegas or on his own TV specials, he exuded confidence and self-assurance. But just a step away from the Elvis extravaganza, he was still that painfully shy kid from Memphis.

And personally, I've always liked Robert Goulet, but every time he was on the show after that, I couldn't help but think, "Gosh, I hope Elvis isn't watching."

*

For some reason, baseball players are the kings of one-liners. Yogi Berra and Casey Stengel probably had more between them than anyone else, never mind baseball or even sports, I mean anyone. Unless he was doubling up on one of his own most famous quips, I think we can take credit for one of Yogi's very best. When we broke for lunch, I said we would go to my favorite restaurant, Bookbinder's. Yogi said, "That place is so crowded, no one goes there anymore."

Casey Stengel had earned his place as a legend in baseball, but I don't think people realize what a wonderful performer he was. If he had never picked up a bat, he could have been a star in Hollywood. In person, Casey was a lovely man, sweet, soft-spoken, and considerate. But he knew his public image was different—the gruff, grammar-bending Yankee and Met manager, jawboning with umpires and firing up his players. That's the Casey people loved to see and he played that role to the hilt every time he appeared with us. One day, he got off on a rant about women and baseball: ". . . they don't know nuttin' about it, nuttin' but trouble for the players, shouldn't even be allowed in the stands." Nobody ever got a reaction like he did for that. The phones rang off the hook with irate female fans out to string Casey up from the nearest scoreboard. I asked him after the show, "Did you mean that, Casey, about women?" He laughed. "Not a word."

*

Casey and Yogi were famous for it, but I discovered during the course of the show that one-liners are kind of a way of life among baseball players.

Mickey Mantle was one of America's all-time favorites and one of ours as well. He wasn't known to be especially glib, but he could get the message across in very few words when he had a mind to. One time on the show, he took questions from the audience. Someone brought up the fact that he had played in pain almost his entire career. In spite of a rash of serious injuries and constant suffering, he still achieved a slew of records and Hall of Fame status. He was asked if he ever found anything that alleviated the inevitable pain. "No," he said, "but I spent a lot of time trying."

Mickey and I managed to schedule a round of golf after one of his appearances. He was known as a fine golfer. I carried a low handicap myself and looked forward to teeing it up with this premier athlete. On the first tee, I hit a big, perfect drive—over 270 yards. Mickey nodded in appreciation, stepped up, and launched one—I mean launched—over 340 yards, as best the dumbfounded caddies could measure. I could only stare. I have played with all the greatest golfers, from Palmer and Nicklaus to Snead and Trevino, and I had never seen a ball hit that far in my life. Walking down the fairway, I asked, "Mickey, you've gotta tell me—what kind of driver do you use?" He just shrugged. "That was a three-wood. I can't hit a driver."

*

Pete Rose was still an outstanding baseball player when we had him on the show. He was not just an enjoyable guest, but a genuinely unassuming man. Less than a year after one of his guest shots, he called me up to ask for a tiny favor. It was shortly after he had made headlines by breaking the all-time hit record, surpassing the immortal Ty Cobb. I picked up the phone and he said, "Hey Mike, this is Pete Rose—remember me?"

Yes, I remember you, Pete. I also remember one of the greatest one-liners I have ever heard. He was on the show for the first time and I happened to run into him backstage as he and his lady arrived. I stopped to introduce myself.

"Hello, Pete. Mike Douglas. Great to have you with us today!"

I turned to the woman standing with him.

"And this must be Mrs. Rose—Hi. Listen, why don't you come on with Pete and—"

Pete jumped in before I got in any deeper.

"Uh, Mike—this isn't my wife. She's a, uh, designated hitter."

Oops. Looking back, I guess Pete was already into serious gambling.

*

Reggie Jackson? Kind of an ornery sort, isn't he? Wrong. Reggie Jackson isn't just a good guy, he's generous and genuine. His spats with George Steinbrenner and Billy Martin made the news, but that wasn't what Reggie was all about. Who wouldn't have a few words with those two anyhow?

The first inkling I had as to what kind of man Reggie Jackson was came the first time I had him on the show, right after one of his spectacular World Series performances. He had earned the nickname "Mr. October," and I decided to probe him on that just a bit. I said that the Mr. October moniker was fitting, and surely one of the great nicknames in sports, but didn't it seem to imply that the only time he gave 100 percent was when it came to the playoffs and the World Series?

It sounds like a tough question, but not really. For most, it would have been an easy fly ball. All he had to say was, "I give 100 percent all year, and 110 percent in October," or some happy talk like that. Not Reggie. He looked me right in the eye and said, "Yes, that's true."

Jaws dropped. Did Reggie say that? He sure did. I was floored. All I could manage was to say that wasn't the answer I expected. Reggie said, "Why not? It's the truth."

Ever since then, I've had great respect for Reggie as a straight shooter. A few years later, one of his teammates filled me in on something else that enhanced that feeling. When Reggie was traded to the California Angels, he managed to squeeze a clause into his contract that provided him with a big bonus every time the home stadium sold out for a ball game. It wasn't the money—his base contract was plenty—it was just a token of appreciation for his considerable drawing power and Reggie enjoyed it every time he stepped up to the plate at Anaheim Stadium and looked around to see a full house. The bonus payment was always made, as scheduled, a few days after. Do you know where it went? You never read about it in the papers, but Reggie made sure there were envelopes of cash in the lockers of all the Angels staff, right down to the locker room attendants. He gave them all a taste, the guys who could use the money. Class, Reggie, real class.

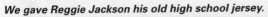

We gave Reggie Jackson his old high school jersey.

*

When you talk about "class" and "baseball" together, the name Ernie Banks inevitably comes up. The man who personified baseball in my Chicago hometown for a generation gave me one of my fondest memories when he not only agreed to appear with us, but helped make arrangements for us to broadcast from Wrigley Field. What a thrill for a Chicago kid to don the Cubs uniform and play ball with Ernie Banks inside the ivy-covered walls of Wrigley. I never wanted to leave. When the show ended and the game was over, all I could think of was Ernie's signature line. "Let's play two."

And I know Gabe Kaplan would never forgive me if I mentioned that day at Wrigley without citing what Gabe called "the greatest moment of my adult life." He was a guest that day and joined us on the field. Gabe may look a lot more like the jaundiced teacher on *Welcome Back, Kotter* than a ballplayer, but he fooled us all. He lashed a pro pitch off the wall at Wrigley—almost four hundred feet—for a clean double. I saw it with my own eyes. After that, Ernie always called him "Gabe Ruth."

With Ernie Banks at Wrigley

*

Class? How about Arthur Ashe? When I asked him what moment in his grand tennis career he would most like to be remembered for, he gave the best answer I've ever heard from an athlete. He said if tennis was all he was remembered for, he would have to consider himself a failure. Pensive and intelligent, he had no interest in talking about his great victories or championship seasons on the court. Arthur Ashe wanted to discuss the innovative programs he was developing for kids. He didn't come on the show to talk about himself, he came to deliver his message about education. Education was his passion. More than any other athlete we ever had on the show, he was completely focused on how he could use his name and reputation to give back to the community.

*

I didn't take up tennis myself until I was over forty, but I loved the game from the first day I held a racket in my hand and spent a lot of time on the court from then on. As it happened, that first time was live on the show with Billie Jean King. We had set up a mini-court on the set and we were batting the ball back and forth when she asked how long I'd been playing. I told her—a couple of minutes: this is my first time. She said I had a natural talent for the game and I took that to heart.

Practicing intensely, it didn't take me long to become a fairly decent player. Of course, that opened the door to a slew of tennis guests who I would prod for tips and impromptu lessons. There are certain advantages to being a TV host, you know.

One of our most memorable weeks was the trip we took to Monaco, with Prince Rainier and Princess Grace acting as co-hosts for the entire week. For me, the highlight was the celebrity charity tennis tournament annually hosted by Princess Grace at the Monte Carlo Tennis Club. Maybe it was the high spirits from just being in that fairyland of a country, but I played the best tennis of my life and was still alive in the final rounds of the tournament. I was looking forward to my semifinal match against no less an opponent than the Prince himself!

The morning of the match, producer Woody strolled over and gave me a great piece of advice on how to handle the Prince.

"Hey, Mike. Lose."

"What?"

"Whatever you do, don't beat the Prince. We didn't come all the way over here to watch you win their tournament."

"Woody! I can't do that! That's—that's taking a dive. I've never done that in my life."

I don't know what Woody was thinking. I'm sure Prince Rainier would have felt the same way. The last thing he would have wanted was for someone to lie down on the court just because he was the Prince. As one of the great sportsmen in the world, he would certainly have insisted that I give it everything I had. Anything less would be a hollow victory.

Of course, I never mentioned it to the Prince and I lost, 6–2, 6–4. It was either Casey Stengel or William Shakespeare who said, "Discretion is the better part of valor," and Woody was right. This was not Wimbledon, this was show business, and the last thing we needed was to respond to the royal family's graciousness by whupping the royal Top Dog on his own court, so I took a dive for the sake of the show and American diplomacy.

At least, that's my story and I'm sticking to it. Woody was so grateful that I kept my competitive spirit in check, I was repaid with numerous production favors for months afterward. Wouldn't it be ironic if he discovered from reading this book that it was all for naught? Do you think Woody would be surprised to learn that, in spite of what he said, I didn't back down an inch and gave it 100 percent, tried my best to overthrow the Prince right there in front of all his subjects, but it just so happened His Highness happened to be a better player and beat me fair and square?

*

Sometimes athletes surprise you. Jim Brown is one. The first time we had him on the show, he was the premier running back in football. As far as I'm concerned, he still is. If you ever had the pleasure of watching Jim Brown on the gridiron, you know what I'm talking about. He may well have been the finest pure athlete we ever had—not *The Mike Douglas Show,* the human race. Speed, power, agility, endurance, determination—he was the whole package.

Jim Brown retired at the peak of his career in 1965 and made an immediate transition to the big screen with his impressive debut in *The Dirty Dozen.* I saw problems with that. Entertainers are often called on to be gregarious and charming and Jimmy wasn't exactly Mr. Bubbles when it came to personality. He was tight-lipped and taciturn, a man

Jim Brown

who kept his own counsel. It wasn't easy getting him to expound on the show when he was a jock, I couldn't imagine he would turn into Howie Mandel overnight.

But Jim Brown did change. He understood the entertainment business included a lot of promotion and he went after it like a rookie in training camp. He learned the plays, studied the rule book, and returned many times to promote other movies. He impressed me with his ability to adjust his personality to the situation. He became far more expansive, at ease, and approachable. I think it was just another sport to him and he was confident he would succeed if he learned the game and practiced.

*

A lot of football players are so physically imposing, they scare you if they get too close. One exception is Joe Namath. He always had more of a stage presence than a gridiron one, and I always admired him. Here was a guy who said what was he was going to do, namely beat the Colts in the Super Bowl, and then went ahead and did just that. What confidence.

Joe was in such demand after his Super Bowl triumph that we couldn't even get him on the show. His people kept telling us there just weren't any open dates. Did that stop us? Oh, no. I told you we had some tricks up our sleeves. We went out and booked his mother, Rose Namath Szolnoki. That got his attention. Rose was a sweetheart, reminiscing about her little Joe growing up in the hills of Pennsylvania. She had some interesting comments, too. For one, she insisted he was born with a full head of hair and sideburns. C'mon, Rose. For another, she said that he was quite shy, and all he did as a kid was "chew on celery." That didn't mean anything to me, but the Celery Growers Association loved it. Celery sales went through the roof. It's too bad I never cared much for the stuff. They must have sent us a truckload as a thank-you.

Joe called while Rose was on the air and we put him on, live. She made him promise to do our show and to call her more often. He did both.

Joe did the show several times after that, and we got to be friends, mostly because of our mutual fanatic interest in golf. He had that wild "Broadway Joe" reputation then—you know, the fur coats and Fu Manchu mustache and nightclubs—but that was a lot more of an act than people realized. Around me, Joe was the furthest thing from a party animal. He was an intelligent young man, a real thinker who didn't go for small talk. I also learned that he was a stickler for the rules and deadly serious about his golf. We played once at a course called Mountaingate in California, just a casual match with a few dollars at stake, but it might as well have been the Masters. Joe always played with that kind of focus and determination.

The match was even when I teed off on a long par 3, about 170 yards. I hit a sweet four iron and stiffed it, about two feet from the pin. I walked off the tee smiling until Joe quietly pointed out that my front foot was a few inches past the tee marker. "You'll have to hit another one," he said, matter-of-factly. At first I thought he was kidding, but he just stared at me, arms folded like a stern referee. I hit another one—into the trap, of course.

Another time, we were playing at Los Angeles Country Club when my ball trickled onto a manhole cover just off one of the fairways. At any other course, a player gets to move his ball away from something like that, but Joe hustled over and noted that the local rule didn't include relief from that particular obstacle. Thanks, Joe. I broke my club and almost broke my wrist blasting the ball off the perforated steel while Joe stood and watched, merciless.

I will say that he held himself to the same exacting standards. Joe Na-

With Joe Namath and Dick Martin

math may have been known as one of the great playboys of the western world, but when it came to the rules of the game, any game, he didn't play around.

*

The biggest surprise of all was this big guy from Austria who could barely speak English the first time we had him on, but he was so congenial we couldn't help but invite him back. I didn't know what good it would do him because he was involved in one of the least lucrative sports going. He was a champion bodybuilder in the days when that was looked on as kind of quirky hobby for guys who got sand kicked in their faces when they were scrawny kids. But this young man was serious about it and had worked his way to world championship levels. He was such an unabashed optimist, I didn't want to be the one to tell him he wasn't going anywhere with the bodybuilding stuff except to the back of some obscure magazine. But he was a great-looking, enthusiastic young man and audiences loved him.

On one show, he mentioned that he was interested in becoming an actor. After the taping, I gave him a little advice. I told him he had to work on the accent. That had to go. Second, he better get himself a new name. There was an old, ironclad rule in Hollywood—if your name has more than seven letters, it's never going to be on a marquee. He was appreciative, but he really didn't listen.

Today, he still has the accent and he still has the fourteen-letter name, which just goes to show you, don't listen to Mike Douglas. Now, they make bigger marquees just so they can fit all of SCHWARZENEGGER across them.

And Arnold is still as warm and genuine as ever. Years ago, Gen and I were attending a huge charity dinner in Hollywood. It was after our show had finally signed off and I was beginning to comprehend that I was no longer important to the promotion of entertainment careers or

With Sally Field, David Soul, and Arnold Schwarzenegger

events that feed the Hollywood machine. In Tinseltown, if they can use you, you're hot, if they can't, you're not. That's just reality.

Gen and I enjoyed all those frantic times, but the recent years with family and friends have been the best years of our lives. Only at the glitziest show biz functions are we reminded of the lofty days of being a ringmaster in the Hollywood circus. It does take you back, a wave of nostalgia that hits you, and for a moment, you miss the excitement, the craziness, and the action.

That's just how I was feeling when we sat down, not at one of the glamour tables, but toward the back of the room. Suddenly, this huge figure comes bounding over. "Mike! Mike Doogloss!"

It was Arnold. He rushed up and gave me a bear hug (almost killed me), then launched into a personal tribute before I could even introduce him around the table, raving about how he owed so much to us for giving him that first wave of national exposure. Still that same huge, happy smile, the same unlimited energy, the same "I can do anything" attitude. One minor difference, of course, was that he had become the biggest movie star in the world.

Sure, I know he didn't owe any of his success to our show. This guy was born to make it big on the sheer force of being Arnold, but what a nice gesture, and so un-Hollywood. Fame and media could wait. Let's go share some laughs with an old friend. It reinforces the old adage "the bigger the star, the nicer the person." They don't get any bigger than Arnold, in more ways than one, and they don't get any nicer either.

*

People think Kareem Abdul-Jabbar is kind of aloof (at seven foot two, it's hard not to be). Nope. He's the kid next door. Just a tall kid, that's all. Very tall. He was on the show once when we did a yoga exercise segment and the instructor told us to step out of our shoes and sit on the mat. Kareem did, and I turned to the audience, "Can you believe how much shorter he is without shoes, folks?" Dumb joke? Yes, but it got a great laugh, including Kareem, who howled the loudest and reminded me of it every time I saw him after that. Kareem was just enjoyable to spend time with, although I could never talk to him for too long at one time because it ruined my neck. Whenever I spoke directly to him, I felt like I should be gargling.

*

The tall guys were all great fun. Something in the genes, I guess. Mead-owlark Lemon, Magic Johnson, Rick Barry, Bill Russell. I played golf with Bill Russell once, and halfway through the round, I picked up one of his clubs just to see how much longer it was than my standard set. I guessed they had to be about double the regular size. I was amazed to see his whole set was standard, not a millimeter in extra length. I asked him how he could possibly play with clubs that didn't go much past his knees. He held out one of those long-range arms that could pat a giraffe on top of the head and let it fall slowly to vertical. I got it. Yeah, he was extra tall, all right, but his arms were so extra long, it all worked out even.

*

Julius Erving, the fabulous Dr. J, joined us once. The crew set up a bas-ket on stage so we could do some basketball shtick. We practiced a little before the show. I think Dr. J. was a little nervous. I made my first three shots. He put up three air balls. With my confidence bolstered, I sug-gested that we play a little one-on-one on the program. "No way," said the Doctor, "I'm not getting beat by some short white guy. It'll ruin my career."

*

In my adult life, golf has been my passion. No surprise, I guess, that every famous golfer on the planet was on the show. (Are you beginning to get the feeling that I did this whole show for my own amusement and was lucky to get some viewers to tune in every now and then just to see how I was entertaining myself?)

In baseball, it's coordination; football, speed and strength; boxing, power and stamina. In golf, the name of the game is concentration. It's just you and that little white ball, and if you lose your focus for a mo-ment, you can put up numbers like a pinball machine before you realize what happened.

The champions all have it, but I don't think there's any argument that the poster boy for golf concentration is Jack Nicklaus. The real reason I invited Jack on the show was to set up a round of golf with him. He came on, we talked, and before he left we made a date to play in the

pro-am round of an upcoming tournament. Did he say anything of interest on the show? I don't remember. All I could think was, "I'm going to
play golf with Jack!"

I could hardly sleep the night before. I got to the course early, hit
some balls, practiced my putting—it was like my personal Masters,
PGA, and U.S. Open wrapped into one. At the time, I was playing the
best golf of my life and looked at the casual outing as a grudge match,
two titans of the game finally going head-to-head. Of course, I never
mentioned that to Jack. As far as he was concerned, I'm sure it was just
another walk in the woods.

I played my heart out. It was the round of a lifetime, with the edge
going back and forth all day. I played way over my head on a tough
course, sank some long putts, hit it like a pro all day. We were even for a

Jack Nicklaus

while, than Jack birdied to go one up. I caught him at the turn, even took the lead on the back nine, then slipped back when he stiffed a four-iron on 17. I lipped out a putt on the eighteenth green to shoot a 73. Jack managed a 72, nipping me by a stroke. By the time we got to the clubhouse, I was exhausted, a little disappointed that I couldn't have squeezed one more stroke out of the round to tie the legend, but proud to have competed so well. I couldn't help but wonder what Jack would say about the match I gave him. As we walked in, I double-checked the numbers on the scorecard and read off the totals: "72, Jack." He nodded without looking up. He always knew exactly what he shot. "And I had a 73."

He stopped and stared at me. "You had a 73?"

He was amazed. He hadn't taken his mind off his own game for over three hours. If I offered him a thousand dollars, he couldn't tell me one shot that I had made all day. It just wasn't in his thought process. That's how focused Jack was on a golf course. While I thought we were in a do-or-die match and watched his every move, Jack was playing all alone.

*

Forgive me for recounting a golf story that isn't very flattering to me, Lee Trevino, or my wife, Gen, but I can't help but laugh every time I think of it.

On one location shoot in Florida, we focused on golf. We scheduled the week around Jackie Gleason's Inverarry Classic Tournament and featured many of the big links names on the program. Every day, after taping was complete, Gen and I headed over to the course to watch some of the late afternoon play and visit with friends.

We were in the clubhouse when Lee Trevino walked in. I should tell you that this was before Gen became an avid golfer. Back then, she wasn't that familiar with the game or its top pro stars.

One of the most personable and popular golfers ever, Lee had just endured one of his worst rounds in years. If you're a golfer, you know what kind of mood that can put you in. Lee sat down, weary and disgusted, and ordered a drink. Gen had no idea who he was, but she saw he needed a little cheering up, and opened with some small talk.

"Do you play golf?"

He didn't know who she was either, but he gave her a look that would melt a titanium driver.

"Do I play golf? Lady, I'm the guy that beat Jack Nicklaus in a play-off for the 1971 U.S. Open! Don't you read the papers? Don't you watch television? You wouldn't know from today, but I just happen to be one of the best golfers in the whole world!"

That's when I stepped in and put my arm around Lee's shoulder.

"Lee, I'd like you to meet my wife, Gen."

"Oh . . . My pleasure."

*

There's one more athlete I have to mention as a way to get something off my chest. There's been a lot of controversy over the years about who had who first. Complaints or criticisms about the show never bothered me. As far as the media is concerned, I think I've gotten off easy. It's open season on famous people nowadays. So personal, so vicious. I swear, if Attila the Hun were disparaged with some of the savagery showered on notables today, some people would rise up and say, "Wait a minute, he wasn't that bad!"

I don't know why, but the media has never laid a glove on me. With so few exceptions that I can't even remember them, I've been treated kindly my entire career. I've got no gripes. Except one.

It's a small matter of pride, but I get irritated every time I see or hear some other host proclaim that they had so-and-so first. From Barbra Streisand and Bill Cosby to Billy Crystal, Phyllis Diller, and Totie Fields, hardly a week goes by without some revisionist media historian assigning credit to the wrong show. It wasn't me in most cases, it was the people on our staff that had an uncanny knack for always finding that needle in the haystack of new talent. They worked hard at that, they were the best at it ever, and they should not be denied the credit they deserve for discovering some of the greatest performers all of us have enjoyed for many years.

I'm not going to argue or go down the entire list, but I do want to mention one athlete as my only rebuttal to any who would dare claim that we couldn't run circles around the others when it came to being first with the best.

I was home in L.A. one night and happened to catch a segment on child golfers on a local news show. It was cute, with lots of little tykes lined up on the range taking whacks at golf balls, but there was one— just a baby, really—who caught my eye. He was shorter than your average putter, but the kid had a swing and he was knocking the heck out of the ball.

I mentioned it at our staff meeting the next morning. A couple others had seen it and agreed that we should get him for a peewee golf demonstration. A few weeks later, the little guy was booked on a show with two superstars, Jimmy Stewart and Bob Hope.

Make that three superstars, because this toddler's name happened to be Tiger Woods. He was already showing a knack for playing under pressure. We set up a mini-range, and he started slamming drives right down the middle, unfazed by the national TV spotlight, with that same flawless swing he has today. It hasn't changed, just grown a little. Bob Hope, probably the most famous golf fanatic in history, took one look and said, "I don't know what kind of drugs they've got this kid on, but I want some." He was two years old.

Beat that, all you revisionists. Maybe somebody had Tiger Woods's mom roll him out in a stroller when he was one, but I don't think so.

It didn't hurt Tiger, either. One of the viewers that day happened to be Mark McCormack, then the standout agent for Arnold Palmer and most of the world's best golfers. Today, Mark is the most influential man in sports, head of the IMG empire, which dominates sports management around the globe. Mark's famous eye for talent didn't let him down. He contacted Tiger's family and began following his career. He waited for the right time—the day Tiger turned pro seventeen years later—and signed him to the most lucrative first contract in pro sports history.

You see what appearing on *The Mike Douglas Show* did for people?

6

Meet the Press

With Your Host, Mike Douglas

Ralph Abernathy * Bella Abzug * Joseph Alioto * Jack Anderson
Howard Baker * Tom Bradley * H. Rap Brown * Jerry Brown
William F. Buckley * Barbara Bush * George Bush * Jane Byrne
Stokely Carmichael * Billy Carter * Jimmy Carter * Lillian Carter
Rosalynn Carter * Cesar Chavez * Shirley Chisholm * Roy Cohn
William Colby * Barry Commoner * John Connolly * Alan Cranston
Richard Daley * Angela Davis * John Dean * Bob Dole * Daniel
Ellsberg * Julie Nixon Eisenhower * John Ehrlichman * Charles
Evers * Judith Exner Campbell * Bud Fensterwald * Jane Fonda
Betty Ford * Gerald Ford * Betty Friedan * John Glenn * Bob
Haldeman * S. I. Hayakawa * Tom Hayden * Alger Hiss * Jimmy
Hoffa * Abbie Hoffman * Hubert Humphrey * E. Howard Hunt *
Imperial Wizard of the Ku Klux Klan * Daniel Inouye * Henry Jackson
Jesse Jackson * Jacob Javits * Lady Bird Johnson * Lyndon John-
son * Robert Kennedy * Rose Kennedy * Ted Kennedy * Coretta
Scott King * Martin Luther King * Henry Kissinger * Herbert Kline
Nguyen Cao Ky * Timothy Leary * G. Gordon Liddy * John Lindsay

Russell Long * Lester Maddox * Malcolm X * Frank Mankiewicz
Eugene McCarthy * George McGovern * Kate Millett * Wilbur
Mills * Martha Mitchell * Walter Mondale * Rogers Morton * Ed-
mund Muskie * Ralph Nader * Richard Nixon * Marina Oswald
Charles Percy * Francis Gary Powers * William Proxmire * Dan
Rather * Nancy Reagan * Ronald Reagan * Elliot Richardson *
Frank Rizzo * Nelson Rockefeller * Jerry Rubin * William Safire
Pierre Salinger * Phyllis Schlafly * Daniel Schorr * Bob Seagren
Bobby Seale * Raymond Shafer * Margaret Chase Smith * Ted
Sorensen * Gloria Steinem * Strom Thurmond * Margaret Trudeau
Harry Truman * Margaret Truman * George Wallace * William
Westmoreland * Woodward & Bernstein * Sam Yorty * Whitney
Young

I had someone on the show who spent lots of time every week with political leaders and activists in the forefront of public affairs during the
most dynamic time in our country's history. You would think this guy
was the insider's insider. He laughed with Jesse Jackson, hugged Betty
Ford, shucked peanuts with Jimmy Carter, danced with Ronald Reagan
(I'll explain later), played golf with Spiro Agnew, had tea with Rose
Kennedy, traded jokes with Malcolm X, sat at the piano with Harry
Truman, and dined at the White House with LBJ. Honest to God, you
would think this guy could engage everyone for hours with the insight of
ONE IN THE KNOW.

He couldn't do it. I don't want to embarrass him, but while everything he knew about the Movers and Shakers of the Universe was intriguing, he never probed the depths of their influence and activities.
They made time for him, catered to him, really, but whenever they were
with him they were on their best behavior and revealed little beyond
good manners and the party line. I like to think it was not his fault, just
the way it had to be, considering his place and theirs. And the main reason I hesitate to identify him is because his name is Mike Douglas.

The names that dominated the front-page headlines of the 1960s, 1970s, and 1980s showed up on our schedule with regularity. Kennedy, King, Nixon, Johnson, Carter, Jackson, Ford, Steinem, Reagan, Kissinger, Daley, Bush, Hoffman, Fonda—Presidents, Vice Presidents, congressional leaders, social and religious icons, radical voices, pioneer women, civil rights legends, New Age gurus—it's a privilege to play host to names destined for the history books. Don't let any talk show host fool you. We stand in awe of the giants like Chicago kids with Michael Jordan. Our show was (hopefully) an enjoyable way to pass part of the afternoon watching television and sell some soap. Some of these guests were making the decisions about global issues. Who were we kidding?

History students take note: this was a milestone in the evolution of modern communications. Before the days of our show, it was out of the question for a person elected to high office to appear on a TV entertainment program. On one hand, I'm proud to take some credit. On the other, it's grown to alarming proportions. Murphy Brown comes into play in a presidential election, Ellen forges national policy debates, the President mugs on MTV, and everyone in Congress is trying to get on *Friends* or *The Drew Carey Show*.

Hey, folks—we're just entertainers, you know, like circus clowns and court jesters! What are you important people doing hanging around with us?

I guess I know why. They started coming on our show for a very good reason that had nothing to do with my thoughts on inflation or strategies in the Mideast. By the mid-1960s, we were an instant afternoon forum linked to a vast gathering of three crucial demographic slices of the America pie—women, working men, and students by the millions.

Many of these guests had spent years of their lives going from coffee klatch to chicken dinner, speaking in front of groups of ten here, a few dozen there, a couple hundred on a big night, trying to catch people's eyes and ears, hoping for a moment of attention. And here were twenty million Americans ready, willing, and able.

People say politicians can be arrogant and abrupt. Not when we talked on the phone about being on *The Mike Douglas Show*. From Abbie Hoffman to Barry Goldwater, Phyllis Schlafly to Gloria Steinem, Malcolm X to Malcolm Forbes, everyone was peaches and cream about spending an afternoon with an apolitical, nonpartisan, outside-the-Beltway, singing TV host. Go figure.

Most people remember our show as TV Lite. No tension, no controversy, just laughs and fun, song and skits. Guess again. On a cumulative
basis, we had the most controversial guest list in the history of television. It just didn't seem that way because we never tried to put anyone
on the spot, never forced a confrontation, never asked for trouble. No
matter who it was, what they stood for, or what they had to say, we
tried to be fair, to give the same unbiased forum to everyone.

I think that was the reason that luminaries from all over the political
spectrum had no qualms about appearing on our show. We had no hidden agenda. You've got something important to say? Okay, let's hear it.

We had a truly ecumenical attitude when it came to serious issues
and political leaders. With actors, athletes, comedians, and musicians,
I was never shy about favoring my favorites. If you're going to have
your own show, what the heck. But when it came to politics, I thought
it would be the height of arrogance to promote any particular issue or
position.

So we promoted them all. The first anti-smoking activist was on our
show in 1963. Wilma Hoede, president of the National Organization
for Women, got blank stares from the audience for saying women
shouldn't be typecast as homemakers in 1968. Seven years before *Roe
v. Wade,* we were talking about abortion law with a biographer of
Margaret Sanger. We had over thirty guests related to the Kennedy assassination, including Marina Oswald and Clay Shaw, right after his
acquittal in New Orleans. Environmentalists came on the show before
anyone knew what the word meant. Animal rights activists got into it
with civil rights activists about priorities. We had Ralph Nader on the
show twenty-six times. You can blame me for all these auto recalls.
Black Panthers, White Panthers, Gray Panthers, Greenpeace, Red
Stockings—it added a little color to the show. The Imperial Wizard of
the Ku Klux Klan stopped by to tell us his group wasn't all bad, they
raised money for charities. I asked him what charities. He didn't know.
CIA, FBI, NSA, MADD, SADD, SDS, NRA, PUSH, NAACP, NAAWP,
Stop the Violence, Worldpeace, Yippies, NORML, Save the Whales,
Save the Dolphins, Save the Gray Wolf, the Bigfoot Society—everybody thinks we were all fun and games and we showcased over eight
thousand hours of political science and sociology. Just goes to prove
our theory that a little bit of entertainment makes the medicine go
down.

*

From the earliest days of the civil rights movement, we featured more black leaders than any show on national television. Some of our efforts date so far back that there were memos cautioning me about "an excess of Negro activists that may not be appropriate for our daytime audience." What was that supposed to mean—you were only supposed to talk about civil rights at night? We had an answer for that one. We booked Stokely Carmichael the following week.

*

We had an unusual rapport with the black leadership of this country.

In a way, we had an important advantage. We knew what to expect of them. Their causes and their philosophies were widely known and we were aware those would be the show's topics, but they didn't know what to expect of us. We established a record for fair play, and that helped, but they didn't know us and didn't know if they could trust us. What they did know was that *The Mike Douglas Show* was a direct line to the heart of middle America. If they had a message to deliver to that audience, here was the podium. That's why they came on, not because Mike Douglas was their favorite guy, but because it was an instant forum in front of a huge slice of white America.

Martin Luther King

What they didn't realize was that we also had the largest black audience of any show on television, but that was an added bonus.

I spent a lot of time with a lot of guests backstage. Some hosts don't see the guests until they're on the air, others stop in to say hello, and that's it. I often visited with guests at length. It raised the comfort level for me and often provided extra insights or avenues of discussion.

I looked forward to actually talking with Martin Luther King, Malcolm X, Jesse Jackson, and others, but it never happened. They were polite and undemanding guests, but it was impossible to get a few moments alone with them. They were always surrounded by advisors, assistants, and security people. Television studios and backstage areas are much smaller than you think. With so many people in such a confined space, there was no opportunity for anything more than a formal hello.

On the air was the only chance I had to speak with most of them. Unlike today, the subject matter and dialogue were unrehearsed. A brief list of topics was exchanged, but the conversation could go anywhere and often did.

As early as 1963, both Martin Luther King and Malcolm X appeared on the show. I don't think we understood then the historic significance of these occasions. It's a matter of great pride for me now. Both these men had enormous impact on our society and you can probably count on one hand the times you saw either of them in less than a very formal setting. I ask you, when did you ever see either of them even sitting down, except for our show?

In my mind, in spite of their divergent philosophies, I found them to be quite similar. Both had a commanding presence—it was difficult to look away from them. Both were meticulous in speech and dress. Both had a rare command of the language. No matter the question, every impromptu answer sounded as if it had been written, reviewed, and carefully edited. Such eloquence is a lost art.

The last similarity I would note is hard to define. It was something akin to sadness, as if they were aware of some truth that they could not talk about and we wouldn't understand if they did.

Martin Luther King was so serious on the show. He had a precise list of the points he wanted to make, but I wanted him to lighten up, relax a little, and just talk to me. It was hard to do. He was so intent on what he wanted to accomplish. The only time I came close was when I surprised him with a question he never expected.

"Reverend King, you've been called many things . . ."

That elicited the only real smile of the interview.

"Yes, I have."

"Some of your critics have even called you a communist. Are you a communist?"

"Absolutely not! It's a charge I have heard and it's a ridiculous charge."

He went right back to his point, unwavering. I tried a few other angles to get past his formality, but he was intractable. He was effective and impressive, but not as personal an interview as I had hoped for.

You'll think I'm kidding when I tell you Malcolm X and I were joking around together. I'm not. He was surprisingly approachable and take it from me, Malcolm X had a real sense of humor.

His friends didn't. The people in his entourage were a grim, stone-faced lot. Every one of them—dark suit, white shirt, thin black tie, sunglasses. A uniform. These fellows made the Secret Service look like happy-go-lucky fraternity boys. But Malcolm—the only time we had to get to know each other were the few minutes during commercial breaks, but there was something ingratiating about the man. He wasn't so dogmatic or anti-white or any of the scary labels that had been attached him. In fact, he had recently been to Mecca on a pilgrimage and said he

Malcolm X

With Jesse Jackson and Sammy Davis, Jr.

had had something of a revelation. He found himself in a sea of people who shared the same Muslim religion and had come for the same purpose, but they were a "rainbow of colors, black, brown, yellow, white." He said it had shamed him, forced him to rethink his beliefs. He was moving away from an anti-white or anti-anything stance to an uplifting message that was pro-mankind. I believed him.

He was also frankly fatalistic. On the air, he said he had white enemies, black enemies, and powerful groups who despised him, but none of the threats would deter him. Off the air, he said, "I'm a dead man. It's only a matter of time."

*

One of our most intimate political shows was with Jesse Jackson. He appeared shortly after the assassination of Dr. King in 1968. Still very young, Jackson was emerging as the most promising of black leaders in the wake of that tragedy. He was impressive, but there was also a profound sense of loss. Martin Luther King had been his personal mentor. He reminded me of Bobby Kennedy after the death of his brother, the President. Speaking to the issues, he was forceful, but at the mention of Dr. King, he had to blink back tears, his body sagging. I think the audience was moved by his emotion.

*

Angela Davis didn't do to many television shows, I don't think she even owned a TV, but she came on ours. I remember Angela as a complicated woman, full of contradictions. She had a striking physical presence, tall and erect with a disarming smile for a woman widely known as a contentious radical.

She wasn't what I expected. I was braced for anger and confrontation. Never happened. She couldn't have been any more reasonable, expressing her thoughts with calm assurance. Even though Angela Davis and I share little common ground, I admired her presentation and enjoyed the conversation.

Afterward, one of the staff came up to me and asked how I did that. Did what? He had seen Angela Davis on other shows that had almost gone ballistic. She comes on my show and it's like a meeting of the Mutual Admiration Society.

That comment was just another reminder that confrontation and hostility rarely start with the guest, they start with the host. If the host has a chip on his shoulder or an angle he's working or a personal dislike for the guest, sparks are going to fly. But if the host is open-minded, you can have a real conversation, maybe even get people thinking.

No matter who the guest was, no matter how little I thought of their politics or philosophies, I didn't think the show was the place for me to grandstand. I wasn't a prosecutor or a judge, I was just a host. The unspoken understanding on every talk show is that all guests will be

**With
Angela Davis**

treated like guests, given a fair opportunity to present their points of view. The people in the audience are smart enough to judge for themselves. They didn't need me to tell them who was good and who was bad. Let the guest talk, let the audience listen, and best of luck to everybody.

That worked for us. That philosophy kept the show accessible to a wide range of controversial personalities who would never have considered doing other shows where they knew the host would be lying in wait, guns loaded. And it kept the hate mail down to a minimum. I never intentionally set up a guest for a fall, never double-crossed one with a loaded question, never sandbagged one.

Oops. I take that back. Yes, I did. I'm not such a nice guy after all. I really didn't mean to, but it happened a few times.

The only time I remember getting that deer-in-the-headlights look from a pol was from Jerry Brown, and that one was an accident. The energetic young governor of California hadn't been on the air with me more than five minutes when I dropped the casual bombshell. The beginnings of his extended relationship with Linda Ronstadt had already been hinted at in the press. He was a single man, a most eligible bachelor, and I thought it was great that he was dating one of the top pop singers. I mentioned that I had heard he had something going with Linda—the whole world knew, didn't they?—and what a great voice I thought she had.

Jerry Brown

I'm glad they didn't have the death penalty in California then. You would have thought I was holding up naked pictures of the governor in a nunnery. A restrained combination of shock and rage flashed across his face. Woody had (accidentally, I'm sure) neglected to mention that the one subject the governor insisted not be brought up for discussion was Linda Ronstadt. For whatever reason, he didn't consider that an appropriate topic for conversation on national television. Sorry, Jerry, I didn't mean to do it. And I still think she has a great voice.

I dropped that subject like a hot Irish potato.

*

Politicians are full of surprises. George Wallace. Trouble, right? Wrong. In 1967, he was one of the most controversial political figures in the nation. His political base in the South was strong enough for him to launch a run at the presidency as an independent candidate but his tune didn't play very well in Philadelphia and our audience gave him the iciest reception any guest has ever received. He came on to a chorus of boos and catcalls. I had never heard that greeting on the show before and it rattled me a little. George Wallace had built a reputation for taking on his opponents and I had visions of an early version of a *Geraldo* show melee breaking out on live national television.

George Wallace

As it turned out, I didn't have to worry. George deflected the hostility. He was soft-spoken and deferential, fielding tough questions with intelligence and commonsense humor. I still wouldn't have voted for George Wallace for dogcatcher, but my perception of him changed in that half hour. The national media had shoehorned him into a tight niche as the racist anachronism, trying to lead the country back to the days of slavery. Given a chance to speak, unedited, he wasn't such a one-dimensional villain. He had something to say about the balance between the states and Washington and individual freedoms. They were worthy topics and Wallace was a well-spoken advocate. But no one was listening. That bitter segregationist label hung on him like an albatross. Maybe that's the way it should be, but I told you the rules of the show. He had manners and our studio audience did not. That was the only time I had to apologize to a guest.

*

I had to apologize *for* a guest once. In the late 1970s, Margaret Trudeau, the young former wife of Canadian Prime Minister Pierre Trudeau, romped across the front pages while playing social butterfly as an encore to her role as First Lady of Canada. She was too interesting a guest topic to pass up. We asked for her, and we got her.

I don't think that rule I mentioned about political figures not imbibing too much before an appearance on TV applied to Margaret. She was effusive, emotional, and way too garrulous for my tastes. I wanted to hear what she thought about her rough treatment from the press, especially the tabloids. She wanted to talk about drugs, nights with Mick Jagger, and problems with Pierre. We made headlines in Canada.

The biggest reaction we ever elicited on a single show was for Teamster leader Jimmy Hoffa. He appeared shortly after his release from prison, looking fit and trim and ready to resume his role as president of the national union. He spoke forcefully for a few minutes and we opened the phone lines for questions. We had five high-tech, high-volume Bell System phone lines ready for calls. The technicians told us they could handle thousands of calls and that it would take twenty thousand simultaneous calls, all incoming at the same second, to short-circuit the system. The phones went down in thirty seconds. All five lines. I'll never know if the callers were pro or con, but a whole lot of folks wanted to talk to Jimmy Hoffa.

*

I was lucky enough to spend time with no fewer than seven U.S Presidents. Every one of them was vividly memorable for me, although I know for a fact it wasn't always vice versa.

George Bush is a fine gentleman and a distinguished American. I noticed him and liked his style back in the early 1970s when he was head of liaison to China. We invited him on the show to talk about the breakthrough in America's developing relationship with China, including the famous "Ping-Pong diplomacy" matches. He seemed to enjoy it and returned when he was in the Senate. Years later, I was at a fund-raising dinner in Ohio for then Governor (now Senator) George Voinovich, who is not only one of my favorite politicians of all time, he is also my son-in-law's brother. Vice President Bush was in attendance at the dinner and I made a point of working my way through the crowd to say hello to him again. I waited in a receiving line for several minutes, then found myself face-to-face with the man I had twice spent time with on the show.

"Hello, Mr. Vice President, good to see you again!"

"Hello, there—I'm sorry, I don't—"

"Mike. Mike Douglas," I said, shaking his hand, a little surprised.

"Mike Douglas. Nice to meet you, Mike."

I don't expect everybody to remember every show, but I was little taken aback that George Bush didn't even remember being a guest on it twice. Please, George, read my lips—*The Mike Douglas Show*.

I hope my encounters with the other six Presidents were a little more memorable. They were for me. Truman, Reagan, Ford, Carter, Nixon, and Johnson.

"I'm Just Wild About Harry" was his theme song, and as far as we were concerned, it fit him to a T. President Truman had to be close to eighty when he joined us for a day, and except for whiter hair, he hadn't changed since his days in the White House. Feisty, funny, and energetic—one of my all-time favorite guests. He didn't care about doing TV, but one more thing about him hadn't changed since his White House days: he was still a solicitous father when it came to his daughter, Margaret. She had been on the program months before and it's Margaret we had to thank for Harry's appearance. We had a fine time when she visited with us. She talked about Dad and wore a witch's outfit to sing "Bippity Boppity Boo." Later, when we contacted the former President, he accepted our invitation. He said, "Margaret told me you're all right. She's a fine judge. That's good enough for me."

*

With Margaret Trudeau

In 1967, we had Liz Carpenter on the show. A fun and hearty woman, she was Lyndon Johnson's personal secretary, and a fascinating guest. I think it may have been the first occasion such a close insider to a serving President had spent time talking informally about the inner workings of the White House on national TV. Liz seemed to enjoy her appearance and promised to take our personal regards back to President Johnson.

A few weeks later we did a special week, a great concept that Roger Ailes came up with. We called it Armed Forces Week, an exciting series of experiences—with me as the guinea pig, of course—meant to give a little pat on the back to our guys in uniform. One day I dove with the Navy Frogmen. The next, I was on the obstacle course at Fort Bragg. Another day I was rescued at sea in one of those astronaut-like recoveries (where I learned that the Apollo crews probably thought the liftoffs and splashdowns were nothing compared to bobbing in twenty-foot waves in a piece of tin the size of a bathtub with nothing visible on any horizon). It was a very rewarding week and we received plenty of laudatory mail and calls.

One morning, my assistant, Lynn Farragalli, rushed in and blurted out that I should pick up the phone right away.

"It's—It's the President!"

"President of what," I said.

"The President!"

"Lynn, I heard you—President of—"

"The President. President Johnson!"

"C'mon, Lynn."

"I'm not—Mr. Douglas, it's the President of the United States."

"Lynn. That's Byner or somebody. The President's not going to call me and—"

"Will you please pick up the phone!"

"Hello."

"Hello. Mike?"

"Yes."

"Mike, Lyndon Johnson. How y'all doing this morning?"

"Mr. President?"

"Mike, I want to tell you, I watched your show last week, and I want to tell you what a fine thing that was. This country could use a little more of that."

Honest, my first thought was, I wish my mother could see this. Her son Mike, gabbing away on the phone with the President of the United States. I have to admit, it was the most impressed I had been on first contact with another human being since the day I met Frank Sinatra.

"Thank you, Mr. President."

"I wish you and your wife would come on down to the White House for dinner sometime . . . Would y'all like to do that?"

"Yes, sir." (So nonchalant.)

"I'm gonna tell Mrs. Carpenter to set that up, y'hear. Real soon, now."

"Thank you, Mr. President. We'll look forward to that." (What a conversationalist.)

"Good talking to you, Mike. I just wanted you to know how much people appreciate what you've been doing."

"Thanks again, Mr. President. That's very kind of you to say."

"You take care now."

"You, too, Mr. President." (What a finish.)

I'm surprised he didn't ask me to join the cabinet after that audition. He did invite us to dinner at the White House, a formal dinner for the Irish ambassador, with music and dancing afterward in the Gold Room. It seems that entertainers have just about taken up residence in the White House in recent years, but back then, they didn't set foot in the door very often. It was a genuine honor that Gen and I both looked forward to. Gen bought a dress, shoes—the whole outfit—just for the occasion, and I have to say she never looked lovelier than when we ascended the steps of the North Portico, striding past crisply uniformed Marine escorts with salutary strings playing in the background. We floated through dinner, applauded the brief speeches, and joined the President and his party in the ballroom.

For me, the highlight of the evening was the receiving line. President Johnson greeted us with Texan congeniality and Lady Bird endeared herself to us forever with her warmth and kindness. As we approached, she opened her arms in welcome. "Ah, at last, a familiar face," she said. We had never met, but she felt she knew me well enough from the show to embrace me as a friend. I'll never forget her brief words or sincere hug.

It was a wonderful evening. Except, of course, for that little incident when I almost punched the President of the United States in the nose.

Lyndon Johnson was a strong and proactive President with many di-

LBJ

verse aspects to his personality, but I wasn't personally aware until that night that one of them was a propensity for turning on the charm with beautiful ladies, and Gen certainly fit the bill that night in Washington. On the third dance, he swept Gen away from our table out to the dance floor, where he led her in a presidential pas de deux.

That's all right, I thought. That's great. Gen dancing with the President. And he obviously likes dancing with her. I can appreciate that.

The music stopped, but Lyndon didn't. As soon as the band started again, he tripped off on the light fantastic again, with Gen still in his arms.

I went blank for a second. Excuse me? What's going on here? Is the President of the United States of America trying to make time with my lovely bride?

I like to think I'm reasonably patient and tolerant in most respects, but I'm a might protective about Gen. I am a little bit Irish after all. As they danced, I started thinking all kinds of terrible thoughts. What was he whispering in her ear? What was I supposed to do if he tried something out of line with Gen? You can't just deck the President of the United States at a dance in the White House.

I was still considering my options as I crossed the dance floor toward Gen and Lyndon. In my mind, he wasn't the President anymore right then, just some jug-eared Texan who enjoyed dancing with my wife a little too much. I must have had a pretty grim look on my face because I noticed one of the Secret Service men gave me a funny look as I approached and tapped the President on the shoulder.

No, of course I didn't hit him. I'm still here, aren't I?

I thought I was quite diplomatic, although Gen said later she couldn't believe I could be so bold.

"Excuse me, Mr. President, but this is our song."

Before he could say anything, I took Gen into the safety of my arms and swept her away. That's right, I cut in on the President of the United States. Maybe it wasn't good protocol, but when it comes to my wife, the guy's just another citizen and one dance is all he gets.

Back at the table, Gen said he had been a perfect gentleman in every respect and she was honored to have danced with him. What a relief. The last thing I wanted to do was ask the President of the United States to step outside. It would have been a real headache doing the next fourteen years of *The Mike Douglas Show* from prison.

*

When it came to Presidents and their families, we had the most fun with the Carters. They weren't just pretending to be down-home folks from Georgia, they were down-home folks from Georgia. Salt of the earth, every one of them, which doesn't hurt when you're in the peanut business.

Jimmy Carter was a good and honorable President and a good man. He had the dignity of a President without any of the airs. He and Rosalynn were also incredibly kind and considerate hosts to us. And Mizz Lillian was one of my all-time favorite ladies. She gave us one of our real moments.

After the 1976 election, we spent a whole week down in Plains with President-elect Carter and his family, down on the farm. In the middle of the week, national issues took precedence when Henry Kissinger let it be known in the press that he was on his way down to Plains to confer with Carter on serious matters. A major player on the Republican-dominated scene, Henry the Great was maneuvering for comparable stature in the Carter administration. The President-elect and First Family's schedule was adjusted to make room for Henry. The coterie of reporters was supplemented with a platoon of national beat writers and crews. Mizz Lillian was asked by a *New York Times* reporter if she was looking forward to the formal luncheon with Secretary of State Kissinger. She gave them a simple answer. For us, it was profound.

"I won't be there, darlin'. I'm havin' barbecue with Mike Douglas at the peanut factory. We set that up a time ago and I wouldn't want to miss it."

We had made the papers many times before for a guest's comment or some funny incident. I think Mizz Lillian's quote was the first time we hit front pages around the world.

We met Mizz Lillian at the Carter home the following day. As we escorted her to lunch, we passed a phalanx of Secret Service men, all in dark suits and sunglasses, just like in the movies. They idled along the walk and around the house. It was a beautiful late autumn afternoon. Leaves cascaded down from the live oak and elm trees, covering the yard in orange, yellow, and red. As we walked by, Mizz Lillian glanced at the cluster of security people, then leaned toward me and said, "You'd think one of 'em might pick up a rake."

*

The Carters were probably the most accessible, but they weren't the only First Family we got to know. We had four members of the Reagan family on the show over a period of several years, including Ron himself, Nancy, Maureen, and Patti Davis. Every one is a story. I have found that political families learn early on that you have to present a united front to the media. The Kennedys, Carters, Fords, and Bushes might as well have spoken in one voice. One never contradicted the other. But the Reagans were a rare exception.

Nancy Reagan was a guest several times. Backstage, off camera, she was great fun, with a wicked sense of humor and a hearty laugh that came from nowhere out of that tiny frame. I wanted that to carry over onto the show, but it never happened. Once the red light was on, Nancy was a different woman, elegant and well spoken, but very protective of her husband and guarded in response to every question. She came across well, but I could never get her to relax and have some fun on the air.

With Mizz Lillian and Billy Carter

When she became First Lady, I read the stories about how "cold" she was and shook my head. People who knew her well would say she's anything but. I believe it's only because no one ever cracked Nancy's hardshell TV persona, and believe me, I tried.

The girls, Maureen and Patti, were another story. In 1968, a very political year, Maureen was a very unpolitical guest. The election? Forget it. She wanted to talk about music, movies, and her own career. Maureen was a surprise but Patti Davis was a shocker. Talk about independent-minded, this young lady sounded closer to Jane Fonda than her father. If Ronald Reagan was looking for vehement opposition, it was clear that he didn't even have to leave the house to get all he wanted. She was so outspoken against her father's positions that I began steering the conversation elsewhere. It bordered on a family feud and I just wasn't comfortable with it.

With Nancy Reagan

It may have bothered me, but you know who it didn't bother at all? Ronald Reagan. He was remarkable. He seemed to be having a great day, no matter what day it was. Some people say he was just a good actor, but he was always like that. He was as accommodating a guest as we ever had. Surrounded by advisors and security people fretting about every little detail, he couldn't have been any less concerned about how he looked, how he acted, or what he said.

We had promised long in advance to review every question with the governor before we went on the air. When it came time to go over the list, he waved it off. Ask me anything. His people made us promise to have him out of the studio at an exact, prearranged time. The deadline came and went and Reagan shrugged. Don't worry about it.

Best of all was our unrehearsed exit. Reagan stayed right through an extra segment, answering questions from me and the studio audience. We finally broke for a last commercial before closing the show. During the break, I leaned over and asked him if he would like to do a little something to end the program. He nodded. I asked if he knew that old vaudeville shtick that the kids had recently brought back into

Ronald Reagan

vogue—the "trucking" routine. He wasn't sure, so I described it.

"You know, that funny walk with the big strides and you wag your finger over your head. You've seen it."

I gave a quick demonstration.

"Oh, sure. Trucking? Is that what they call it?"

"That's right. Like 'Keep on truckin'.'"

"I can do that. I'll follow you."

So we came back on the air, said our goodbyes, got up and walked off stage together as the music played, high-stepping, fingers wagging, Ronald Reagan and Mike Douglas truckin' off into the sunset. My kind of President.

*

The Kennedys have a magic aura. In the entire history of *The Mike Douglas Show,* the loudest, most prolonged ovation was given to Ted Kennedy, just for walking on the stage. That was in 1971, only two years after the Chappaquiddick incident that almost ended his career and in the midst of a Republican administration that had left him in the shadows of national affairs. It didn't matter. The audience would not stop and would not sit down.

That smile didn't hurt, or the movie-star good looks, or that unmistakable Kennedy profile. Still, the thunderous applause surprised us both. I had wanted Ted on the show for a long time and was pleased to have finally landed him as a guest, but I was unprepared for the kind of reaction he elicited. I had been looking forward to a spirited conversation about issues, but that all changed when I heard that response. For our audience, this man was beyond issues, beyond mundane politics. He wasn't just Ted, but the personification of every good thing the Kennedys meant to so many.

My staff had a list of serious questions for Ted. As the applause continued, I quietly slipped them into my pocket. We talked about the family and memories of his brothers.

I don't regret it. My audience wasn't interested in hearing about the war in Vietnam or inflation or the price of oil. This was the standard-bearer of the Kennedys, and all people wanted was to enjoy a few nostalgic minutes with him.

*

Despite his standing as a senator and presidential hopeful, Ted wasn't the toughest Kennedy to get on the show. That was a distinction reserved for the matriarch of the clan. We had tried for years to get Rose Kennedy as a guest, and when she finally agreed to a date, I learned firsthand why those Kennedys are such overachievers. This was one iron-willed lady.

In 1967, Rose got on the phone herself with our producer and said yes, she watched on occasion and would be happy to be a guest. There were a few qualifications, however.

"I want to meet that young man, Mike Douglas. You tell him to come over and have tea with me tomorrow afternoon."

She was staying at the Warwick Hotel and the flustered staff member tried to explain that I never left the studio to go visit with guests and probably couldn't work it into my schedule even if I wanted to. Mrs. Kennedy had only a brief reply.

"Tell him one o'clock sharp."

Where do you think I was early the next afternoon? On my way up to Mrs. Kennedy's suite for tea. And I don't even like tea.

My first impression was surprise at how tiny she was. She was already in her seventies then, but looked and acted about half that. Tea was served promptly at one, and by one-fifteen she had taken over as executive producer of *The Mike Douglas Show*. She had a list of questions, wanted to rehearse how I should ask them and how she would respond. She had underlined certain things to be emphasized and another

Rose Kennedy

list of subjects that were prohibited. She knew how long she wanted to be on, where she should sit, and what camera angles to use. I suppose I could have said, hey, wait a second, lady, this is my show and I'll make the decisions. Well, maybe you think you could have taken her on, but I wasn't about to talk back to Rose Kennedy.

The show went exactly as she planned it. No other guest ever did that to me. None even tried. It was a good show, too. I swear, if she wasn't so busy raising that huge family, Rose Kennedy could have been head of a network.

I saw her again, years later. I was performing at a charity thing at a country club in Hyannis Port and I had to be there early in the morning for sound checks and preparations. As I arrived, I noticed the golf course, a fine layout with shades of the links clubs in Scotland. The mist was rising and I noticed a figure in the distance, a solitary woman on the course. She was hardly more than shadow against the morning light, but I recognized her, even at that distance. It was Rose Kennedy, playing alone, carrying her own clubs in a canvas bag slung over her shoulder. She was in her nineties then. Hats off to you, Rose Kennedy. I don't know about politics, but that's what golf is all about.

*

Here's a political footnote. Did you know that Roger Ailes's career as the most influential political media advisor in modern times began in the back room of *The Mike Douglas Show*? You might say that one show of ours helped make a President, and it certainly cost me a producer.

Richard Nixon was a guest at a crossroads in his career. This was in January of 1968, just as the run for the White House was getting underway. A "new" Nixon was emerging from his defeats in 1960 and 1962,

Richard Nixon with Mike and Gen

one far more willing to make informal television appearances, and our show was a first step in that direction.

Mr. Nixon had arrived at our studio and was in the dressing room while producer Roger Ailes and I reviewed the upcoming show. Roger suggested he visit briefly with the former Vice President and go over material with him. I agreed. I didn't know it then, but Roger used that opportunity for a tête-à-tête with Nixon that changed both of their lives. Roger had some media ideas he thought would be helpful and he wasted no time expressing them to his preferred presidential candidate. He told Nixon, straight out, "The camera doesn't like you." He was bold enough to say that television had already cost him one presidential race because of the 1960 debates with Kennedy. Roger told him he needed help if he was going to be effective on TV and that the battle for the presidency would be won or lost there in 1968. Nixon believed him.

On the show, he was more enthusiastic than I had remembered him to be. Always a master of facts and data, he had a tendency to come across as kind of stiff, but he was already responding to Roger's advice. Even made a few jokes. Afterward, he huddled again with Roger before departing.

Within days, Roger came to my office with a shocker. He was leaving us. He had received an offer to join Nixon's campaign staff and decided to take it. He loved the show but his heart was in politics and this was a golden opportunity. All I could do was wish him good luck.

I don't know if people realize what a difference Roger Ailes made on that election and subsequent ones. Quickly rising to the upper echelons of the staff, he reshaped Nixon's media image, surely the deciding factor in his narrow victory over Hubert Humphrey in November. He went on to become a major influence in Republican campaigns, right through the Ford, Reagan, and Bush years. Sometimes I wonder, does that mean I can take some of the credit for the resurgent economy and ending the Cold War?

*

The last President I'm going to mention is Bill Clinton. He was an up-and-comer as governor of Arkansas the last few years our show was on, and we had discussed having him as a guest, but scheduling conflicts prevented it from happening. I never got a chance to meet him. But our paths crossed indirectly, years later, and I have to tell you, President Clinton has gotten me in a lot of trouble. It has to do with sex, it's a real problem, and it won't go away, and I'm not going to keep quiet about it anymore.

Do I have your full attention?

Here's the story. No doubt, you're familiar with that whole Monica Lewinsky scandal that erupted in January of 1998. Didn't know I was involved? Neither did I.

Weeks into the scandal, the radio talkers were having a field day, covering every conceivable angle. Rush Limbaugh was leader of the pack. He hammered away relentlessly, excoriating the President for hours a day. At one point, he began discussing the possibility that the President was a "sex addict," and perhaps he could get counseling for the problem. He even went so far as to mention that other famous people had been known to have similar problems and had been successfully treated by some sort of specialist in sex therapy. He even identified some famous patients. Where he got the names and how credible the information is, I have no idea.

One of the names he offered up to his listeners was "Mike Douglas." He dutifully reported that "Mike Douglas" had a serious sex addiction problem, but that he had dealt with it successfully and moved on with his life.

Let me mention here that I don't even know how all this works. I don't know if there's a listing in the Yellow Pages for "Sexual Addiction Counseling" or where you sign up. I don't know if you go to meetings with a bunch of other sexual addicts (although I think that might be a little dangerous), stand up in front of the room, say "Hello, my name is Mike and I'm a sex addict," and go on to recount your experiences, then sit back down to donuts and coffee. I just don't know anything about it.

All I know is, late one day in Palm Beach, I walked in from a round of golf and people are looking at me, uh, differently. Kind of cocking their heads to one side (if you'll pardon the expression) when they say hello and giving me strange, half smiles. It wasn't until the following day when I met some friends for lunch and everyone applauded when I walked in that I knew there was definitely something up. Before lunch was over, I had gotten the whole story. "Rush Limbaugh told the whole world that you were a sex addict." I didn't know whether to laugh or cry, but I was pretty sure the next conversation I had with Gen was going to be fairly interesting.

Keep in mind, this was right after I had gotten some attention in an Eddie Murphy movie, his *The Nutty Professor* remake. I've always loved Eddie Murphy's comic talents, but I never had him on my show either, never met him. We left the air just before he exploded into stardom. But I have to admit, he gave me a major boost with a whole new generation. In the film, a family gathering of very large black people are exchanging small talk over a bountiful dinner. For no particular reason, the talk turns to TV, then to my show, with the matriarch of the family volunteering that "I loved that Mike Douglas. He's the only white man that made me wet."

Between that and the Rush Limbaugh thing, I was becoming a topic in chat rooms on the Internet and at swingers' conventions.

What to do? In my entire career, I've never been connected to anything sordid or scandalous. I don't go to parties with Charlie Sheen, never dated Madonna, and the last guy I punched was in a boxing ring when I was nineteen. I don't even cheat at golf. A decent lifestyle may not be as exciting as some, but one thing it gets you is a decent reputation. And now, here I am past seventy, publicly branded one of the most notorious sex addicts in America. Thanks, Rush.

So what do I have to say for myself? Is the secret finally out?

I don't think so. The problem was, Rush Limbaugh wasn't talking about me. Right or wrong, he was talking about actor-producer Michael Douglas. If Rush had seen my show about fifteen years ago, he would have known better. Michael was a guest, and he explained how it had been necessary for him to use "Michael Douglas" when he first registered with the Screen Actors Guild and forever after. I was already "Mike Douglas" so he became "Michael Douglas." Throughout his stellar career, he has always been "Michael" Douglas, never "Mike." Even his friends don't call him "Mike." That is, until Rush Limbaugh came along, trying to be a Hollywood guy, I guess, repeatedly referring to "Michael Douglas" as "Mike Douglas" in his salacious stories.

Some people tried to call Limbaugh and have him issue an on-air correction, but you try getting through to him. You're on hold forever behind two million dittoheads who want to talk about Vince Foster's suicide. So here I am, over a year later, and people are still winking and nodding at me in restaurants and stopping me on the street to give me an encouraging pat on the back and say, "One day at a time, Mike."

No, I'm not going to sue Limbaugh. I know it was unintentional and I have gotten flattering offers from younger women lately. But excuse me if I agree with another former guest, Al Franken: Rush, you are a big fat idiot. Don't pretend to know people you don't and don't give people nicknames they don't have. That's all. I have nothing else to say on the subject and I don't want any revenge. I never even believed that rumor about Rush Limbaugh and Jerry Springer and the donkey.

And President Clinton—I don't know what goes on in the White

House, I don't want to know, but please, keep me out of it.

Finally, as to the vicious rumor that I am or ever have been a completely out-of-control sex machine, if there's one thing I've learned from spending time with all these politicians, here it is—

No comment.

7

You Are There

With Your Host, Mike Douglas

SOMETIMES, even today, I wake up in the middle of the night. We're two minutes from airtime. Something's wrong. The set's not finished. A guest is missing. The microphone won't work. I'm not wearing my pants. The second hand on the studio clock is sweeping, sweeping—1:30, 1:29, 1:28. I start to run for the control booth, knowing I have to get there and back before the red light goes on, but my legs are moving through unseen Jell-O in ultra slow motion. I'm not going to make it.

I've had many different versions of the dream, all basically the same. An insurmountable crisis, no time left. I always wake up before the disaster happens. It's not really a nightmare. I know what it is. It's the subconscious rerun of the latent concern that lurks just beneath the surface of a show like ours. What if we just can't do it? What if we don't solve the sudden problem, can't find a way, no one steps up for the last-minute save? All we knew was, we could never, never let that happen. That red light will flash, the show must go on, and no excuse will do. From an audience point of view, it may not be that big of a deal, hardly more than a curious omission—"Hmm, no *Mike Douglas Show* today, wonder what happened?" For us, it would be the end of the world as we know it.

It never happened. But if you wonder why there are no daily, ninety-minute, live-action shows today, there's your answer. In spite of the advances in technology, it's impossible.

Television has no immunity to Murphy's Law. If anything, it's more susceptible. The things that can and do go wrong are legion. Guests get sick or stuck in airports. Sets fall down. Microphones go dead. Lights explode. Wires get crossed. Videotapes are lost. Props are stolen. Someone in the audience gets a sudden attack of whooping cough. It's not bad planning, errors, or incompetence. It's just life.

Today, huge staffs spend millions of dollars a week to generate a single hour of programming. Our budget was a tiny fraction of that and we were cranking out seven and a half hours every five days. Sometimes I wonder why my wardrobe today isn't mostly straitjackets.

It's hard to explain. There were so many considerations, so many moving parts, the show was like a giant Swiss watch designed by Rube Goldberg.

I think the best way to give you an idea of exactly what happened on a typical week of *Mike Douglas Show*s is to walk you through it. Every week, we custom-built the show around the co-host. Okay, let's say this week the co-host is YOU. That's right. Everyone else got to be co-host for a week. Why not you?

Are you up for it? Good. We're on a very tight schedule, so let's get started.

*

Six weeks to two months beforehand, our people call your people and your fate is sealed. Maybe your agent has been lobbying for years to get you on. Maybe you're so big, we've been chasing you. Doesn't matter. The deal is struck and you're booked.

As soon as your name is penciled in on the schedule, our researchers go to work. You are going to be on camera for the better part of 450 minutes during your visit. That's a lot of time. We need a lot to talk about and a lot for you to do. We know you're a star, everybody knows that. But who are you, really? What about your family, your background, hobbies, likes and dislikes? We don't know, but we will. Over the course of a few weeks, we're going to perform the equivalent of an FBI background check. We'll talk to lots of people. Old newspaper clippings, family photographs, and memos from friends and associates will start piling up in our office. Most of it won't go anywhere, but there will be some nuggets we can use.

We would love to sit around and talk with you for weeks to get some real insight, but that's not going to happen. You're busy and we're busy. It won't be until the Wednesday before you're scheduled to appear that things start getting serious. You'll get a call from Woody.

Now, let me tell you about Woody, our genius-madman producer who created the concept and runs the operation. I love Woody, he's like a brother to me, but the man is certifiably crazy and by agreeing to appear on the show, you have placed your career in his hands. You are about to get the most public exposure you will ever have at one time. About one hundred million people will see you in the course of the week. And Woody's in charge. Good luck.

*

Woody and I go way back. In fact, he was on *The Mike Douglas Show* before I was. It was his idea to have a talk-variety show with a host who was more catalyst than star. Woody realized that earlier versions of that kind of show often got in their own way. The guests were there to feed the host, and that could get pretty stale after a while. He wanted to turn that around, have a host that was willing and able to showcase the guests. That way, the show was constantly fresh, renewing itself every week. Simple enough, but not as easy as it sounds. The host had to be a performer and performers have sizable egos. It's the nature of the beast. They don't like playing second fiddle to anyone. Woody spent months looking for a host who was talented enough to carry the ball when he had to, but ever willing to listen more than talk, direct the focus to his guests, and showcase them before himself. No surprise, he couldn't find one. He had already gone through the entire alphabetical Talent Directory and had gotten to Frank Zappa before he thought of me.

Once we got together, it just clicked. Never in my career did I work so closely and so in sync with anyone the way I worked with Woody. I can remember all the way back to before the show started, when we were working out the kinks, doing some audition shows up in Windsor, Canada. Westinghouse had sent us up there so we could tape a week of pilot shows while not drawing too much attention.

We worked so hard all week. Nonstop. Everything was riding on these shows and we gave them our all. At week's end, Woody and I crawled back to the single hotel room we shared, giddy with exhaustion. I remember lying in bed, too tired to sleep. The adrenaline wouldn't stop

Woody Fraser

pumping. Woody was tossing and turning in the next bed. For some reason, it struck me as funny that neither one of us could sleep. I began laughing and couldn't stop.

Woody wanted to know what was so funny, but I couldn't catch enough breath to tell him. Then Woody started, and the two of us laughed ourselves sick. A couple of complete lunatics.

It had to be half an hour before we settled down. Then one of us would erupt and the whole thing started over again. Finally, I don't know how, I suppose from lack of oxygen, we passed out.

When I woke up, I went into the bathroom and took a shower. We both had flights scheduled that morning—I was heading back to California and Woody was returning to Cleveland. The next thing I knew, Woody was tugging at the shower curtain.

"What the hell are you doing?" he asked.

"What does it look like, you idiot, I'm taking a shower."

"Why are you taking a shower at four in the morning?"

I was so disoriented, I thought it was about eight. The laughing started again. We were absolutely goofy. Around the bend.

At the airport the next morning, we were like a Laurel and Hardy routine, stumbling around, bumping into each other, still deep in the throes of sleep deprivation. Every time we'd look at each other and see what a couple of zombies we were, we'd start again.

We decided to separate. We had to. I went to the newsstand to pick up a paper, killed some time looking at magazines. Twenty minutes later, some weird character with a severe crew cut walked up to me and asked if I was ready. It was Woody. He looked like an escaped convict. He had gone for a haircut and fallen asleep in the chair. The laughter started again. People must have thought we had martinis for breakfast. I boarded my plane with tears running down my cheeks.

*

That's pretty much the mode Woody and I stayed in for the next decade or so. Everyone at Westinghouse could look on this venture into broadcasting as serious business, but we just couldn't do that. This wasn't the *United Nations Hour,* it was entertainment. And if we were going to kill ourselves all week every week to do this thing, by God, we were going to have some laughs.

That attitude carried over to the show. We knew the core of it was inevitably going to be standard talk show fare—actors, singers, authors with new books, comedian monologues—but Woody was intent on spinning off into creative madness, and I was crazy enough to say, "Go for it!" Thanks to Woody, there was always something new and nutty lurking around the next commercial break to keep the guests and me on our toes and keep the audience at home watching for the next mad moment.

*

And that takes us back to you, our next co-host. Sorry to keep you holding on the phone so long, waiting to talk to Woody. But here he is now.

Woody is going to welcome you to the show and promise an interesting week. Oh, by the way, he has a few more questions on your Broadway show or your last album or your next movie. He wants to know if you have any suggestions for other guests to join you during the week, any friends in the business you particularly like or family members with unusual talents, And isn't your birthday coming up?

Watch out. It's a trick. While you're trying to be helpful, Woody's hatching skits and bits in that mischievous, three-ring mind of his, planning stunts and surprises. As soon as he has enough inside information on you, he's going to parcel it out to associate producers like Rich Ludwin and Burt Dubrow, and they're going to scramble to make Woody's dreams come true. Among them, they'll come up with about eight special segments, just for you. This is your week on *The Mike Douglas Show*. Woody wants to make sure you never forget it.

A lot of what you tell Woody may come back to haunt you. Whatever you do, don't mention you have a fear of flying. We'll be doing Tuesday's show from the cockpit of a biplane. And please don't tell him you don't like elephants. There might be one sitting in with the band playing trumpet when you step over to do a song on Friday.

*

We're going to fly you in to Cleveland or Philadelphia or L.A. on Sunday afternoon. Let's say it's Philly. A limo will be there to take you to the Warwick Hotel. You're a VIP guest and Woody himself will be there to meet you. The two of you will go over a few notes, but nothing formal. Unlike nowadays, there aren't going to be any set pieces, no series of questions and answers, no specific lines for you to deliver. We want the show to have a spontaneous feel. Too many shows pretend to be spontaneous, but the sequence and the dialogue are fixed and rigid. The audience can pick up on that and it's deadly. We're not pretending. We're going to wing most of it and so are you.

If you want Woody to stick around for dinner, he'll oblige. If you have other plans, he won't ask, won't tell, and will quietly disappear. Get a good night's sleep. We'll see you Monday morning.

Monday, 8:00 A.M. Woody and I will join you for breakfast, just to meet and break the ice. Again, no specifics. Just like Woody was kind of circumspect the night before, I'm not going to get into heavy conversations with you either. Keep it fresh, keep it light.

The limo will pick you up at 10:00 A.M. The staff and crew have been working for hours. Launa Newman is on the phone, making sure the scheduled guests for today are on board and finalizing details with others for the remainder of the week. You'll get a list with some notes so you know who's who. The audience wants to see a big star like you interact with others, so we'll make sure you know the author's book and what it's about, a few details about koala bears so you can chat with the zoo lady, and some of the key planks in the senator's platform.

Watch out for that cable and don't let the gaffer hit you in the head with the ladder. Don't step in the paint. Rocco Urbisci has designed a set just for you and he's getting it just right himself. He loves giant letters, so I hope your initials aren't an acronym for anything distasteful. He spent three days putting up a huge "V.D." When I saw it, I scratched my head.

"We're doing a segment on veneral disease, Rocco?"

His shoulders sagged in despair. Three days wasted for Vic Damone. Same thing happened with Bart Starr and Peter Ustinov.

*

We're going to do a few songs, of course, so the band is running through the music. We've got to rehearse. You and I are doing a duet in the third segment. Here—memorize the words to "Moon River." They'll be on cue cards, but you'll come across better if you're not staring slightly off camera.

Sound check time. What a headache. Sound is important. Bad sound can destroy the finest performance. When a singer or a group performs a concert, their sound people spend most of a day fine-tuning the system, sometimes longer. We have more complications, three primary systems in play. One for broadcast, one for the studio audience, and one for the performers. It's almost impossible to sing or play if you can't hear yourself. Also, our equipment, the best in the business, is primitive compared to what's available today. But we only have about twenty minutes to make it perfect. "Testing, 1-2-3 . . ."

*

Sit down. Relax. Have a cup of coffee. Read your notes. Here's the quick synopsis you'll need in order to talk coherently with the engineer from NASA. You can review that for all of five minutes. Uh-oh, time's up. Here comes Woody.

He wants to tell you about the bit we're going to do in segment four. It's a goof on fashion, and he wants you to wear a zoot suit. Now, don't get testy. Maybe you'll look like an idiot, but it's all in good fun.

Some of our guests didn't take so kindly to Woody's antics. Don Ameche was the nicest gentleman in show business. Woody was explain-

With Roy Rogers and Neil Sedaka

ing to Don and myself this sketch he concocted that involved us both wearing a series of funny hats. Woody was going into this detailed explanation of how we change from one goofy hat to the next.

"I don't wear funny hats," said Don.

Woody pretty much ignored him and carried on.

"You're not listening, Woody," Ameche repeated. "I don't wear funny hats."

That got his attention. Woody took his diplomatic tack. He understood, but he was sure Don would break that rule just once because this was so funny, so outrageous a bit that—

"Woody. I'm not wearing any funny hats," Don said with crisp finality.

Now Woody was turning crimson, about to blow. Woody Fraser is a gentleman, too, but when he loses it, look out. He can make Roseanne sound like Donna Reed. We were headed in that direction, but I think he knew that would only make things much worse. He turned to me in desperation, looking for some help with our reluctant guest.

I just shrugged my shoulders. "I don't wear funny hats either." Yeah, I double-crossed him. I had been waiting for that chance for years. It didn't take him long to get his revenge, though. Two days later, he brought in Roy Rogers. We had to wear hats in every segment.

*

Okay, it's almost noon. How are you doing? Hungry? Let's go to lunch. Careful, watch out for Ken Philo. He's the art director and he's putting the final touches on one of the backdrops for today. He's whipped up enough sets over the years that if you put them all together, you'd have a city about the size of Hong Kong, but don't get in his way. Bump his elbow and he'll cut off half your foot with that jigsaw.

Let's go to Bookbinder's, my favorite place for lunch. Here's a menu, anything you want. Me? I think I'll have the scrod and stewed tomatoes. Get used to it. We're going to lunch at Bookbinder's every day, and every day I'm having scrod and stewed tomatoes. I had that dish so much, I'm surprised my picture's not on the scrod package in the frozen foods section right next to Mrs. Paul. I don't know, maybe it's because the show was so unpredictable, I needed an anchor, one consistent thing. No matter what else happened, I knew I was going to Bookbinder's for scrod and stewed tomatoes.

*

Back to the studio. Remember those notes? Tear them up. Here's the revised version. Only a half hour till airtime, but you can read them in makeup.

Okay, you look great. Now, there's another rare consistency. Just before we kicked off, I would stroll into the makeup room and exclaim how wonderful the guest looked. It only backfired on me once. Hubert Humphrey was there. His wonderful and witty wife, Muriel, was with him. I walked in as they powdered his face and patted his hair down.

"Hubert, you look great. Doesn't he look great, Muriel?"

"He looks like Whistler's Mother," said Muriel the comedienne.

*

Countdown. The floor producer is hushing the audience. Lights up. Camera and boom operators at their stations. Band members in position. Instruments ready. Stagehands, crew, that's it. Get off the set. Now. And we have ten . . . nine . . . eight . . .

I give you a pat on the back for good luck. You stay backstage for a minute while I go out, open the show, and do the first song.

Three . . . two . . . one. Here comes the downbeat. Hit it. We're on.

*

Four minutes in. I sang "The Best Is Yet to Come." Joe and the boys nailed it. Great tune. Nice response from the audience. Good group today. Now it's your turn. Starting to sweat? Wonder what that thump-thump-thump is? Only your own heart pounding. Don't worry, you'll be fine. Besides, I already knocked off a big chunk of time. You only have to be your very best in front of millions of people for eighty-six more minutes. How many people exactly? Look at it this way. If they all came to the studio and you took just ten seconds to say hello to every one of them personally, you'd be here for twenty-six years.

"I can't tell you how pleased I am to introduce our co-host for this week. One of my favorites of all time, and I'm sure, one of yours. So please, join me in a warm welcome for . . . YOU!"

You're sitting in the hot seat now, and they don't call it the hot seat for nothing. How about those lights? You could use some sunblock. And now you know how it feels to be out there on a wing and a prayer. No script, not sure how much time is gone or how much is left, some guy with a headset off camera giving strange hand signals like a third-base coach, cameras gliding across the floor headed for another angle. The audience so close they're almost breathing on you, staring, daring you to be interesting or funny or something. Which light is on? Where do I look? Someone is talking, but who? Oh, it's Mike Douglas, and he's talking to me.

"So, I understand you're working on a new film with Meryl Streep. That's got to be a kick. How do you like working with her?"

What? What film? Who's Meryl Streep? Why am I here? Who am I?

It's all right. The first few minutes are always the hardest. A few more seconds and words will start spilling out of your mouth and everything will be fine. Once, we had a kid on who made headlines for a day pulling a prank at Cape Kennedy. He snuck past security to get a front-row seat at a space shuttle liftoff. What he didn't know was, he had gotten so close, he would have been killed, fried to a crisp, if the launch had proceeded. Lucky for him, it was postponed for weather. It was one of the quirky human interest stories that people enjoy, so we signed him up to talk about it. He was fine in the pre-interview. Nice personality, nice kid.

On camera, I asked him the first question and he froze up stiff. Couldn't talk, couldn't even blink. I asked him another question. Nothing. I mean, I was talking to petrified wood. That wouldn't do. We were eight minutes from a commercial. I hit him on the shoulder, pretty hard, and yelled at him.

"Hey! You pull the biggest stunt in NASA history and now you're not going to tell us about it?"

That did it. He came out of the coma, laughed at the joke, and started rolling.

You, you're a pro. You'll be fine.

And you are. We're talking, we're laughing. The audience likes you. Before you know it, you're into the flow and the time is flying by. You

Robert Goulet and female impersonator

hear the band swing in to some bumper music, somebody says "Okay, one minute fifty," and we've put the first segment to bed.

That was easy, eh? Forty-four more of those and you're out of here.

*

You're a singer, right? Okay. Woody has a swell setup for your first song. He used this one to perfection with Robert Goulet. You walk into the audience and sing a nice, romantic ballad to a very pretty young lady there, handpicked by Woody. No problem. You take the mike, stroll on out, and there she is. You give her your rendition of "I Can't Get Started with You." It's perfect. She's even getting into the act a little, swooning and cuddling against your shoulder. At the end, she gives you a smooch. Nice touch. As you finish, the audience applauds, and she pulls off her wig to reveal that she's a he. A female impersonator. The place goes crazy. And you didn't even see it coming. Don't look at me. I had no idea. I warned you about Woody, didn't I?

*

Okay, you make it through the entire first show. Spent but exhilarated, you're ready to go again tomorrow. Back in the limo, back to the hotel. Please don't ask me if I want to go to dinner. First of all, I try not to do that because we'll have a conversation and, inevitably, we'll have it again on the air and it will sound rehearsed. Second, the rest of us have work to do.

Like Ernie. Ernie DiMassa's the advance man, also one of the creative writers, setup men, and coordinators. He spent last week setting things up for you—working out the music and dance numbers, putting together the comedy sketches, making any special arrangements you needed, promoting your appearance to the other media. Now he's fine-tuning everything, one day at a time. He's back up in the office, working on a comedy routine. Woody drives everyone to their limits, but Ernie doesn't seem to have one. He'll go sixty, seventy hours like it's part-time. He only hit the wall once, after two solid weeks of back-to-back re-motes. The following Monday he was in his office, typing up a sketch. In his sleep. True story. He was sitting in his chair, eyes closed, generating pages of crazy non sequiturs. Woody read it at the staff meeting and had everyone on the floor.

We want the whole world to know about your appearance, so Ernie will have a lot of help with the PR. Owen Simon, Group W's vice president of creative, will pull every string he can to get you a mention in this column or on that radio show. Owen was constantly coming up with new promotion gimmicks. He was the one who had the clever idea of getting Phil Donahue and me to trade appearances. First I did his show in Chicago, then he came over to Philly to do mine. A win-win concept. The only hook was that we were with two different syndicators and appeared directly opposite each other in some markets. When his show came up for broadcast with me as guest, his own flagship station in Chicago bridled at the thought of promoting the competition. It took Phil himself reading the riot act to the station manager to get the thing aired.

*

Rick Rosner's another associate producer who's going to help get the word out about how great you are on the show. You remember him, you met him in the hallway. You thought he was a high school kid. He's just

With Phil Donahue

a baby, but he's got the savvy of a twenty-year veteran. A few years back, he was trying to get *Look* magazine to do a story on me. They weren't listening. He was pestering one editor who said the magazine was having a huge cocktail party and he had to get off the phone. Rick hung up, threw together a package of bio material and 8 x 10 glossies, and jumped on a train for Manhattan. He crashed the party, button-holed the editor, and sold him on the pitch. The next month, I was on the cover of *Look*.

Rick Rosner was so good, he would defy me to give him a task he couldn't accomplish.

"Okay," I finally said, "get me the Pope, Rick."

I thought that would be the end of that. The next day, walking by his office, I heard him speaking rapid-fire Italian. He was on the phone to the Vatican. He had already jumped through the first dozen hoops and was having a heart-to-heart with Paul VI's personal secretary, Cardinal Somebody. I swear, he almost made it happen. I think his only mistake was mentioning that His Holiness would be on with the Muppets and Minnie Pearl.

With people like that, everyone will know what a great week we're having with you as co-host. You just go back to the hotel and relax.

*

It's only Wednesday, you're completely exhausted and you're starting to wonder how you got yourself into this. Your agent just called and mentioned that, at the end of the week, you get your check for a little over a thousand dollars. Now you're starting to think he's lost his mind and you have, too. Five ninety-minute shows for a grand? You got more than that in high school.

Don't be like that. Sure, you're well known, but now you're a household word. Everybody's talking about your song to the he-she. Do you know how much a good PR firm would charge you to generate that kind of publicity? You should pay us.

Besides, we wanted you and we got you. That's how it works. Talent coordinator Launa Newman is quite a talent herself. Woody once told her he had to have Tony Bennett and she had to get him. She tracked him down to a hotel in New York, but he wouldn't take her calls. That night, she showed up at the hotel in person. The next morning, Woody got a call from Tony Bennett. He told Woody he was going to do the show. Launa had apparently told Tony she would be fired if he refused to appear and Tony had an earful for Woody.

"You want to know why I'm doing it? I'm not doing it for you. I'm not even doing it for Mike. I'm doing it for this sweet woman, this Launa, who tackled me in the lobby and told me she was going to lose her job because of me. Me?

"Listen Woody. You set it up, I'll be there. Just one condition."

"Anything," said Woody.

"You're gonna give Launa a hundred-dollar-a-week raise, starting to-day."

She got it, too.

*

Enough stories. You've got a lot more show to do. Today, we bring in your ninety-year-old drama teacher from high school, except she doesn't fly, so poor Rick Ludwin has to stay on the phone half the day making sure she made it on the train from North Dakota.

Don Rickles comes on and insults you for ten minutes, but then we get him back. You and I don special-effects caps so we look as bald as he is. Another killer with the audience. Your Q-rating has climbed five points.

*

Thursday, we hit some snags. Nobody's perfect. You've been working from 10:00 A.M. till 4:00 P.M. every day and you can't believe everyone's not as beat as you are. If you only knew. They've been going from six or seven until eleven or midnight. And they'll do it again next week and the week after. Thursday morning, we have the wrong set for our duet and Woody blows his stack. You don't want to be around for that. After-ward, some of the crew will go to my personal assistant and the show's den mother, Lynn Farragalli. She'll listen to the tales of woe, march over to Woody, and make him apologize. Everything will be room tempera-ture again by the time you get there.

Thursday is animal day. I told you not to mention animals with Woody. You said you wanted to sing that "Unicorn" song, so Woody has a donkey rigged up with a horn glued to his forehead.

Consider yourself lucky. When Robert Goulet co-hosted again, he told Woody he would be singing "Eye of the Tiger." Woody went right

With Gunther Gebel-Williams, the tiger, and Rex Reed

to production supervisor Ron Little and told him we needed a tiger. (I think Woody was like Elvis: he had a lifelong grudge against Goulet.) He wanted to have someone bring in a tame tiger on a leash in the middle of Robert's song.

Ron Little was amazing. The more absurd the request, the more he took it as a point of professional pride to get it done. Ron went out and signed a tame tiger and his trainer, sight unseen. On the day of the show, the tiger's late. Ron kept insisting he'll be there. Woody asked him ten times if it's safe, if the tiger is completely tame. Ron promises he's a pussycat.

We're already on the air when Timba the Tiger and his trainer arrived. They hustled the big cat and his handler backstage and barely got them into position before Robert started the song. It wasn't until they started to walk across the stage that anyone noticed the trainer is missing one arm. Now if that didn't give rise to second thoughts about this tiger's temper, I don't know what would.

Robert Goulet was singing his heart out when he heard the audience cry "ooooooh." Robert thought he was wowing them with his performance until he looked up to see Timba and his trainer. I don't know the trainer's name, but ever since that day, we just called him Lefty.

The tiger was a shock, but when Robert saw the one-armed man, he stopped in mid-note and bolted like the Fugitive with Lieutenant Gerard on his trail. Only the tiger himself can top that. He hoses down the stage and the first two rows of the audience. Two ladies fainted, Goulet is gone, and Woody's done it again.

Your animal show is a piece of cake. The donkey trainer has all his limbs and everything goes like clockwork.

*

Throughout the week, the talk segments get better and better. You sound relaxed, confident. The timing is perfect. Once again, you can thank Woody and his production staff. Bob LaPorta probably stopped by several times over the week to give you encouragement, slip you a couple good jokes that would fit in anywhere, and tell you you're one of the best guests we've ever had.

During the show, Woody will always be there, hovering around the stage, just off camera. He's giving me signals all the time. This is working, keep going with it. That isn't, cut it short. Find a punch line and close, we're going to a break. We're fading, cut it off and intro the next guest early. I'll catch his eye for a fraction of a second and I know what he wants.

Just be grateful we're not on the road. The studio is tough enough, locations could be chaos.

Ernie Sherry was the show's first director. He was a dedicated, talented man who left us way too early, but he set a pace and a quality standard that every director that followed was hard-pressed to match. Ernie sat in on every production meeting and called the shots during the show. It was his job to figure the camera angles that made you look your best and the sequence of shots and sounds that kept the audience glued to their sets. And he was good. He could make a stamp collection look thrilling.

There were times when the show got too thrilling, especially on the road. The very first remote broadcast we ever did was from Cypress Gardens, Florida. It was a great choice. Beautiful scenery, lovely weather, enthusiastic crowds, and every conceivable water stunt and sport. Woody planned a segment on water-skiing with beautiful girls in bikinis doing jumps and spins off ramps, weaving all over the water. Wouldn't you know that Woody came up with a twist? He found a blind water skier who could run the entire slalom course. I wasn't crazy about the idea at first, but we did a rehearsal and the blind skier sailed through the course without incident. He said he'd done it a thousand times. Fine. Let's do it.

The next time, it was on air, live. Ernie called "Action" and there was our daring young man on his flying skis, gliding effortlessly around the hairpin turns. Ernie Sherry had three cameras following him, including one on close-up. It was exciting television.

To this day, no one knows what went wrong, whether it was the skier, the boat, the boat's pilot, or something else altogether. Whatever the case, our skier took a turn a little too wide and ran smack into one of those beautiful banyan trees. Wham! I mean, he didn't graze the tree, he kissed it head-on at what had to be twenty-five miles an hour. And this was no "cut tape" situation, this was live.

Thank God the skier lived. Miraculously, he wasn't even hurt beyond a few cuts and contusions and a badly bruised ego. But we didn't know that at the time. Poor Ernie Sherry was at a total loss for the only time in his tenure on the show. Go to a close-up? Get the audience reaction? Fade to black? He finally yelled, "Go to Mike! Go to Mike!"

Thanks, Ernie. What am I supposed to say? "We'll be right back after these words from Blue Cross?" Half the audience thought it was a trick, the other half thought he was dead. I mumbled something about getting him some medical attention and started asking some of the tourists in the audience if they were enjoying their trip to Florida. I'm sorry, but there's nothing in the TV Host Manual about "What to do when the blind skier hits a tree."

Oh, by the way, since this is your week, I'd go with that stamp collection.

*

Okay, it's Friday. You're gonna make it. By the time you come in, the production staff has wrapped up the 9:00 A.M. meeting. Brad Lachman and Rick Ludwin have added some twists and Bob LaPorta contributed a great bit that kicked a little stunt into a full-blown sketch. Associate producer Susan Winston had two costumes overnighted from L.A. so we can do that *Star Wars* bit. The show's on cruise control. Most of our guys are already working on next week, wondering what to do for five days with Pia Zadora.

You look around and I'm not there. Don't worry. I had to meet with some of the Group W suits and listen to them worry about costs (not you—you were cheap; it's the production budget they keep fretting about). But I'll be there. I'm always there. I never even took a vacation in all the years on the show except the one week I had this nagging fever and a pain in my abdomen that wouldn't let up. I managed to get to midweek before calling a doctor. It took him all of five minutes to determine my appendix was bursting. I was off to the hospital and off the show for the one and only time.

Thank God for Alan Alda. Alan wasn't a doctor, but he played one on TV. He also played a darn good talk show host in my absence. If I had my choice of substitute hosts, Alan Alda would be my number one draft choice. I think he's a perfect fit for the show, although I would have liked to have given him about two months' notice. As it was, he

With Alan Alda

only had two hours, but he stepped in like an all-star relief pitcher and saved us for five days, the only substitute host in the history of *The Mike Douglas Show.*

*

The last show was great. Is Jonathan Winters a funny guy or what? All those props? Oh, that's just George Yokum, the property master. He's got a million of 'em. The guy's been around since vaudeville.

And you are really into it now. It's too bad you're just hitting full stride because we have to say goodbye. We'll show a few highlight clips from earlier in the week, give you a keepsake album of photographs and a *Mike Douglas Show* mug. You didn't think a lousy thousand bucks was all you'd have to show for a week with us?

*

After the red light goes off for the last time, we go backstage together and you take the time to let me know how much you enjoyed yourself and what a great bunch of people we have here. You don't know how right you are. It's a lot easier to prove my case with several years of hindsight on my side, but the collective achievements of the team we had working for us are nothing short of astounding. I hope you have time for a few examples.

Woody Fraser didn't have anything else to prove, but he did anyhow. He has produced dozens of successful shows, including *That's Incredible!* and *Good Morning America.* He's considered the best live-action producer in the business.

Roger Ailes didn't do much in television, unless you want to include his credits as America's number one political media advisor and his invaluable contributions to Presidents Nixon, Ford, Reagan, and Bush. I like it that, after me, Roger worked primarily for Presidents of the United States.

The talented Launa Newman is now Launa Newman-Minson, director of special programming for ABC.

Ernie DiMassa went on to produce for *Alan Thicke,* then over to King World and *Inside Edition.*

Burt DuBrow produces *Sally Jesse Raphael.* Barry Sand graduated to producer for *Late Night with David Letterman.* Jack Wartlieb heads up production for Paramount Television.

Bob LaPorta became vice president of entertainment for the Sea World empire. George Yokum joined him as arts manager (still a propman, he had it a lot easier working with whales and dolphins—they never complain and never step in the paint).

George Back was a key coordinator with Group W. He made similar contributions to the *Today* show, the *Tonight Show, Real People, Love Connection, David Letterman,* and *Entertainment Tonight.*

Rick Rosner created the *CHiPs* series, then took the helm as executive producer of the new *Hollywood Squares*. Chet Collier, the Group W exec who helped get us off the ground, went on to serve as CEO for Metromedia. Debbie Miller is vice president at William Morris. Michael Rollens is president of Josephson Communications. Vince Manze is the PR director for KNBC. Joe Harnell wrote the scores for several TV series and feature films.

Michael Krauss is a veteran producer. He worked on the *Today* show for years, now he's his own boss, generating specials for all three networks.

Barry Blaustein became one of the top writers in the business. He came up with some of the best of *Saturday Night Live,* then wrote *Coming to America* for Eddie Murphy and contributed to a slew of other big-screen comedies.

Art Forrest put his producer skills to work for Rosie O'Donnell, helping her show to hit the ground running in 1997. Sherry Coben created *Kate* and *Allie.* Fred Tatashore was *Dinah*'s producer before forming his own production company.

Rocco Urbisci put down his hammer and picked up a pen. He has been writer-producer for TV specials for Lily Tomlin, Richard Pryor, and over a dozen others.

Becky Greenlaw is associate producer of *Days of Our Lives.* Eric Lieber was producer and owner of the *Love Connection.* Rick Ludwin is NBC's vice president in charge of all special and variety programs. Brad Lachman produced *Solid Gold.* Sonya Selby-Wright produced for *Good Morning America,* along with Amy Hirsch and Rick Gaffney.

Sherry Grant owns Sherry Grant Enterprises, producing short films and videos. Rift Fournier produces *Close-Up* for the USA Network. Adrienne Meltzer is the co-host of *2 on the Town* in New York. Joe Goldfarb is senior VP for Lorimar. Ken Philo is in great demand as an independent art director. Peter Calabrese produces for Jay Leno. Ken

Johnson produced *The Incredible Hulk*. Bob Loudin is director of *Hollywood Squares*.

Merrill Mazuer, Larry Einhorn, and Linda Brown took their talents on the road. All are successful independent talent coordinators or production associates.

Vince Maynard was a local parish priest in Philadelphia. We talked him into joining our staff. He's still in the business and still in the priesthood, a talent director and spiritual counselor.

I could go on, and I know I've omitted several important names that I'll be sorry for later, but you get the idea. I don't think any show in the history of television has ever assembled a more talented and diverse conglomeration of achievers.

And you thought I did *The Mike Douglas Show* all by myself.

8

The Greatest Hits of
The Mike Douglas Show

THE best shows ever? Don't think it's easy. I started this book a long time ago. First, I had to review all the tapes. That took many years. Now, I should go back and review them again to double-check my notes, but by the time I get that done, Willard Scott will be wishing me Happy Birthday. We'll have to do this the way we did the show—go with what we have.

"Monkey Goes Bananas on Douglas Show"

One of our most memorable incidents actually included two shows about a week apart in 1975. It was the most bizarre and frightening thing that ever happened.

It started off innocently enough. We had Roddy McDowall on the show and came up with a great gag playing off his recurring role in the *Planet of the Apes* movies. The makeup wizards from the film came over and transformed both Roddy and me into movie apes. They did a wonderful job. I hosted the entire show as Ape-man Mike Douglas. I just wish we would have had Charlton Heston as a guest. That would have been memorable enough, except you know Woody. He brought in a real chimpanzee as a guest on the show and that's when the trouble started.

The chimp took a seat next to me and fell in love. That's how good the makeup was. He started caressing my arm and staring deep into my eyes. The only simian talk I know is that grunting "oooh-oooh-oooh" stuff, so that's what I did, in kind of a friendly chimp-to-chimp tone. I don't know why the chimp took it so hard. I suppose it lost something in translation. Anyhow, that set this chimp off like a rocket. He was out of the chair, shrieking and grunting and flailing all over the stage. Before anyone could react, he was off the stage and into the audience, completely out of control, bouncing through the seats, kicking, scratching, pulling hair—it was awful.

At least a half dozen crew members started chasing after him but the chimp was so fast and so wild, no one could grab him. It was getting to be a truly dangerous situation when we broke for a commercial with the chimp still terrorizing the entire studio.

By the time we returned, the home audience thought that order had been restored, but that was anything but the case. The crew closed in on him in but he eluded their grasp, escaped through the studio door, and

With the chimp and David Steinberg

continued his rampage backstage. While we carried on with the show, the chimp was destroying the entire office and production area. You cannot believe the amount of damage one chimpanzee can do. Try it sometime in your office. This little guy smashed lamps and furniture, tore curtains and shades, emptied drawers, turned over the water cooler, and threw a typewriter out a window. His meek trainer and a dozen crew and staff people never came close to corraling him. We finally had to call someone from the Philadelphia Zoo to come to our rescue. The zookeeper showed up with a tranquilizer gun and dropped him with one dart while the chimp was ripping out ceiling tiles and throwing them at anyone within thirty feet.

In the aftermath, the chimp was fine but we weren't. He woke up refreshed from a short nap, uninjured and oblivious to any problem he had caused. Our offices looked like a train wreck. Over $20,000 worth of damage. We managed to get things back together, although I can just imagine the look on the insurance adjuster's face.

The whole event was such a big deal and enough of it had been captured on film that we made a nice splash in the papers: CHIMP GOES BANANAS ON *DOUGLAS SHOW*. I thought that was the end of it.

No such luck.

About a week later, I was interviewing Walter Cronkite for the first time on the show when two burly men showed up out of nowhere. They were huge, with long beards and longer, unwashed hair and unkempt clothes. Before I could even guess what they were doing on camera, one of them grabbed my arm and handcuffed me to the nearest TV camera stand. And remember, this is live, on the air.

The audience giggled, figuring it was some stunt. So did I. It had to be Woody up to his old tricks. It was only when I looked off stage and saw the frightened look on Woody's face that I knew this was no joke.

The cameras were still rolling when one of the men said something about being from MOVE. That didn't mean anything to viewers around the nation, but MOVE had established a local presence in Philadelphia and it wasn't good news to us. They were a very mysterious organization, founded a few years earlier by a man who called himself "John Africa." He had picked up several followers and MOVE had grown into a multiracial collective of dozens of adults and children, all committed to their leader's stated principles of animal rights, a completely natural lifestyle that prohibited bathing, and an aggressive political attitude that protested against police repression. I wish I could give you more details to help make sense of all this, but I don't have any. I do know that about ten years later, the MOVE group was involved in one of the most horrifying incidents in Philadelphia history when police were repelled trying to serve an arrest warrant and ended up dropping a bomb from a helicopter onto MOVE's midtown headquarters, killing eleven people and destroying an entire city block.

That catastrophe was years away. All we knew at the time was that these people were unpredictable and potentially dangerous.

As one of the intruders demanded to be given airtime to protest our treatment of the chimpanzee, our crew members started to close in. He started into a lengthy diatribe about cruelty to animals on television when we cut to a commercial.

That's when the real tension started. Walter Cronkite sat there, mesmerized. Woody and the production staff stayed back, unsure what action would minimize the risk of any harm to me. I stared at the intruders, silent. I would have run for it except I was handcuffed to a two-thousand-pound TV camera. You could have heard a pin drop in the audience. They stared at the scene in awe, not sure if they were part of some protest, a kidnapping, hostage drama, or worse.

One of the intruders demanded that we go back on the air so that he could make a statement about animal rights. He started getting belligerent about it. Both men were wearing heavy coats and it was impossible to tell if they were armed or not.

Finally, several of the crew edged toward them. These were the union stagehands and they were husky guys as well. Hauling sets and heavy equipment all your life will do that to you. Most of them had been on the show for years and they were a loyal and protective bunch. One of the gaffers decided to speak up.

"You better take the handcuffs off Mike."

The MOVE delegate flinched, but just slightly. He insisted he was going to get his time on TV and they better back up.

In seconds, the crew had the two intruders completely encircled. The crew foreman spoke now, inches from the MOVE man's face.

"Listen, pal. You're gonna take those ******* handcuffs off right now and we're gonna let you walk outta here or we're gonna ******* break every ******* bone in your ******* body right here on this ******* stage."

With Walter Cronkite

I didn't care that much for his language, but I liked the message. The MOVE man stood there for a moment, then pulled out a key and released me without another word said. No one interfered with the intruders as they hurried out of the building. The police picked them up later, but we didn't press charges. It was over. No harm, no foul.

By the time we came back from commercial, everything was back to normal. I resumed my interview with Walter Cronkite and the show proceeded as planned, with just a brief comment from Walter before we went back on the air.

"Tell me, Mike, is it always like this around here?"

Tony Orlando's New Dawn

One of the hottest acts in the country, starting in the early 1970s, was Tony Orlando and Dawn. Most people don't know that Tony had been in the business since he was about twelve and paid his dues for many years before "Knock Three Times" made him an overnight sensation in 1970. His career took off, but those years of struggle proved to be a real benefit in the long run. They added a humble dimension that many stars lack and they gave him time to hone his craft. By the time he made it, he was already a veteran. He knew how to handle himself on stage and he knew how to handle an audience.

One of our most frequent guests, he also became a close friend. More than most, I knew Tony, including the touching story of the handicapped sister who had been the catalyst of his career. Severely limited, physically and mentally, she had responded to Tony's singing and playing. It inspired him to make performing his life's work.

He was also very close to Freddie Prinze, the talented comic who had landed a hit TV series, *Chico and the Man*, at the precocious age of nineteen, and was headed to the top of the comedy mountain before the

With Tony Orlando

complexities of stardom entangled him in a web of drugs and depression. He died a suicide at twenty-three in 1977. No one was hit harder by Freddie's death than Tony. That tragedy doubled when his precious sister passed away at twenty-one a short time later.

The 1970s were wild times in show business circles and Tony was not immune. He had dabbled with drugs, but the sudden deaths of two of the most important people in his life sent him into a drug-laden, manic-depressive free fall.

Tony was in life-threatening trouble. To his credit, he pulled himself together, went into treatment, and came back a better man.

He was welcomed back to the show in the fall of that year. It was good to see the real Tony again. In rehearsals, he was in fine voice and better spirits.

The show was meant to be a celebration of Tony's comeback, personally and professionally. It turned into one of our most poignant hours.

Tony poured his heart out before the nation. He recounted his trip to hell and back, blaming no one but himself, pleading with every kid in the audience to avoid the temptations that had devastated his life, his marriage, and his career.

Once he opened that door, I followed him in. I asked and Tony responded to questions I wouldn't ask a close friend in a private conversation. Tony was painfully honest. There was a sincerity in his final soliloquy that elevated those moments to among the best our show ever offered. I'm proud to have been a part of it and prouder still of Tony's courage. It was powerful and life-affirming.

He brought tears when he spoke of Freddie dying in his arms. He had the guts to describe his traumatic first days in an institution when other patients ridiculed him for his stardom. Before the nation, he apologized to his wife, Elaine, then thanked her with a rendition of "You Are So Beautiful" that brought more tears.

Can you imagine that happening today? You might see a hundred phony versions but I doubt if you will see anything that authentic on any of those five hundred channels. Agents, managers, and lawyers would be howling. Sponsors and network executives would be jumping out of their Armanis. Sure, they'll joke about getting busted for drugs or whatever, but stars don't talk in any depth about serious personal crises. This is entertainment. Somebody hit the LAUGH button.

Maybe they're right. Maybe it just doesn't work anymore. But there was a day when Tony Orlando stood tall, told it like a man, and I'll never forget it.

The Big Mix

"The Mix." Take an assortment of stars from diverse fields, mix well, serve up hot in the late afternoon, and see what happens. Woody Fraser made it up, we perfected it, and it stood the test of time for twenty years. Those daring pairings turned up snake eyes once in a while, but it worked like a charm a few thousands times, too.

Samples? Oh, I enjoy those. Did anyone see the show with Madalyn Murray O'Hair, the poster girl for atheists? She was a controversial lady, all right, but so morbidly serious about ridding America of its affiliation with God that she rarely made for good television. We took care of that. She was joined by the Reverend Robert Hughes of Citizens for Prayer. That got us up there. Then Carol Burnett joined in to lighten things up. Later, Nancy Wilson changed the tone with some sleek jazz. Meanwhile, Ravi Shankar was in the background with his trusty sitar. I'm sorry, Madalyn, but I thought the whole show was divine.

Do you like variety in your music? One time, we had James Brown, Roberta Peters, and Jimmy Dean sing back-to-back-to-back. Or how about Sonny Bono singing with octogenarian banjo player Pearl Pepper? They loved each other. Frank Sinatra, Jr., sang with the Turtles. The Four Tops did a duet with the Muppets. Judy Garland and William Safire, although I don't remember them singing together, just talking. It's not such a stretch to imagine Dustin Hoffman and Peter Fonda together, but where else are you ever going to see both of them with Pete Fountain, Chita Rivera, and London Lee? And how many times have the Beach Boys appeared with William F. Buckley? You've seen Duke Ellington, you've seen Phyllis Diller, but together? Nancy Reagan and Cybill Shepherd weren't close, but they were side by side on our show. Tommy Lasorda and Pia Zadora sounds like a good match, and it was, on the same show with Jimmy Cagney, Don Rickles, and Charley Pride. One strange cluster was Sean Connery, Buffalo Bob, Natalie Wood, and Dottie West. Not much in common? They all went to lunch together. Billy Crystal and David Copperfield were a magical pairing, at least until David made Billy disappear. Benny Goodman and Maynard Ferguson was magically musical. Sylvester Stallone and Helen Reddy didn't work:

**With
Burt Reynolds**

she couldn't take a punch. Lillian Carter and Leon Spinks worked for me. Whoever matched Jane Fonda and Charlton Heston was looking for trouble. Michael Jackson and Shecky Greene were never meant to hang around together, either. I knew we were in for it when Shecky showed up wearing one sequined glove.

My holiday favorite was the Christmas show that featured Burt Bacharach, Bo Derek, Phyllis Diller, the Captain & Tennille, Danny De-Vito, Santa Claus, and the rock group War. Now there was a show that had everything. The only problem was that one of the rockers took a swing at Santa in the Green Room. They didn't call them "War" for nothing, I guess.

There are so many more wonderfully odd couples that came together

for a once-and-once-only appearance on our show—Ronald Reagan and
Lily Tomlin, William Shatner and Patti Smith, Gerald Ford and Ricardo
Montalban, the Lennon Sisters and Johnny Paycheck, Woodward &
Bernstein and the Smothers Brothers—but this is the Greatest Hits chap-
ter and I have to name the number one lineup we ever assembled. Once
you whittle it down to about thirty finalists, it's almost a lottery pick.
Still, I think that honor belongs to the broadcast of January 22, 1979.

We were on location, with Burt Reynolds as co-host and Kenny
Rogers booked as the leadoff guest. Burt was riding high, the number
one box office star in the world, filming the sequel to *Cannonball Run*.
Kenny Rogers was not just the number one country singer, he was all
over the charts—country, pop, rock, contemporary, easy listening, you
name it.

I don't know why the staff thought that would be a good day to have
the number one female singer in the country, too, but Olivia Newton-
John was also on the roster.

Okay, you guys, enough is enough.

No, it wasn't. Burt had invited Hal Needham, so we had to make
time for the number one action director. And Jerry Reed was coming,
too. Another leading country singer and composer and Burt's co-star.

We had enough star power to do Jerry Lewis's telethon and we only
had ninety minutes. About ten minutes in, Jackie Gleason decided to
visit for a few laughs. That made for an even half dozen heavyweights.
The last thing we needed was Dom DeLuise, but there he was. I needed
to keep my composure on a day like this and having Dom was like
someone tickling me for an hour and a half. And wouldn't you know
who he would have in tow? America's heartthrob, Farrah Fawcett, looking better than her ten-million-selling poster.

What a show! I wish I could say I accepted the challenge and managed
to present a coherent ninety minutes of entertainment, juggling superstars
with cool aplomb. I lost it as soon as Dom DeLuise started grinning at me,
Burt couldn't stop laughing, Kenny hardly made it through one song,
Olivia couldn't even try, Gleason stole the middle half hour, Jerry jumped
in with some perfect one-liners, and Farrah sparkled through.

Hal Needham kept looking at his watch. He had a movie to do.

Just when I thought we would never top this, two more uninvited
guests crashed the party—Dean Martin and Sammy Davis, Jr. That did
it. Put it in the record books.

We closed that day with an easy question for our last two guests: what single word would you like on your tombstone? Sammy had a good answer. "Entertainer." Dean took a sip of his drink and went him one better. "Dead."

Most people plan months in advance, make arrangements, and get all dressed up to go to a party they'll remember for a long time. I just had to go to work.

The Bull and the Bear

I told you producer Woody Fraser tried to kill me several times. I love the guy, but if I brought him up on charges, the best he could do would be to plea-bargain his way down from attempted murder to manslaughter. I've got more proof than Kenneth Starr.

Back in the mid-1960s, Woody was into animal acts. I think he really wanted to produce *Animal Kingdom*. Monkeys, llamas, parrots, dogs, snakes, camels—there were times when I felt like Noah doing a show from the Ark. The two classics were the Wall Street quiniela Woody foisted on me about six months apart—the Bull and the Bear.

The Bull was bad enough. Trini Lopez was the co-host one week in 1968. Trini was huge for years with his Hispanic twist on folk songs. A good guy, he was always up for anything. Trini is Spanish, so Woody conjured up a bullfight shtick, made arrangements for us to dress up like matadors and sing a duet in an improvised bull ring outside San Diego with a huge but harmless bull in the background. I was a little concerned when the crew insisted on staying on the safe side of the high-walled arena, but Woody insisted there was no danger. The bull was old and feeble, could barely stand up. Okay, Woody, whatever you say. Trini and I climbed in and approached the gentle giant.

Trini Lopez was very athletic, with powerful shoulders and legs. He was built like a halfback. I was a little older, forty-something, but I liked to think I kept myself in pretty good shape. As we approached the bull, we discussed what to do on the remote chance that the animal posed any danger. Trini said something, but I didn't really get it because Trini had that thick accent and was difficult to understand. I just nodded.

We were about halfway across the arena when everything went wrong. It wasn't an old bull, as advertised, it was young and energetic. Eight hundred pounds of prime beef. The bull looked up warily, caught

Mike and Trini Lopez as bullfighters

scent of something in the air (Trini's cologne? My fear?), and started scraping the ground ominously, tearing up huge clods of earth. I turned and called out to Woody.

"What's he doing?"

Woody waved us on.

"It's okay. Don't worry!"

We took a few more steps. The bull snorted, put his massive head down, and charged, the twin stiletto points of his horns glistening in the sun. There was no time to think. Trini let out a string of Spanish epithets, which the bull may have understood but I didn't, and the two of us ran for our lives.

It was about forty yards to safety. It all happened so fast, there are only two things I remember. Trini had a slight head start on me, and he yelled some encouragement as we ran. He was suddenly speaking more perfect English than Laurence Olivier. Must have been the adrenaline.

I also remember being impressed at how fast Trini was running, right up until I passed him like a speeding bullet. I was at the fence and over it in a single bound, dusting myself off and yelling at Woody by the time Trini made it over, a few yards in front of the bull, who crashed into the fence like a runaway tank. My only regret is that no one had a stopwatch because I'm certain I set the world record in the forty-yard dash.

If you think I was rough on Woody, you should have heard Gen. For a gentle lady that never raised her voice, she chewed on that man's ears like Mike Tyson.

The bull was bad, but the bear was worse. Woody was certain that putting me in apparently dangerous situations that he knew were perfectly safe really heightened the dramatic value of the show. He couldn't help himself. He booked Bernard the Bear Trainer for the show along with his prized pupil, Rudolph the Red-Nosed Bear. Rudolph was so well trained, we were going to do this bit with me wrestling Rudolph, who would succumb to my enormous strength and go down for the count. When he finally brought it up the day before, I didn't want to do it.

"I'm not wrestling any bear, Woody. Forget it."

"Mike. C'mon. He's a puppy dog. You touch him, he'll go down."

"Oh, no. That's too dangerous. I'm out."

"Mike. It's a trained bear. He grew up with this Bernard guy."

"Well I hope they're happy together but I'm not doing it."

"C'mon. Hey, Grizzly Adams works with bears every day, never had a scratch. Gentle Ben? This bear is gentler than Gentle Ben. And Bernard'll be right there the whole time. Keeps the bear on a short leash . . . I mean, chain."

"He stays right there in the ring?"

"You, Bernard, and the bear. Bernard never lets go of the chain."

"I grab him, he falls down?"

"Like he's shot through the heart. Does it every time."

"If he so much as growls, I'm outta there."

"You're my hero."

Show time, and here comes Bernard, right up center aisle, with Rudolph loping along behind like a friendly, eight-hundred-pound dog, secured by a chain you could use to anchor the *Queen Mary*. I was a little anxious when I saw the huge teeth and the claws that looked like a row of machetes, but I felt better when Rudolph lumbered up on stage, bored and benign. If you've ever been close to a bear (and I hope you haven't), you know that the odor will probably kill you long before the bear does. This poor guy needed a bath and a couple hundred pounds of Right Guard, but he didn't act like he was looking for trouble—at least not until the noise and the lights started getting to him.

I've seen it happen before, but never with a bear. Stage fright. He got to the middle of the makeshift ring where Bernard was supposed to start off by demonstrating how to wrestle a bear, but Rudolph didn't want any part of it. He stood there, frozen in his tracks, staring at us both. When none of his trainer tricks worked, Bernard stepped up to the beast and slugged him right in the snout. I guess that's where he got the "red-nosed" moniker. I'm sure Bernard really is a professional trainer and not just some suicidal maniac Woody hauled in off the street, but that was not a good idea. The enraged bear slugged him back with a nice left hook that knocked Bernard right out of the ring into an offstage wall, out cold.

I was thinking that was probably the first time someone had been knocked out on live television outside a boxing ring when I heard the screams and noticed the audience was smart enough to start running for the exits. The crew backed away. Now it was me and the bear, alone on stage, *mano a bearo.*

This wasn't good. The chain was still dangling from his neck, but no one was holding the other end. Rudolph turned to me, growling and flashing those four-inch teeth. I hoped he'd had a big lunch.

I yelled for someone on the crew to grab the chain. I was keeping my eye on the bear, so I didn't see the smart guy who yelled back.

"He's your guest!"

Unlike with the bull, there was nowhere to run and nowhere to hide. All I could do was grab the chain and try to herd him back toward the open cage we had stashed backstage to transport him after the show. I can't tell you how pleased I was when I took the chain, tugged gently, and the furry monster didn't bite off my head. Good bear, Rudy! A few seconds later, the crew rushed in and joined me in nudging him off stage. Docile as a puppy again, he ambled meekly into his cage and we flipped the lock.

It was over in seconds and no one was hurt, but I never had so much as a bear cub on the show ever again. It was years before I would even book Bear Bryant.

And Woody? From then on, the only nonhumans Woody was allowed to invite on the show were birds. That slowed him down, but it didn't stop him. It wasn't long before Woody had Dom DeLuise and myself saddled up on twelve-foot ostriches, racing through Las Vegas at forty miles an hour, hanging on for our lives . . . but that's another story.

Martha, My Dear

By 1974, we were no longer broadcasting live. After years of working "without a net," the logistics of production and scheduling mandated the transition to tape delay. It had to be, for a number of reasons, and I never regretted it. Except once. At the height of the Watergate scandal, we managed to get Martha Mitchell, the outspoken wife of Attorney General John Mitchell, to co-host the show for a week. In the summer of 1974, the entire nation was focused on the intense events unfolding in Washington and Martha Mitchell was one of the most intriguing and most enigmatic players involved in this political drama. Although the White House had tried to muzzle her, she was too much for any spin doctor to handle. Martha made her own decisions, and she decided to do our show just as the House of Representatives was preparing to vote on the impeachment of President Nixon.

The announcement that we had scheduled Martha Mitchell for an entire week hit Washington like a bombshell. What would she say? What would she do? We even got a call direct from the White House asking us to cancel her, then scolding us as irresponsible for putting "that alcoholic" on the air. We didn't budge. There was a gaggle of reporters clustered outside the studio from the first moment she arrived. They didn't know what to expect and neither did I.

Contrary to the leaks and innuendoes in the press, Martha Mitchell was not the zany, unpredictable chatterbox she had been portrayed. In fact, I found her to be an incisive observer of the Washington scene who knew what she was talking about and said exactly what she meant. She had been accused of embellishing what little information she had to pique the interests of the press. Nothing could be further from the truth. Martha didn't exaggerate one bit. She didn't have to. She knew things, firsthand, that could blow the lid off most of Wash-

With Martha Mitchell

ington. The only one she was interested in protecting was her husband, John. She believed he was an honorable man being dragged down by some bad actors who surrounded the President, and she wasn't happy about it at all.

Martha and I spent hours together, before and after the shows. And she talked. No subject was taboo, and there was nothing in Washington that she didn't know a whole lot more about than Woodward & Bernstein ever dreamed of. I wish I'd had a tape recorder running that whole week. Then again, I guess President Nixon proved that's not such a great idea.

She gave me chapter and verse of the special White House "plumbers" who didn't work for John Mitchell, the Justice Department, the FBI, the CIA—no one. These people were out of control. She claimed that certain White House higher-ups had turned Watergate into a "tar baby" for Nixon, and that it was no accident. Weeks before it was revealed to the nation, she told me there was a voice-activated system in the White House and "everything anybody said was on tape." She even claimed to know who "Deep Throat" was. She insisted that "Al Haig is the talking puppet and Kissinger is pulling the strings. He's the biggest phony in Washington. The only English word he never learned is 'loyalty.'"

Wow. Martha was something else. I sat there with my mouth open all week while she dropped the Beltway secrets like she was telling knock-knock jokes. Some of it made it on the air, but a lot more was left in the Green Room. In the end, it didn't matter because the tape delay put the broadcast on in mid-August for most areas of the country, a week after the sudden resignation of President Nixon. Watergate was effectively over by the time Martha used our show to tell her story.

"I like you, Mike, and I don't want to get you in trouble," she told me one day before a taping. "It's too bad your show's not live anymore. We could make history together."

She wasn't kidding. As the years passed, more and more of what she told me proved to be true. Every time, I would shake my head and think of Martha Mitchell. Her husband was never President, but she'll always be the First Lady of politics in my book.

One for My Lady

One memory on my personal list is special only because it involves my silent partner for every minute of *The Mike Douglas Show,* my bride, Gen.

Harry Belafonte is a wonderful guest. He's always up, always on, and brimming with talent. It doesn't hurt that he's one of the most handsome men on the planet and has been for—wait a second, that's way too long to be that handsome. Somebody should check that out.

Harry came on the show in the early 1970s. He was his usual ebullient self. I didn't expect anything more than the usual good conversation and great songs, but Harry did me a big favor that day, something that I had been trying to do for years with no success, and I have to thank him for it.

I introduced him to the audience. We started to talk. But there was something on his mind, and it wasn't more than a minute before he brought it up.

"Excuse me—Mike?"

"Yes?"

"I'm sorry but, there's something—there's a splendid woman backstage and I really think we have to bring her out here right now."

I didn't quite catch on yet.

"Who's that?"

"I believe you know her well. I was just speaking to her, and I asked

Mike and Gen Douglas

her to come out here with me and she turned me down. Adamant. And I don't think we can accept that."

Now I knew. He was talking about Gen. Good luck, Harry. For more than a decade on the show, for my entire career, Gen had worked harder and provided more emotional and professional support than anyone in my life, but the one thing she would never do was spend one moment in the sun. She had never been a guest on the show, in spite of a thousand requests. She would not even stand up in the audience and wave. She was backstage every day, only a few feet from the spotlight, but she wouldn't set foot in its glare. That was for me, not her. No matter how many times I implored her to share, she declined. No way.

At least, not until Harry Belafonte came along. After a lengthy warm-up, extolling Gen beyond measure, he had the audience applauding, then chanting for Gen to come out. Who could refuse?

Gen, that's who. Harry didn't know who he was dealing with. But Harry Belafonte is an irrepressible man and simply would not take no for an answer. He finally got up, walked off stage, and literally hauled Gen out in front of the camera to the delight of the audience. Harry was beaming.

"Ladies and gentlemen, Mrs. Genevieve Douglas!"

I led the standing ovation.

Finally, there was Gen. It wasn't hard to tell she had been ambushed. She looked bashful, embarrassed—and radiant.

Harry Belafonte made that happen. I don't think anyone else could have managed it. I certainly couldn't. But Harry did, and I thank him for it.

The Men in My Little Girls' Lives

One more personal indulgence, if I may. My three little girls—Michele, Christine, and Kelly—mean the world to me. It's hard to believe they're not so little anymore. All grown up, two are mothers themselves, one even a grandmother—I don't care, they're still my little girls.

This show business life of ours might seem enviable to other kids, but the truth is it wasn't easy on them, especially the twins, Michele and Christine. They grew up in our most difficult years, always traveling, life always unsettled. Even the success of the show wasn't such a blessing for them, with the demands on my time and the endless buzz of activity. There were precious few moments just for family. They were real troupers, though, never complaining, going with the flow. But I always regretted the time lost and wanted to do something special.

It was 1966. The twins had sprouted into young adults right before our eyes. They were in college already. After her freshman year, Christine returned home one day escorted by a young man named Paul. They wanted to get married. Oh my God, I thought, you kids can't do that. You can't be more than ten.

I was off by a few years. Christine was almost twenty and Paul Voinovich was a few years older. Still, it was way too much too soon, never mind that Gen and I were even younger when we cast caution to the wind and eloped to say our vows.

Mike with Gen, Michele, Christine, Kelly, and granddaughters

I tried my best. I told Paul that, if they would only wait until after Christine graduated, I would buy them a house. Yes, it was a bribe. He had a classic reply, "I don't want your money, Mr. Dowd—[he even used my real name]—I want your daughter." What could I say? They were married shortly after.

About a year later, I received a copy of a song with a note that said a fan had written it with me in mind. It was more of an ode from a father to a daughter, but the words touched me so deeply, I made arrangements to record it as soon as I could get a few minutes away from the show. I only did it for my own girls, but the studio thought it had some potential and started sending it around for airplay right after it was pressed. The reaction was unbelievable. "The Men in My Little Girl's Life" shot up the charts, toppled the Beatles from the number one spot, and stayed there for months. The song turned into a phenomenon that I still can't believe. Nothing else in my entire career can compare to the personal satisfaction I've gotten from the heartfelt messages of appreciation from so many fans, the fathers who tell me how much it means to them, the mothers and daughters who thank me for adding the perfect touch to a wedding or family reunion. Touching people's hearts like that—all I can tell you is, it's what a singer lives for.

That same year, Christine and Paul were expecting their first child. Our show was still being broadcast live, and I knew if she had the baby in midweek, I couldn't be there. It broke my heart. Show business in the way again. It was Gen who came up the idea of getting Christine on the phone, live, on the show, and singing my feelings to her in front of the world.

Our first grandchild, Deborah, was born in the early hours of November 5, 1966. On the show that very day, through a phone hook-up to the hospital in Cleveland, I gave the most important performance of my life, singing "The Men in My Little Girl's Life" to Christine, to Deborah, and to Michele, Kelly, and Gen. All the girls in my life. That was my Carnegie Hall. I put everything I had into it. The studio audience, the TV audience—they didn't exist at that moment. It was just me and my girls. I don't know how I made it through, but I did. Of all the songs, all the performances I have ever given, that was the one that counted most.

The One That Got Away

None of you will include this as one of the unforgettable memories of *The Mike Douglas Show,* but I have to, whether I like it or not.

Frank Sinatra called himself a "saloon singer." Well if that's what Frank said, it's good enough for me, but he was the best saloon singer of all time. I don't claim to be an expert at many things, but I know a little bit about saloon singers. I've been singing in saloons since I was nine years old. I've seen all the great ones, but there was only one Sinatra. As a singer and a personality, Old Blue Eyes will always be in a league of his own.

I had wanted Sinatra on the show since Day One. Literally. When they first asked who I would like to have for a guest, I said, "Sinatra." Of course I knew it was impossible, but that's who I wanted. You might as well start at the top. At that time, the only television Frank ever did

was a rare prime-time special of his own.
Nothing else. So I put it out of my mind
until we managed to land Sammy Davis,
Jr. Sammy did the entire ninety minutes,
put on a spectacular show, and brought a
tidal wave of positive reaction. That gave
me a glimmer of hope that someday,
maybe, we could get Frank. My formal
lobbying efforts began with Sammy. I
mentioned we were pretty tenacious when
it came to getting guests. Sinatra was a
ten-year program. Sammy appeared on the
show over thirty times, and I'm sure the
only thing he didn't look forward to was
the conversation with me at the end of
the day.

Frank Sinatra

"You were great, Sam. Hey, have you talked to Frank lately?"

"Don't start with me, man. You gotta talk to his people."

"Sammy, you're his people! C'mon, you can do it. He'll do it for
you."

"He's Sinatra, Mike. He'll do what he does when he does it."

I had already had the pleasure, as if granted by a genie, of hosting virtually every major performer of the times and many of the living legends
of days gone by. There was not a singer, musician, or composer of note
who hadn't been on *Mike Douglas,* except Elvis and Frank Sinatra. Elvis
was impossible, hadn't done guest shots since the 1950s. I wanted Sinatra.

"Woody, we gotta get Frank."

It was impossible. I tried everything. I sent gifts. I made supplications
through mutual friends. I had Frank Junior on the show. Several times. I
had Tina on more than once and not only featured Nancy Sinatra as co-
host, I doubled up by adding son-in-law Tommy Sands. Frank liked
Shecky Greene? Shecky does a week. Frank's pal Pat Henry is available?
Several guest shots and a week in the co-chair. Frank is dating Mia Farrow? She's on three days later.

Will Frank do the show?

No. Too busy right now.

No. Recording in the studio.

No. Mad at the whole media over that thing in Australia.

No. Maybe some other time.

No. Leaving for a film in Europe.

No. Has to do Vegas.

No. He'll talk to you about it sometime.

No. Upset about the coverage of that fight at the Desert Inn.

Maybe. Try this summer sometime.

No. Doing that thing in Houston for the astronauts.

No. His throat hurts.

No. Try in the spring.

Frank, what else can I do? Who else is there in the family?

Finally, miraculously, I ran into Frank myself at a benefit we were both appearing at in New Jersey. He was in great spirits and we spent some time together backstage. Just before he went on, he asked if I had any good Italian jokes and I gave him two fresh ones. Frank used them both in his short set and laid the audience out. He did a few songs, bowed before his usual standing ovation, and walked off stage beaming, looking for me.

"Mike, those were killers! I owe you a big one, pal."

No time to be bashful.

"Any time, Frank. Listen, why don't you do my show and we're even."

He smiled that Sinatra smile, blue eyes twinkling.

"I've been waiting for you to ask. Next week okay?"

That's how easy it was. All those years, and all it took was two Italian jokes. The only thing he asked was that we invite his buddy, comedian Pat Henry, to join us on the show. I was so grateful, I called Pat the next day and booked him as the co-host for the week.

Our people firmed up the details through a phalanx of Frank's agents and Mr. Frank Sinatra, the Chairman of the Board, was booked on *The Mike Douglas Show* for the following Friday.

Monday and Tuesday with Pat, a genuinely funny man and a nimble co-host, were great. Everybody was up, sky-high. We spent some time reviewing notes for Wednesday and several hours in early preparation for Friday, adding pieces to the orchestra, making sure the sets would be perfect, going over questions for Frank. Everyone went home happy. I had no premonitions, no sense of impending doom. I never felt better in my life, dressing for dinner with Gen, absently watching the evening news. Co-anchor Trudy Haynes on local WKYC in

Philadelphia moved from a hard news item into an entertainment tid-bit, something about ". . . even congenial TV host Mike Douglas isn't immune to being snubbed by the unpredictable Frank Sinatra. Old Blue Eyes was scheduled on *The Mike Douglas Show* today, but failed to appear, leaving Mike and co-host/best friend Pat Henry in the lurch . . ."

What?

Frank wasn't scheduled for today, he's not due until Friday. She's got that one all wrong. Gen mentioned that someone on the staff better call and straighten them out. At least it's only a blurb on a local Philly sta-tion. I'm glad Frank's not in town. If he heard this, he might be of-fended—

The phone rang.

"Hello?—Pardon me?—Who did you—yes, I saw it, and I'm—but we didn't—now if you just hold on a minute—I'm sorry, but we—Listen, I'm going to call—Hello?"

Frank had heard about it, all right. Apparently within minutes of the broadcast. And I don't think I'm exaggerating when I report that he was not happy. He seemed to understand that neither I nor anyone on the show had anything to do with the bogus report, but it didn't matter. He canceled his Friday appearance.

Frank didn't speak to or communicate with me in any way for over two years after that. That's Frank. I understood.

A few years later, I was out for a modest birthday dinner with Gen and a few friends at Chasen's in L.A. Across the booth behind me, I could see Steve Lawrence and Eydie Gormé and waved hello. There was someone else with them, but his back was to me and I couldn't tell who it was. After the meal, as my companions broke into the mandatory cho-rus of "Happy Birthday to You," the man with Steve and Eydie rose and turned to me. It was Frank. He reached out, shook my hand, then hugged me.

"Happy Birthday, Mike."

That was great, a moment to remember. But he never did the show. We never spoke about it after that. I never asked. He never offered. I still regret it. He's the one that got away.

I don't know what happened to Trudy Haynes but she was never in-vited on our show and I doubt if she was ever invited to the Columbia School of Journalism either.

With John Lennon and Yoko Ono

The Ballad of John & Yoko & Mike

Since their earliest days, the Beatles had displayed a strategic sense of limiting their appearances to massive concerts and brief press conferences. By the mid-1960s, after breaking every concert record in the world, the group had withdrawn to the recording studio. You heard the Beatles on their zillion-selling albums, but rarely saw them in a live setting. A generation of Americans had come to idolize them, but didn't know them well.

Yoko Ono was even more of an enigma. She had been demonized by many as a disruptive influence on the group and remained a mystery to the rest. What did John see in this woman? Why did he choose her over the most successful group in music history?

It was our show that finally afforded the first extended opportunity to answer those questions. We felt privileged and challenged. The most sought after guests in the entertainment world had agreed to do a week of shows with us and we were determined not to waste it. In 450 minutes over five shows, we planned to present the real "Ballad of John and Yoko," let them shine through in their own words and music, and let America assess this remarkable couple for themselves.

I think we accomplished that, but it wasn't easy. It was one of the most interesting, most trying, and, in the end, most rewarding week of shows we ever produced.

Not only did we have to deal with John and Yoko and their idiosyncrasies, but that particular set of shows drew more interest from disparate groups of people than any other in our history. Media requests alone could have filled the audience. We could have sold a hundred thousand tickets to Beatles fans. Westinghouse executives who hadn't been near the set in years showed up with family and friends. And, although I didn't find out until years later, at least a half dozen of the conservatively dressed men in attendance every day were FBI agents dispatched by Director Hoover to keep an eye on the suspiciously radical Beatle.

They didn't have to worry. John Lennon proved to be a most benign, talented, and likable young man. Yoko Ono proved to be, well, Yoko.

We were well aware that these were very special guests, and we wanted to treat them that way. Even that was a problem.

Long before their arrival, we had renovated a backstage area as a separate dressing room just for John and Yoko, with new finishes, decorations, furniture, carpeting—the works. For me, that room came to illustrate the paradoxical behavior of this preeminent couple of rock. One of the themes of the week was John and Yoko's concern about the environment. When they departed, the first thing we had to do was gut the John & Yoko Room. It had been trashed beyond recognition. It looked like a horde of vandals had been trapped in there for a week. Now I think that was a mistake. We should have kept it intact. It may have been one of those "performance art" things and we just didn't get it.

Word was that John and Yoko had put the drugs behind them, but I think that the rumor was a little premature. Bandleader Joe Harnell can attest to this. He had to deal with a whacked-out monkey running amok, leaping on the instruments, and attacking band members after John decided it would be fun to blow some marijuana smoke in the animal's face. (What was it with monkeys and *The Mike Douglas Show*?)

But the headaches were relatively minor and I will say that John was

John Lennon, Yoko Ono, and Chuck Berry

as joyful a guest as we ever had. He was smart, funny, gregarious, and beguiling. He was as good a listener as a talker, with a genuine compassion for other people and respect for other philosophies.

Yoko was every bit as sincere as John, but where John was soft-spoken, Yoko was strident. No one was ever harder for our staff to please. Many of them came to me completely exasperated over the days of working on those shows. Yoko wanted it warmer. Yoko wanted it colder. Yoko said there wasn't enough of a certain color in the dressing room. Yoko wanted it quieter. Yoko wanted it louder. Yoko wanted it brighter. Yoko wanted it darker. Another week and Yoko wouldn't just be responsible for breaking up the Beatles, she'd break up *The Mike Douglas Show,* too.

In spite of it all, I have to tell you that, by the end of the run, I think I came to understand something about John's affection for this woman. She was strange and she could be difficult, but she was a powerful character, unswerving and unapologetic about following her own unique path in life and if you don't like it, too bad. Do your own thing. She's going to do hers.

We offered to include a number of John and Yoko's selections on the guest list throughout the week. We provided this courtesy to most of our weekly co-hosts, but never to the extent that we did for John and Yoko.

John's first request was Chuck Berry. If you're a rock 'n' roll fan, that show belongs in a time capsule. One of the founding fathers of rock playing side by side with the Beatles' leader, and the result was spectacular. They kicked off with "Memphis" and closed the show with "Johnny B. Goode." It was a powerful set, a pairing of legends, but for John it meant even more than that. Chuck Berry had been his idol. As he told me after the show, he didn't care what happened the rest of the week. Those few minutes on stage with Chuck Berry were "worth the whole gig, 'ey?"

Yoko's top draft choice was Jerry Rubin. Jerry was well known as an unrepentant anarchist and antagonist and I advised against inviting him, but John—and especially Yoko—wanted him badly. They mentioned he had recently come out strongly against drugs and I could emphasize that. Okay. I relented. Maybe it wouldn't be so bad.

Oh, yes it was. Jerry Rubin came on and started right in about how everyone should rise up and overthrow all the Washington warmongers who had made America the most oppressive nation on earth. My temperature was already rising when I tried to steer him into more agreeable territory.

"Jerry, I understand you've made a real turnaround and taken a stand against the use of drugs?"

"That's not true. I'm not against drugs. Just heroin, because heroin is a tool used by the Gestapo police of this country to subjugate the black man."

Not what I was hoping for on the drug issue.

I can count on one hand the number of times a guest, any guest, really got to me. It was unprofessional and unfair to the guest. But on rare occasions, something was said that shattered my carefully constructed objectivity, and I would fire off a round or two. The show with Jerry Rubin was an extreme example. He just got on my nerves. It sounded like this guy hated the President, the Congress, everyone in business, the military, all police, and just about everything America stands for. Worse, here I was giving him a forum to spout off to twenty million people. The only way I could think of to make things right was to poke some holes in his venomous balloons.

Jerry and I were going at it pretty good when who do you think stepped in as ombudsman to calm things down and restore order? John Lennon. John picked up the mantle of Kind and Gentle Host and he did it quite well, reinterpreting Jerry's comments to take some of the sting out and adding a little humor to help keep things cool.

I was still exasperated after the show ended, at both Jerry and myself, but twenty-five years later, I see it in a different light. Rather than regret what happened, I appreciate it. It was great confrontational television, a harsh exchange of ideas. But there were no chairs thrown, no noses broken, not a single word bleeped out. It was emotional but not offensive, with the added bonus of allowing people to see what a genuinely nice fellow John Lennon was.

The real surprise of the week was Bobby Seale, leader of the Black Panther Party, another John-Yoko nominee for guest. After the trying experience with Jerry Rubin, I was hardly looking forward to Bobby Seale. The general public viewed the Black Panthers as heavily armed, white-hating militants. Talk about the perfect way to alienate my core viewing audience. I had visions of the announcement in the press at the end of the week:

After scoring a television exclusive with co-hosts John Lennon and Yoko Ono, *The Mike Douglas Show* was abruptly canceled today in response to protests by millions of viewers and a recent FBI report that named Douglas one of the nation's most dangerous radicals.

It was starting to look like the price for having John & Yoko was going to be my career. I was braced for a firestorm the following day when I introduced ". . . the chairman of the Black Panther Party in America, Mr. Bobby Seale."

All I can say is, God bless Bobby Seale. There was no trace of the rancor I anticipated. He didn't want to talk about "pigs" or that "up against the wall" stuff. He discussed programs that collected shoes for the needy and provided breakfast for inner-city kids who had been going to school on empty stomachs. He brought a film clip of the Panthers handing out bags of groceries in poor neighborhoods. And Bobby Seale wasn't playing the saint, either. He readily admitted that part of the group's generosity was based on pragmatism: "If you expect a crowd to turn out and listen to what you have to say, you better give them something for it."

I could identify with that. We had been doing the same thing for years.

We enjoyed some silly segments, too. I still have to laugh when I think of John, Yoko, and Louis Nye calling strangers at random on the phone to say, "We love you" and pass it on. It was Yoko's idea for a wonderful way to spread "unconditional love," but it didn't quite work. The first five people all told us to do something to ourselves which was physically impossible. The rest didn't believe, didn't understand, or didn't care. I finally had to step in and find a way out. I got the studio operator to ring up David Frost's office and closed the segment by informing that world that I loved David, and pass it on to Johnny and Merv.

One day, Yoko introduced a baffling performance art piece, a small box lined with mirrors for everyone to smile into. She called it "Collecting Smiles." As we circulated the box and the audience sat there mystified, John turned to me and said, "I live with her and I still don't get a lot of this stuff." You had to like the guy.

After taping the last show, I gave John Lennon a big hug. It was a pleasure to have gotten to know this gentle man better than all but a handful of Americans. He was pleased enough to promise to do it again sometime and I told him I would hold him to that.

Years later, I did, and that leads to a chilling postscript. John Lennon went through many more changes in the 1970s, but by the end of the decade he returned to the studio, reenergized, for his first new album in years. That gave me reason enough to invite him back on the show. He quickly agreed and we scheduled him for December of 1980, when we would be on location in Hawaii.

Unfortunately, the studio sessions dragged on, the album was not quite complete, and John called to postpone.

A few weeks later, we were in Hawaii. I can recall the exact moment when a grim staffer gave me the tragic news that John Lennon had been shot and killed in front of his Dakota apartment house in New York. It was the day of his scheduled appearance. In a bizarre coincidence, his assassin, Mark David Chapman, had traveled from Hawaii to stalk and slay him. There was no sense to be made of it. All I know is, we lost one of the most creative forces in music that day, and an exceptional man.

And Away We Go!

We had many theme shows and often featured the entire cast of hit sitcoms like *All in the Family, Mary Tyler Moore,* or *Welcome Back, Kotter.* That format provided a unique look at the synergy that made those shows click and always ranked among our most popular programs. I enjoyed them all, but one of my favorite guests switched that concept around and gave me one of my favorite television moments.

After numerous appearances as a guest and countless rounds of golf, Jackie Gleason announced he was going to do something to return the favor. They didn't call him the Great One for nothing.

The Honeymooners had been one of the nation's favorite shows for years before we went on the air. Ralph and Alice in their tiny walk-up, trying to make something of a small life in the big city with best pals Norton and Trixie. Was there ever a more hilarious or heartwarming show on television? Maybe that's why it's still in reruns today.

Jackie's gift to me was something that no one else could do, and even if they could have, I doubt if anyone would have had the imagination and audacity to try. After *The Jackie Gleason Show* had moved to Miami and incorporated *The Honeymooners* as a stand-alone segment, he instructed his writers to create a special episode, with Ralph and Norton and their wives following an unlikely series of events that culminated with their appearance on *The Mike Douglas Show.*

For one glorious week in Miami, *The Mike Douglas Show* was reincarnated within *The Honeymooners.* It was a fantasy come true for me. I may not be the most objective critic, but I think it was also one of the finest *Honeymooners* episodes ever. Jackie and friends were never better, and I hope I'm not out of line by admitting I think I did rather well in one of my rare dramatic roles, capturing the subtle complexities of a television talk show host named "Mike Douglas."

I felt like I had that role down pat. The only disappointment was that I was overlooked at that year's Emmy Awards. I wasn't even nominated. I hate to complain, but—and this is no exaggeration—I worked on that character for years.

Saint Teresa

One of the most impressive guests we ever had on the show couldn't sing or dance or tell jokes very well. She had never been elected to anything, never appeared in films, lived in a tiny shack, and didn't have any money.

I'm not sure why we expended such effort to get Mother Teresa to come on the show. This was the late 1970s. Although her work was admired, she had not yet received the extraordinary media attention that would make her world-famous in the 1980s and 1990s. But I had read Malcolm Muggeridge's stirring account of her life and I urged the staff to explore the possibility of having her come on and talk with us.

It was difficult at first because she was so busy. That was not an uncommon excuse to defer a booking, but in her case it was remarkable. She wasn't busy on tour or writing a book or making an album or making personal appearances. Mother Teresa was too busy ministering to the needs of the poorest people in the world, the dying and destitute of India. Helpless and hopeless, they had nowhere to turn, no chance for

With Mother Teresa

the least solace in the last days of their lives, except for the loving arms of Mother Teresa. We wanted to fly her first-class to Los Angeles, put her up in a luxury hotel, and cater to her in every possible way for a few days around a brief appearance on our show. She was too busy. It made me take a hard look at my own priority list.

She finally agreed to do the show. People she trusted convinced her that we would provide an opportunity for her to get a message across to millions of American viewers. She reluctantly agreed to take some time off from her important work.

I cannot tell you what it is like to be in the presence of a living saint. Regrettably, I don't think it comes across very clearly on the small screen either. You have to be there. In person, Mother Teresa was tiny, a wrinkled waif of a woman with absolutely no pretenses, yet she exuded such an aura of peace and contentment. She was disarming and somewhat disorienting because her demeanor was so contrary to that of most guests on the show.

In this business, everyone has an agenda, everyone wants something and is desperate to get it, eager to have you help and worried that it won't happen. Mother Teresa didn't have anything and she didn't want anything. She wasn't trying to find out what life was about, she knew. And it was wonderful. It seemed that she was trying to tell the rest of us, as gently and simply as possible, but we were too busy to listen, too busy trying to find out what life was about.

In the presence of this tiny woman, I felt small. She would look up at me with that beatific smile and I couldn't keep my mind from wandering into strange territory. Who am I? At the end of my life, am I going to stand before God and say—what? We were number one in the ratings? You spent five minutes with this lady and things that mattered so much didn't matter at all.

No, I didn't run off to Calcutta right after the show and spend the rest of my life comforting lepers. I didn't give away all my worldly possessions and join a monastery. I didn't even quit the country club. Mother Teresa was a saint. I'm not. But the brief time I spent with that special woman changed my life in a way that I still can't quite explain. For all my life, I had been driven by an inborn need to succeed, a drive to excel, to win, to be the best. Even after years of affirmation in the form of accolades, ratings, and monetary rewards, I was still compelled to work harder, do more, reach higher. One day with Mother Teresa taught me a lesson I had long neglected. You can't reach high enough. You can't run fast enough. You can't earn enough money. Not ever. Don't be ashamed of your worldly accomplishments, but don't be too proud of them either. They are not meaningless, but if all you have to show for a lifetime on earth is a bunch of toys, you're not a winner, you're a loser.

Mother Teresa shared a secret with us. I asked her, "What's the biggest problem in the world today?" She answered in one word: "loneliness." She said she had overcome that by helping others. She didn't think she had sacrificed or suffered. She had been blessed. It gave her so much joy. Of all the guests we ever had, all the wealthy, famous, beautiful, and spectacularly successful people that marched across our stage, Mother Teresa was clearly the happiest, the most content with her life. What does that tell you?

I know this. If I had it to do all over, and they said I could only do one show with only one guest, it would be Mother Teresa.

9

TV Guide

With Your Host, Mike Douglas

William F. Buckley ✳ *Johnny Carson* ✳ *Dick Cavett* ✳ *Chevy Chase* ✳ *Connie Chung* ✳ *Katie Couric* ✳ *John Davidson* ✳ *Hugh Downs* ✳ *David Frost* ✳ *Joe Garagiola* ✳ *Dave Garroway* ✳ *Arthur Godfrey* ✳ *Virginia Graham* ✳ *Merv Griffin* ✳ *Charles Grodin* ✳ *Bryant Gumbel* ✳ *Arsenio Hall* ✳ *David Hartman* ✳ *Magic Johnson* ✳ *Jenny Jones* ✳ *Ricki Lake* ✳ *Jay Leno* ✳ *Jerry Lester* ✳ *David Letterman* ✳ *Jerry Lewis* ✳ *Joan Lunden* ✳ *Bill Maher* ✳ *Chris Matthews* ✳ *Dennis Miller* ✳ *Deborah Norville* ✳ *Keith Olbermann* ✳ *Conan O'Brien* ✳ *Rosie O'Donnell* ✳ *Donny & Marie Osmond* ✳ *Jane Pauley* ✳ *Maury Povich* ✳ *Sally Jesse Raphael* ✳ *Regis & Kathie Lee* ✳ *Geraldo Rivera* ✳ *Joan Rivers* ✳ *Roseanne* ✳ *Dinah Shore* ✳ *Tom Snyder* ✳ *Jerry Springer* ✳ *Jon Stewart* ✳ *David Susskind* ✳ *Barbara Walters* ✳ *Montel Williams* ✳ *Oprah Winfrey*

Now here's a chapter guaranteed to get me in trouble. When we sat down to talk about this book, one of the first things my editors requested was a critique of all the prominent talking heads on television, past and present.

"Oh no, I'm not doing that."

"Mike, you have to. You were the first in daytime, you had the longest-running, highest-rated show—who else is more qualified?"

"I don't care. You're talking about people that I know. I'll be happy to talk about the ones that I like, but I don't want to go near the shows I don't care for. That's not my style. I'm not a hatchet man."

"A little controversy won't hurt. You know more about this than anyone. There's a whole new generation of talk show hosts and people are going to want to hear your thoughts. You owe it to your fans."

"No, really. I just—there are some shows out there now . . . it wouldn't be pretty."

"We know there's the good, the bad, and the ugly. It's important that you take a stand on which is which. The book's not complete without it."

"Fellas, please—I just can't."

"We'll double the advance."

"Do you want them ranked chronologically or alphabetically?"

*

When we started *The Mike Douglas Show* in 1961, we were doing something unique. Nothing like it. Today, there are over 140 programs on network and cable that could be classified as talk or talk-entertainment TV, from Leno and Letterman to that little old nun that holds forth on the religious channel and the talking chefs on the gourmet channel.

We might as well start at the top. Maybe I'm showing a little generational bias here, but in my mind, Johnny Carson will always be the Gold Standard. And you know what? I'll bet most of the talking heads on the tube today would agree with me. He's an icon to them and to millions of Americans, including myself.

Johnny Carson had a range of talents like no one else, before or after. If the talk show format was a sport, his mantel would be sagging with MVP awards. For openers, he could play both offense and defense—

carry the load himself all night or sit back and spoon-feed straight lines to a hot guest, whatever the game plan called for.

Johnny defined what the opening monologue should be—up-tempo, quick-hitting, current as the headlines, but not too much, just enough to bring you back for more after the first break. Over the years, he sharpened the monologue into a fail-safe, two-edged sword. If the material was good, his timing—the best since Hope or Benny—took it over the top. If the writers had an off day, not to worry. Johnny Carson floundering through the opening was better than most other hosts with their A stuff. He turned it around and invited the audience to enjoy watching him crash and burn. With Ed McMahon—the best sidekick in the history of TV—leading the lynch mob, Johnny could milk bad jokes for so many laughs, you would think they did it on purpose.

Johnny Carson also understood two concepts that so many new kids on the TV block don't have a clue about. Number one is ego. If you want to endure as a host, ego is the first deadly sin. It's killed more shows than Nielsen. Johnny knew it better than anyone. You're the host, your name is on the show, you are unquestionably the star, and as soon as you get all that out of your head, the better, because if you don't, you're through. The paradox is, the show is not about you, it's about everybody else.

Johnny never dropped names, never talked about who he was playing tennis with or what he did last night. He deflected the focus to his guests, to Ed, to Doc Severinsen, to Freddie De Cordova, to the audience—to everybody and anybody but himself. If you're going to be there every night, there's no reason to hog the camera. Sooner or later, you'll get more airtime than you know what to do with. A good host is gracious and deferential. A good host doesn't interrupt, doesn't top a guest's story with one of his own, doesn't jump in with a punch line, doesn't get in the way of his own show. That's rule number one and Johnny Carson wrote the book.

Number two, enjoy yourself. Whether it's a great show or a terrible one (and if you're on long enough, there will be plenty of those), everything will be all right if the host doesn't lose it, and Johnny never did. As soon as the audience senses that you are uncomfortable or unhappy, they squirm in their seats or reach for the remote. Talented people have gone down in flames when the audience picked up on the fact that they weren't enjoying their own shows. That's what sent Pat Sajak spinning back to *Wheel of Fortune,* packed off Chevy Chase to another vacation, and made Magic Johnson disappear. If you don't like the heat, get out of the talking kitchen.

Johnny Carson was made of asbestos. He could rise from the ashes of the most dismal show with a one-liner out of nowhere to save the whole night. Or he could invite the audience to "feel his pain," basking in the droll humor of a show that had no redeeming entertainment qualities.

Above all, Johnny possessed an empathy that crossed over all demographic groups. Because he was so self-effacing, you never really knew his agenda, if he had one at all. Was he a Democrat or Republican? Liberal or conservative? Protestant, Catholic, or Jew? You couldn't tell because Johnny wasn't there to lecture, he was there to entertain. And he did that better than anybody in this business for over thirty years.

*

I think it's fair to say that there are only two modern hosts contending for Johnny's heavyweight title—Jay Leno and David Letterman. Both were on our show when they were up-and-coming comics, and we invited both of them back because they were obvious talents.

I have to take my hat off to Jay and David. They are very good, they work very hard, and both carry their respective shows on their backs.

That said, I think they both have a way to go before they can match the 24-carat standard of Carson. It's not even a fair comparison yet. Johnny didn't spring from the womb a full-blown talk show host. He had many years to hone his craft. These two are going to be around for a long time, too. Check back in a few years and see if one hasn't risen to a level where people will start saying, "Now who was that guy who used to do the late-night show a while back?" Could happen.

Jay Leno has the strongest opening monologue on television. I don't know who his writers are, but I'll bet he is paying them a fortune because they deliver fresh, cutting-edge pages night after night. The quality is so good, if he didn't have his show, he could take the jokes from any night, go on tour with them for a year, and knock 'em dead in every club in the nation. Killer stuff, and he takes it deeper into the show than anyone else. There's only about fifty people on earth who know how hard that is to do, night after night.

Jay's stand-up material is so strong, it tends to overshadow the rest of the show, setting a pace and a pattern that is hard to break away from.

With Jay Leno and Gabe Kaplan

Once the guests start arriving, the format should transition to conversational and away from line-joke, line-joke. Too often, Jay's locked into the jokes. The guests become straight men. It keeps the laughs coming and the energy up, but it doesn't allow us to get past the surface or get to know anything worthwhile about a guest. Plug a movie. Joke. Plug the new series. Joke. The book's out tomorrow. Joke.

It doesn't have to be. I'm hoping that Jay will relax a little now that he's settled in and the ratings are so strong and let some minutes go by without a punch line. I think that would make the show more intriguing and endearing. If he goes that way, I believe Jay could end up ranking with the all-time great hosts. Right now, it's only the funniest, highest rated, most profitable show on late night TV, so I hope he heeds my advice before it's too late.

*

David Letterman is an enigma to me. He was always out in left field when it came to comedy. Even years ago, when he was on our show, I

Ricky Schroder, Meadowlark Lemon, David Letterman, and Jon Voight

couldn't tell you why he was so funny. He just was. He didn't do one-liners or voices or any kind of recognizable shtick. He just thinks funny. And although he never looks like he's trying and you have the sneaky suspicion he might not even care, he does a very effective interview. He comes up with one of those freaky questions out of the blue, and before you know it, very famous people are saying things to him on national television that they wouldn't tell their psychiatrists.

Dave made his mark on his *Late Night* show with the Top Ten List (has any concept ever been borrowed by so many others in the history of comedy?) and the most outlandish bits on the small screen. When it comes to inventive comedy, David Letterman is Thomas Edison, a TV hybrid of Jerry Lewis and Rod Serling.

If Dave has a problem, it's one of the most common ones known to man—women. He seems to be getting better, but he has difficulty interviewing women. He is visibly altered by the presence of a female in the guest chair, like a kid who accidentally walked into the ladies' room and can't wait to get the heck out of there. Like it or not, about half the guests are going to be women and you better get used to it, Dave.

His own success has taken a little wind out of his sails as well. Part of David's charm has always been his irreverence, but it's hard to maintain that maverick persona when you're one of the highest paid performers on television. I guess it's a tradeoff he'll have to live with.

Last thought on Letterman: Long Live Paul Shaffer.

*

Jay and Dave may rule that hour after the eleven o'clock news that *The Tonight Show* carved in stone as the defining hour, but with cable has come the deluge of talk. The broadcast day is twenty-four/seven now, and the talkmeisters are everywhere you turn.

Let's go to daytime, my favorite place. If Johnny Carson is the King of Talk, Oprah Winfrey is the Queen. Not just today—ever. And not just of talk shows—all of television.

Whenever I watch Oprah, and that's as often as I can, the same thought occurs—this is what television was meant to be. The lady is in a class by herself. She consistently appeals to our better angels. The low road is never an option. Her show has spontaneity and humor, but there's never any "wandering" or downtime. Every show, this is a woman on a mission. And most of the time, it's mission accomplished.

I don't know how she manages to come across as a leader, an innovator, and the girl next door all at the same time, but she does it so well that I'm sure one of her biggest problems is perfect strangers coming up to her on the street to give her a hug. She's probably the most approachable superstar we have ever had.

They tell me Oprah makes over a hundred million dollars a year. That sounds like a lot, but as far as I'm concerned, it's not enough. Her shows on family issues have helped people heal wounds. Her shows on race relations have added to the positive dialogue and raised the awareness level. Her book club has probably done more for literature and literacy than anything else in media history.

I don't know Oprah personally, but then again, I guess I do. We all do. I'm convinced that the Oprah you see on TV is the same as the Oprah at home or out with Stedman. He may think he knows her better than the rest of us, but he just gets to spend more time with her.

That's the key. When you're on five days a week, it doesn't take long

Oprah Winfrey

for people to know if you're being yourself or putting on an act. And if you can't be yourself, your act better be spectacular. No matter how strong your guest lineup, production values, or writing staff, a talk show will live or die with the host.

There's no better example of this than when Oprah dared to take her whole show down to Texas when the cattlemen hauled her into court to face charges for slander. It's a testament to the power of this woman that when she said a few disparaging words about hamburgers, she brought down the whole bull market.

Talk about winning over hearts and minds. She took the bull by the horns, faced the whole issue head-on, and held it up on her show for all to see. She let the cattle folks have their say and told her side, too, fair and square. Instead of twelve people in Texas, she let the nation be the jury. It was vintage Oprah.

We're lucky to have her.

*

If you're looking for trouble in a talk show, here's two words to keep in mind: permanent co-hosts. It's hard enough to find one person with enough of what it takes to anchor a successful show. Try finding two that can work together, complement each other, and not end up in an endless battle of one-upmanship. If you would have asked me years ago if it could ever work, I would have said no. The plains of television are littered with the wreckage of co-hosted shows.

Wrong again, Mike Douglas. I've had to revise my thinking because

Regis Philbin with Carmel Quinn, in the days long before Kathie Lee Gifford

of one show and one show only. The exception to the rule is *Regis &
Kathie Lee.*

There's one word to describe this winning combination and that's
chemistry. They've found the formula. People forget that both Regis
Philbin and Kathie Lee Gifford were around for a good while before
they found each other, and it became one of the most perfect pairings
since peanut butter and jelly. I don't know if this show was the intentional design of some genius producer or just a happy accident, but these
two mesh their considerable individual talents into a near-perfect TV
machine that's as fresh as flowers and as comfortable as old shoes.

I go way back with Regis Philbin. He's been one of the good guys in
this business for as long as I can remember. There was never any doubt
that he could be a valuable TV commodity, but it seemed like shortsighted producers were determined to shoehorn him into places he
didn't belong. His talents were completely overlooked on the old *Joey
Bishop Show.* Joey was a fine comic but he struggled as a host, especially
in the suicide slot opposite Carson. Regis was a willing and able second
banana, determined and loyal to Joey. Instead of leaning on Regis for
support, Joey used him as a whipping boy. That was a big mistake and I
think it hastened the demise of the show.

Kathie Lee is a born entertainer, a gifted singer, and an inexhaustible
woman. Anyone who knows her can tell you it was easy to predict she
would be a star. She could make it on sheer willpower.

All they needed was each other. Regis's affable pessimism is the perfect foil to Kathie Lee's bubbly optimism. They remind me of the best of
George Burns and Gracie Allen. There's not a better team on television.

And one more thing. At the risk of putting myself in the tabloid line of
fire, why don't you vultures find someone else to pick on for a while?
Kathie Lee Gifford has given more time, effort, and money to more chari-
table causes than another hundred entertainers I could name, and you
can't let a week go by without pouncing on her? I won't even ask you to
lay off Regis. He's a thick-skinned Irishman. But isn't there some worthy
target you could spend a few paragraphs on every now and then and give
Kathie Lee a break? Where was Jerry Springer last week anyhow?

*

Excuse me, did I get off on a little rant, there? Sorry. But at least it's a
good segue to another host I think a lot of, and that would be the King

of the Rants, Dennis Miller. You might think Dennis is a wee bit racy to be my cup of tea. Well, I wouldn't mind if he'd tone down the language a little, but it's the 1990s, I'm used to it.

Dennis Miller is so smart, he's almost hard to watch. Acerbic with a capital A, his glib acidity is unmatched today and I doubt if anyone in TV history could run with him when it comes to mixing wicked humor and cutting-edge commentary. This young man's wit is so razor-sharp, it should probably be classified as a lethal weapon.

And don't tell me he doesn't do all of his own material. Maybe he's got a few writers to help with the polish, but who is he going to get to come up with that stuff if he doesn't—Robin Williams and William F. Buckley working together?

*

The only one out there with Dennis is Bill Maher. He was on our show when he was just getting started as a stand-up. He managed to lampoon the powers-that-be with a disarming style that was more Will Rogers than Mort Sahl, and I figured he was something special. It didn't surprise me at all when he landed as host on *Politically Incorrect*. Perfect fit. Intelligent, daring, and the best use of the eclectic "Mix" concept since we closed our books years ago. It's not easy handling the combustible guest combinations they put together every night, but Bill handles it deftly. The risk on a show like that is that it can get nasty, or worse, bogged down in boring polemics, and Bill is always there with a timely quip to lighten things up. He makes it look easy, and it's anything but.

*

Barbara Walters? The best interviewer on television. Case closed. No songs, no dances, no jokes, just Barbara and her guest, one-on-one. She has a sixth sense for asking the right questions and she doesn't waste any time getting there. No use trying to hide anything. Barbara's going to get there, one way or another.

I'll never forget her interview with Katharine Hepburn. Her relationship with Spencer Tracy had been widely known and speculated about for decades, but no one dared to broach the subject with Miss Hepburn. Forbidden territory. Not for Barbara. She asked very personal questions about their famous affair, but so well crafted that even the great Kate couldn't help but respond. It was a classic, one of Barbara's many.

With Barbara Walters

How about her week with Fidel Castro? Or the exclusive with Anwar Sadat when he kept calling her "Barbie"? This lady's not just talented, she's got a whole lot of clout and no shortage of feminine charm that she can use as a secret weapon. When you can turn heads of state, well, that's a bonus that even Edward R. Murrow didn't have.

*

Of course, charm isn't limited to the ladies. Geraldo Rivera knows how to turn it on when he has to. He's got more wiles than a tomcat and just about as many lives. It wasn't so long ago he was considered almost as unrepentantly low-brow as Springer, but, as he has before and will again, he reinvented himself right before our eyes.

There was Geraldo the rising network star, Geraldo the anti-network rebel, Geraldo the investigative reporter, Geraldo the carnival barker, Geraldo the street-fightin' man getting his nose broken, then Geraldo the ombudsman and peacemaker. This guy's got more reincarnations than the Dalai Lama.

Some people have a problem with his advocacy style but I find it refreshing, whether I agree with him or not. Rather than lie back and feign objectivity, Geraldo is always willing to jump right in and take a stand. It may border on recklessness, but it sure makes him watchable.

*

I have to mention another gentleman that has been underrated for most of his distinguished career. Tom Snyder. He's been playing this game a long, long time, and he consistently delivers a first-class, in-depth interview, whether he's talking to a baseball player or a prime minister.

He's also a good man and a unique character, and I have a personal story that might tell you a little bit about him.

A few years ago (don't ask), Gen threw a surprise party for my sixtieth birthday. There were lots of family and old friends—just a wonderful night. It wasn't intended to be a roast, but Don Rickles started in on me, Shecky Greene had to top him, and before you knew it, everybody was getting in on the act. Someone else might have taken offense, I suppose, but I know I'm an easy target. The jokes might have been at my expense, but they were very funny jokes and it made for one hilarious evening.

After getting tattooed for the better part of an hour, I was glad to see Tom Snyder step up to the podium just so I could catch my breath.

Well, Tom Snyder didn't take any shots at me. Not only that, he had taken umbrage for me at all those who had. It took a moment to realize he was serious, but soon the entire room grew quiet while Tom Snyder scolded them all. He told them I had accomplished something that no one in the industry ever had, that he had nothing but respect for me, and that everyone else present should show a little more.

Of course, these folks weren't being disrespectful, they were having fun. Besides, I wasn't the Pope, I was just a TV host and my career was hardly worthy of his solemn appreciation. Still, Tom walked up there and took on a whole roomful of Hollywood heavyweights because he thought I needed someone to stand up for me, and I'll never forget that. On top of everything else, I received a lot of wonderful gifts that night, but the one I remember most was from Tom Snyder.

*

Rosie O'Donnell

You think I'm going to have a chapter on talk show hosts and neglect to mention Merv Griffin? Are you crazy? Everybody's been telling me all my life that I remind them of Merv and Merv reminds them of me. It's time I had my say.

I think Merv Griffin is one of the nicest human beings and one of the greatest talk show hosts who ever lived. He's talented, funny, amiable, and handsome. No wonder people get the two of us confused.

*

When Merv and I were riding herd on daytime, it was a man's game. It was many years before Dinah Shore finally broke through, and even that wonderful lady was restricted to such a feminine format her show might as well have had the label "For Women Only." They kept Dinah in the kitchen so much, she did more cooking segments than Graham Kerr.

Today, women rule daytime. We talked about Oprah. I guess it should come as no surprise that the only one even close to her quality standards is another lady of the day, Rosie O'Donnell.

The good thing is, I don't even see the two of them as competitors.

Entirely different styles and approaches. Oprah is theme-oriented. Rosie is guest-oriented, and I guess that's why I like her so much. Her show is the closest thing going to ours.

No one knows how to treat a guest like Rosie. Like me, she considers herself a fan, first and foremost. She's so excited, so happy to have you on her show. No wonder she gets the biggest names in the business. Even Oprah. Who could turn her down?

Rosie also has so much little kid in her. Who else would just burst out singing jingles to old commercials in the middle of her show? I mentioned how important it is for the audience to believe the host is enjoying the show. Rosie's show is like an amusement park and she's got the only season pass.

*

Phil Donahue was king of the 1980s and rightfully so. Daytime talk grew up with Phil, got beyond the laughs and recipes and moved on to real people, real issues, and real depth. People found his show entertaining enough to keep him at the top of the ratings year after year, but the real service he provided was to raise the bar for all of television when it came to serious subject matter and in-depth information.

One of my favorite things about Phil Donahue, and the one that defines his character, was his refusal to conform to ratings dictates and degrade his show to compete with the carnival barkers. If only a few others would follow his example.

*

Conan O'Brien has been on for years now, and he still looks very much like an amateur who happens to be filling in because AFTRA is on strike. I don't think he is exactly well prepared for every interview he has ever done. I get the feeling he's reading the information on his own index cards for the first time on the air. He looks like he hates wearing suits. He seems surprised every time he has to go to a commercial. (A what? A commercial break? Oh. Okay.) The whole show is chronically out of control.

So why do I like this Conan so much? I don't know. Maybe it's because he does the most creative bits since David Letterman was a pup. Maybe it's because you can't not like him. Probably, it's because of Andy. I love the guy.

*

By now, most readers probably believe I can't bring myself to say anything genuinely critical of anyone who's ever had a talk show. So far, this
chapter is so syrupy, it might as well have been written by Mrs. Butter-
worth. Wait a minute. I'm not through yet. I've talked about a lot of the
great ones, but the talk show circuit is not heaven on earth. I guess it's
time we took a look at the darker side.

Sally Jessy Raphael seems like a nice enough lady, but why does this
woman have a talk show? Have I missed something, or shouldn't she be
running a real estate office in a small town somewhere in the corn belt?
The format is old and tired, the guests are an embarrassment, and Sally
herself never seems to have anything to add one way or the other.
What's the point?

*

Roseanne has a talk show now. Kind of. I know she has an enviable
track record in television but I'm sorry, I don't get it.

I saw her debut week of shows and haven't seen it since. You get a
marquee name like Whoopi Goldberg, a wily veteran and one of the best
guests in the business, and you make her shout to be heard? Roseanne
looks uncomfortable and so do all the guests. The comedy bits are an
embarrassment. It hurts to watch. Other than that, I loved it.

*

At least no one has died from being on Roseanne's show. I'm sure the
last thing Jenny Jones ever wanted was to see anyone come to harm as a
direct or indirect result of her TV cash cow, but it doesn't do any of us
any good to pretend it didn't happen. There's a price for reckless irre-
sponsibility on television and there's a limit to what you can do for ratings. What happened to Jenny Jones was the worst nightmare of any
media personality, and I sympathize, but the honorable thing would
have been for her to sign off the day it happened. That she stayed on the
air says something chilling about Jenny Jones . . . and her audience.

*

Jenny Jones is not the worst. My guess is, if someone was killed on one
of Jerry Springer's alleged programs, he would have had the tragic seg-

ment deleted from the tape, then use it on his next video and raise the price. "JERRY SPRINGER SNUFF VIDEO—TOO HOT FOR TV!" He'd sell a million of 'em.

You know, I really wish I could say I like Jerry Springer. I know how tough it is to get ratings, to establish yourself, city by city, across the country, to fight for time slots and meager promos to get the word out. I know those things. It's an uphill battle and I salute anyone who has made it through that gauntlet. And I know Jerry Springer is not only the star of his show, he's the mastermind who made it happen.

The problem is, he took the lowest conceivable road to success. I cannot find any justification for what he passes off as television.

I'm not going to kid anyone. Eradicating Jerry Springer will not save our children from TV trash. With cable and satellites and new networks sprouting up like weeds, there's no stopping it anymore. The range of programming has expanded exponentially. The best programs ever produced are being aired right now. Inevitably, so are the worst. If Springer disappeared today, that wouldn't change.

The Jerry Springer Show is simply bad television, disgraceful television, intentionally brought to you by a very intelligent man who has opted to make us all pay for his singular greed. I cannot think of another person in media history who has stooped so low with such relish.

His shows are dishonest and lazy. They portray a false image of an American culture that doesn't even exist to an impressionable audience. There's a danger in that. Real danger.

Jerry's "guests" are not guests at all. They are victims, willing or not. They are there to be mocked and made fools of. Contrary to his bleating sermonettes, they are not representative of anything. They are aberrations.

So is Jerry. When I see him standing there holding his limp microphone and smirking while the stage erupts in preplanned violence over lurid disputes, I see contempt in his eyes. Contempt for his guests. Contempt for his audience. Contempt for all of us.

The only thing that interests me about Jerry Springer is how this ugly chapter in television will end, and I have a hunch it's going to work out all right.

It may sound crazy, but I'm telling you, in spite of the money, this is not a happy camper. Read the stories. I believe that Jerry Springer is near the end of his rope and that a dramatic change is not too far off.

With Donny and Marie Osmond

Underneath it all, he's probably not such a bad guy, and he's going to see the light. I can't wait for that glorious day when America turns on Jerry Springer to see a contrite, bespectacled man in sackcloth and ashes, saying: "I'm sorry. This is so wrong. Forgive me for having done this as I forgive you for watching."

He'll go from there right to the religious channel and be an even bigger hit. It could happen. I just hope it happens soon.

Talk Show Quickies

LARRY KING. An institution. There was a time when America had a number of media voices who spoke for the people, the face in the crowd, the man on the street. Today, that breed has almost disappeared, except for Larry King. He's a fan and a concerned citizen. He asks the questions that people want asked, without pretense or prejudgment. Salt of the airwaves.

THE VIEW. The Barbara Walters All-Star Team of Talking Ladies. High concept. Who would have thought you could do a show with five co-hosts? And that it would work? I'm impressed.

MONTEL WILLIAMS. A polished, highbrow host with gritty, lowbrow guests. What's wrong with this picture? The show's direction is a waste of his talents.

DONNY & MARIE. As appealing as an ice cream cone on a hot summer day. Big hit.

MAGIC JOHNSON. One of the nicest men on the planet, but not a talk show host. You didn't see me try to play basketball for the Lakers, did you?

CHARLES GRODIN. One of the most considerate gentlemen in show business, a fine actor, and a wonderful wit. His show comes off as unpretentious, quirky, and unique. It might as well be broadcast from his living room. This is Charles Grodin, they gave him a show and he's going to say whatever is on his mind. He'll never have the biggest ratings, but he doesn't care any more than you do.

CHEVY CHASE. He forgot to do my show. Twice. What goes around, comes around. He forgot to do his own show every night.

THE JOAN RIVERS SHOW. Too much Joan Rivers, not enough Show.

STEVE ALLEN. He could do a show, be his own sidekick, and play all the instruments in the band. He could do another show today as entertaining as anything on the air.

RICKI LAKE Too shallow for me. Know what I'm sayin'?

JOHN DAVIDSON. Okay, everyone wanted me to make some comments on the fellow that Group W decided to replace me with. I don't mind admitting that it hurt at the time, but I got over that long ago. John Davidson was a personable, eager, and handsome young man when Group W tapped him with their magic wand and said, "We're going to make you a talk show star." It takes more than that. John's show didn't last very long. I'm not going to go into any details, but I will share with you one anecdote that made my day many years ago.

One of my old friends at Westinghouse sent me a copy of a videotape, about a year after John's show had been anointed as our replacement. There was a cryptic note with it that just said, "I think you'll enjoy this." It was an excerpt from a *John Davidson Show* that was excised, never broadcast. Gen and I tossed it in the VCR.

John was talking to Jesse Owens, the great Olympian. In the course of the conversation, they played a clip from the 1936 Olympics that included Jesse sprinting to victory. The footage was originally produced by Leni Riefenstahl, the Nazi propagandist filmmaker, and also included the carefully staged scene of a little girl handing a bouquet of flowers to a smiling Hitler. When it ended, it was back to John and Jesse. John Davidson turned to the camera, beamed that smile, and added a comment: "You know, we never really got to see that side of the man, did we?"

It's like I've been trying to tell you. Not everyone can do a talk show.

10

Queen for a Day

Is it possible to know one thing, the truest thing you ever knew, and know it so well for so long that over time you can forget it?

Yes, it is possible, and you should never let it happen. The one thing I knew through a show business career that spanned a half century was that, in the beginning and at the end, it all came down to one woman—my bride, Gen.

I'm not talking about my life, you know—real life, that time away from set and stage when you have real relationships with real people, fall in love, raise a family, and meet those suspicious-looking boys that say they'll have your daughter home by eleven, and all the things that make you flesh and blood instead of some two-dimensional ghost in a box of circuit boards. In real life, Gen and I were always one.

I'm not talking about that. What no one knew except our family and our TV family, the staff and crew, was that *The Mike Douglas Show* was really the *Mike & Gen Douglas Show,* except I got all the credit and the fame and Gen got the headaches and the hard problems.

Worked for me.

And Gen never complained, never asked for credit, and begged me not to mention her name on the show. I told you I was lucky and now you know—I'm a walking four-leaf clover.

Gen didn't miss a minute. In her own way, she made everything possible. From the clothes I wore to the make-or-break career decisions, to suggestions for keeping the show fresh and vital, and the endless series of tiny components that make the difference between success and failure, she was always there.

Her line about the lean years, and they were long ones, is that she was too young to know enough to be afraid. I never bought it. She was so very young, but she knew enough to be petrified. There had to be times, like the years we spent crisscrossing the country in a well-worn Cadillac Fleetwood with destination unknown, when she said to herself, "What am I doing bouncing around with this so-called singer? I could have married a mailman in Oklahoma City and had some real security." She just never let on she was the least concerned.

"It'll be all right, Mike. I know it will," is what she always said.

When everyone said, "There's no way you two can get married!" it was Gen who said, "It'll be all right, Mike."

When everyone said, "You'll never make it in this business," it was Gen who said, "It'll be all right, Mike."

When everyone said, "A television show in Cleveland is the worst idea we've ever heard!" it was Gen who said, "It'll be all right, Mike."

And it was. It always was.

*

Flash forward about thirty years. I had finally gotten the hang of a lifestyle that evolved around the four Gs—Gen, the girls, the grandchildren, and golf. Okay, once in a while golf came before the grandchildren, but I've been making up for that in recent years by golfing with my grandchildren.

I know it may sound ungrateful to talk about "adjusting" to a life of leisure, but I've always been a driven sort. When you've spent a good part of your life in bright lights, fighting to stay there, and thriving on the demands, the intensity of it all—well, it takes a little adjusting to ease back into the shade.

At first, I did the best I could. I learned to bring the pace down a few notches, and, with Gen's help, to enjoy some simple pleasures. Family, friends, travel. Reading. Watching television. I never watched it before. I scrutinized and analyzed, compared and evaluated, but I never just watched. It's pretty good.

Life was pretty good, too.

Then came the first jolt.

It was 1990. We were still living in Los Angeles when I was sitting in bed one night watching—what else?—a little television. One of the network newsmagazine shows was doing a segment on prostate cancer. I was hardly paying attention.

Gen and I had been blessed with good health for so long, we didn't even think much about it anymore. In all our married years, neither Gen nor I had ever spent a night in a hospital, except when the girls were born. As the years moved on, we tried to take good care of ourselves, stayed active, got our annual checkups. We just never expected any bad news, and there wasn't any. Until that night.

Whatever number one was on their list, I nodded absently in affirmation. Number two? Yes, I thought, that's me. Three? Ditto. Four? Absolutely. By the time they got to number seven, I was starting to feel like a hypochondriac. Seven for seven. That might be a great statistic in baseball, but when it comes to cancer, they were lousy numbers.

Now, I'm not one of these guys that call the paramedics every time there's a show on heart attacks because I start noticing a pain in my arm and an irregular heartbeat, but I thought I better get a doctor to tell me I had too much time on my hands and I shouldn't be looking for things to worry about when there weren't any. I was at UCLA Medical Center a few days later.

After my examination, the good doctor gave me the bad news and three options. One was to do nothing and hope to outlive the cancer that would likely take years to extend beyond the prostate area. Two was extensive chemotherapy and radiation. Three was the knife: prompt surgery to excise the tumor.

Excuse me, Doctor—is there a Door Number Four?

No such luck. It didn't take me longer than five minutes to choose option three. We consulted with the surgeon. His next available date happened to fall on Gen's birthday. I booked myself as a guest at the UCLA surgery clinic for one of my least favorite appearances. But the date was a good omen—I have always felt that the day Gen was born was the luckiest day of my life.

I'm happy to report my luck held. The procedure was successful, the cancer eradicated, and Gen was there every minute to see me through.

That was a rough few weeks, but it was nothing compared to the sim-

ilar scenario four years later when we were back in Cleveland, closer to
the girls and their families, and Gen and I spent an uneventful afternoon
at the renowned Cleveland Clinic getting our annual checkups. I was in
the waiting room reading old magazines for an hour because Gen had
been delayed. That's when I got the loudest wake-up call of my life. It
wasn't Gen who came out of the examination room. It was a stranger in
a white coat.

"Gen has cancer, Mr. Douglas."

That one line of news, delivered with genuine concern by a sincere
young doctor, sent me into a tailspin unlike anything I had ever experienced. Here I was, a guy who had made a living singing songs and sling-
ing words, practiced in the art of never letting anything that anyone said
rattle me one bit, and that one word knocked me to my knees. The way
I was brought up, there's only one thing to do when you find yourself on
your knees—you pray.

I never made a display of my faith on the show. I've said it before, the
show was not about me, personally, and there is nothing more personal
than religion.

But this was not show time, this was real, and I was having a hard
time rising above a state of total shock.

I loved Gen. I needed Gen. I had spent my life with Gen. In the last
fifty-three years, we've only spent two nights apart. And I didn't like either one of them.

I couldn't imagine a time without her at my side. But the first hard
lesson from this shattering news was that I had come to take her presence for granted. The weather will be here tomorrow, and so will Gen.

Not necessarily, said the young man in the white coat.

Gen stayed in the hospital and I went home alone for the first time in
my life. It was a hollow feeling, wandering through empty rooms, my
head spinning. One thing I knew, and kept repeating over and over to myself—it was MY turn now. My turn to be the rock. It was so important to
be more than a brave face and a hand holder, but I groped for ideas. I had
to laugh at myself. I had watched her play that role forever, and when the
time finally came for trading places, I didn't know what to do.

I don't mind admitting, I was a wreck. There were sleepless nights
and waking hours of anguish. When I wasn't on the phone to doctors,
specialists, and our daughters, I spent most of my time trying not to
think about what I would do without her.

Only one thing helped. I would play the movie of our lives together over and over again in my mind. Part drama, part comedy, part romance—it was, for me, the equal of anything created on the silver screen. No, it was better. It was real.

*

I was working as a singer at an Oklahoma City radio station, back in the days when radio stations had live singers. Only seventeen, I had already toured most of the U.S. several times with Bill Carlsen's Band of a Million Thrills. And it was for me, too. A bunch of starry-eyed cool cats, playing and singing at dances, parties, state fairs, shopping centers—if they were paying for some swing music, we were there.

A Chicago agent heard me sing and offered me a full-time job as staff singer at radio WKY in Oklahoma City. I was more than ready to unpack my suitcase. Besides, who could turn down that kind of money? I would be making all of seventy dollars a week.

For me, going to the same place every day and signing off at six o'clock was easy and fun. The folks were easygoing, too. I struck up a quick friendship with Charlie Purnell. Just a few years older, he was the station's continuity man, tearing the wire service reports off the ticker and reworking the news items into broadcast form. Charlie invited me to his family's house for Thanksgiving. I showed up in my best and only suit, Charlie opened the door, and the last thing I remember was a disembodied voice saying, ". . . and this is my sister, Genevieve."

I was gone. Over the moon. Don't let anybody tell you there is no such thing as love at first sight. I can testify. "Genevieve Purnell," I repeated like a mantra, over and over, for days. "Genevieve Purnell." I floated to the station and back. When I was on the air, I sang to her, only her, no one else in the world. I wanted to see her again, walk down the street with my arm around her, take her dancing, sweep her off her feet. There was only one small problem. Gen was all of sixteen years old, the only daughter in an upright Christian family that considered dating something more suitable to ladies in their thirties. In Oklahoma in the 1940s, rules like that were not arbitrary, they were cast in stone. There was nothing for me to do but bide my time.

When Gen was finally allowed to socialize, it wasn't with me. I was a working lad and Gen a high school girl. She went out a few times with boys in her class, but I didn't dare come calling. The only highlight of those days was Christmas at the Purnells'. I wangled another invitation and spent every moment with Gen.

Months crawled by. I spent my days working at the station and my nights dreaming of Gen. Then came the most extraordinary day of my young life.

I was full-time at the station, on equal footing with the staff people like Charlie. Above us were the managers and beneath us, in the radio caste system of the day, were the pages. Like today's interns, they were meagerly paid, part-time youngsters who handled menial tasks for a few bucks a week and the greater glory of being a part of the radio business.

One afternoon in 1944, one of the pages strutted through the studio with his new girlfriend, showing her the station and showing her off to everyone there. You couldn't blame him. She was gorgeous.

On second glance, I realized she was a lot more than that. She was Gen.

I cannot describe the rush of emotions I experienced in the next fraction of a moment. Surprise. Envy. Anxiety. Suspicion. Alarm. Despair. Hope. Confusion. Love. When I regained control, I decided that I better do something and do it fast. This was a sudden and shocking development. Apparently, Gen was now allowed to go on full-fledged, unchaperoned dates, and there she was with some despicable human being whom I can only describe as "not me." That was unacceptable.

I came up with some excuse to send the page back to the mail room for a minute. Alone with Gen in the sound studio, I confronted her.

"Genevieve."

"Yes, Michael?"

"When this war's over, will you marry me?"

Sure, it was ridiculous. We had never been on an official date. But as far as I was concerned, this was a dire situation. I wasn't about to let her join the ranks of eligible young women, fair game for any of the fifty million or so eligible bachelors in America. Proposing to her right then and there was all I could think of. Of course she would say no, but at least she would know that my intentions were serious and honorable.

To my astonishment, she said, "Yes." Barely above a whisper, but an unmistakable "Yes."

That wonderful word changed everything for me. From then until now, with more good fortune and good grace than any man has a right to, the word that has defined our lives together has been "Yes."

*

Except for telling Gen's parents, we kept our marriage pact entirely to ourselves. I told no one. We were engaged, we knew we were engaged, and everyone else would have to wait to hear about it until we worked out a few minor details like how we were going to get married when she was only seventeen and how we were going to live, and a few other incidentals.

Another complication arose a few weeks later when I was classified 1-A. We were in the middle of World War II. It was my turn to serve. I signed on for naval officers' training, but I wasn't happy about the timing. Gen and I needed time to work things out. Still, it was no use arguing with Uncle Sam. I was getting ready to report for duty when I got a lucky break. Literally.

Gen and Mike when he was finishing boot camp.

Mike and Gen judging a dog show.

I broke my ankle. It wasn't the easiest way to get a reprieve from military duty. I was headed home from the station one night when I came
across two gents in an altercation. They were both in their cups, swing-
ing wildly. I separated the brawlers, but not before one stumbled into
me. I caught my foot against the curb going down and my ankle just
snapped. So much for Good Samaritanism.

I was 1-A but not A-1. The draft board gave me ninety days to recuperate. I was in a cast, on crutches for weeks, but it was a blessing in disguise. Gen nursed me like a wounded hero and we spent many hours together. When I was back on my feet, we even dated a time or two, enough to convince us both that our commitment was no impetuous mistake. We were in love. We were meant for each other. We wanted to spend the rest of our lives together.

Might as well get started. One afternoon, we borrowed a car, drove forty miles to a country justice of the peace in Norman, Oklahoma, and took that giant leap of faith. Gen and Mike got married.

Hardly scandalous by today's standards, it was absolutely crazy then. A boy singer on his way to war and the prettiest girl in Oklahoma City.

Two weeks later, I was in the navy. First at boot camp at the Great Lakes Naval Training Station in Chicago, then on to Madison, Wisconsin, for officer's training as a naval radioman. Typical government logic—since I was a singer on radio, it made perfect sense that I should transmit coded radio signals from warships on the high seas.

I've forgotten most of the codes, the technology, and everything else I learned in my accelerated course of naval indoctrination. What I do remember vividly is climbing down the drainpipe of my second-story barracks and racing off in the middle of the night to spend a few hours with my new bride, who had borrowed just enough from her family to come to Madison and rent a tiny room a few blocks from the base. This was wartime, and going AWOL was technically a capital crime in the military. I could have been shot if I'd been caught, but it was worth it to spend a few fleeting hours with Gen before I shipped off to a combat zone.

So shoot me. It was all I could do.

Weeks later, we were forced to part for what proved to be the only time in our lives. I headed for Long Beach and a berth on the S.S. *Carole Lombard,* commissioned in honor of the movie comedienne and wife of Clark Gable who had been killed in a plane crash while touring for the USO. It was a good ship, but the crew didn't consider it such a great honor to be on board. The *Carole Lombard* was a munitions transport headed out on the long Pacific route to Australia. My first day on board, I asked my CPO where our destroyer escorts were. He got a good laugh from that question.

"Escorts? Son, we are one big floating stick of dynamite. If we get hit, everything within a mile is going straight up to Kingdom Come, and it don't take more'n a warm match to do it neither."

I figured my chances of ever seeing Gen again were about one in ten.

Just to end the suspense, I have to tell you the *Carole Lombard* didn't go down with all hands. We never took a hit. Never saw a single enemy craft. In fact, on that first nail-biting round-trip excursion, we didn't have a casualty, unless you want to count the men laid low by rolling seas. Seasickness was epidemic. The most prevalent skin color on board was greener than Kermit the Frog.

There were only a handful of exemptions to this awful curse of the sea and I happened to be among the lucky ones. The undulations of the waves that turned the stomachs of most of the crew just made me hungry. I would take my watch on the ship's radio, saunter over to the mess, eat my own meal, and then snack on sixty others left untouched by sailors who couldn't stand to look at food. I sympathized with those poor guys, but there was nothing I could do and it was a shame to see good food go to waste. It's a good thing the war ended when it did or I would have come home looking like Dom DeLuise.

*

After the war, I was recruited for a most enviable position—lead singer with the country's top radio show, Kay Kyser's Kollege of Musical Knowledge. Kay didn't just change my life, he changed my name. He never liked Irish names, and Michael Delaney Dowd was way too Irish for him. One night, as I strolled to center stage to start a set, Kay informed the audience they were about to hear ". . . our own singing sensation from the heartland, Michael . . . Douglas!"

I looked around to see if someone was joining me for a duet, then realized he meant me. It happened that fast, off the top of his head, but I guess he knew what he was doing. People have been calling me that ever since.

The Kollege was great, but I was forced to graduate a few years later. For Gen and me, it was the beginning of hard times.

For a while, I worked the L.A. club scene. I remember Gen constantly pressing my one and only tuxedo so I would look good doing three shows a night.

We saved enough to buy a tiny house in the valley. We needed the room. Gen and I were already the proud parents of beautiful twin girls, Michele and Christine.

Live radio and the nightclub circuit were swamped in the wake of

Mike singing on Kay Kyser's show. Kay is telling the audience that Mike is to have twins.

television's rush to dominance of the nation's leisure hours. Like many of my show business peers, I saw TV as the enemy. It was Gen who saw it as an opportunity and urged me to try my hand on the tube. Our first forays into television didn't last, but Gen saw the promise of what could be. When the offer came from Cleveland, I was hesitant to risk what little we had on a local show in the Midwest with an unproven format. Gen said, "It'll be all right, Mike," and off we went. The rest, as they say, is history.

*

Show business is risky business. It's difficult to stay on that edge—make the audience comfortable, but surprise them, too; establish a solid routine, but still keep growing and changing as a performer. I was lucky to have Gen to give me a commonsense perspective. She was my biggest fan and most severe critic. She knew entertainment. She could read people, all kinds of people, and wasn't dazzled by fame. She had a sixth sense for what worked and what didn't. And she was always right.

Mike's mother and dad (Mr. And Mrs. Michael Dowd Sr.) as they appeared on Mike's show in 1970.

When *The Mike Douglas Show* lifted off, Woody Fraser was the engine, but Gen was our wings. You never saw her or heard her name, but she lived and breathed every minute of the show with me.

And she was just a country girl from Oklahoma. Gen was never comfortable with the way show business people always greeted each other with a kiss. Perfect strangers smooching like part of the family? She never did get used to it. I think she invented that "phantom kiss" they all use now, where you just kiss the air.

Every TV host in history has had a staff assistant who takes care of miscellaneous personal things, like cleaning and laundry. Not me. Gen wouldn't allow it. Have some secretary see your pajamas and underwear? Don't be ridiculous!

That's how she is.

We did a week from the Grand Ole Opry once, except almost not. As usual, the whole staff and all our guests geared up for a location shoot. We were road veterans by then, and we arrived in Nashville ready to go.

This time was unusual because we made a major blunder our first day. Frankie, one of our staffers, got out of line with a few of the Opry people, acting like we were the big fancy national TV show and they were a bunch of hillbillies. The Grand Ole Opry is a proud institution. They have a wonderful heritage that dates way back. When you're on their turf, you are going to behave and do things their way or hit the road. They didn't take kindly to Frank's attitude and were ready to tell us to start packing. It would have been a major embarrassment. Kicked out of town by the Grand Ole Opry.

They were already pointing their fingers at the door when Gen stepped in and calmed the troubled waters. The Opry folks were past talking to any East Coast city slickers, but they were willing to give an ear to a soft-spoken Okie girl. Gen apologized, pleaded for understanding, promised cooperation, and quietly spirited Frankie away from the set.

Crisis averted, we spent an enjoyable week in Nashville.

Gen saved us that time, and many others. Even the staff doesn't know about most of them because she wouldn't talk about it and made sure no one else did. She wasn't being coy, she just knew she could contribute most from behind the scenes.

And she did, day after day for twenty wonderful years.

November 5, 1981. Dateline . . . Hollywood

The Mike Douglas Show was on another run. One Monday after the show, I returned to my office to find a dog-eared memo on top of the usual stack of mail and paperwork. The corporate memos were treated with the reverence of orders from the Pentagon by the Group W execs in L.A. and this one was a summary report on the latest Nielsens, hot off the presses. The show was pushing its dominant afternoon ratings still higher, breaking new records. Number one in New York. Number one in Boston. Number one in Philadelphia. Cleveland. Chicago. Houston. Miami. San Francisco. The highest ratings in the show's history. We were soon to celebrate our twentieth year on the air. It was the best of times.

It was the worst of times. Something had changed in recent months. Some tectonic shift of the bedrock of television had been rumbling beneath our feet since the torch had been passed in the hallowed high offices of Westinghouse. My friend and mentor, Don McGannon, had retired. A new generation of executives had taken over, with new attitudes, new philosophies of programming, and a new set of buzzwords like "power demographics," "show velocity," and "Q ratings." They knew all about television. They had earned MBAs in mass media and communications from fine universities, doubling up with accounting degrees from Wharton and Carnegie-Mellon. The new breed, eager for a new beginning.

I think it was the end of the era. When our show started, national television was still an adolescent, flexing new muscles, struggling for the right voice, groping for the right place to be. In those formative years, it was instantaneous and unpredictable, without historic standards to set a firm direction.

I believe we helped set some of those standards and directions. We were allowed to be creative, to invent things you could do on TV, how to do them and how to act. Nothing pleased us more than to see other shows pick up on something we did and use it themselves. It meant that we were right. It worked. It was good TV.

Television grew up in the 1960s and 1970s, right through the time we were on the air. From live to videotape, from black and white to color, from vacuum tubes to computer chips. By the 1980s, TV had become a full-fledged member of the business establishment. A corporate entity. A profit center. Television generates so much money, I suppose it was inevitable. I'm still not sure that it's good.

*

The day we got the all-time Nielsen ratings, I went back to my office, picked songs for the following week, read the new guest list, and went home to tell Gen the news. She was pleased. We had a nice dinner and went to bed early. I had to be at the studio for a production meeting before rehearsals the next day.

I knew when I arrived the next morning that something was going on. Group W vice president Frank Miller was outside the door waiting to greet me when I pulled into my parking space. Frank was one of several executives who occupied parallel offices on the second floor, but we didn't see them often. They were busy with corporate stuff, advertisers and syndicators, and rarely got involved with the show itself.

I couldn't think of any good reason Frank would be outside waving at me when I arrived unless the building was on fire.

Maybe the company was going to do something special in appreciation of the record ratings. I didn't think so. We had passed a lot of ratings milestones over a lot of years and stopped the celebrations long ago.

So it had to be something else. But what?

Frank greeted me with a hollow heartiness that sent a chill up my back. "Good morning, Mike. And how are we doing today?"

"We're great, Frank. What's up?"

"Listen, there's something I wanted to talk to you about. You got a few minutes?"

We walked in together, in silence, all the way to my dressing room. He closed the door behind us. Uh-oh.

What he said was news to me, although it had somehow escaped from the corporate offices earlier and swept the building like a flash fire. The entire staff knew already. Even the crew and the band already knew the secret.

"Mike, I'm sorry to have to be the one to tell you this, but I wanted you to know before it was released to the press. The board has decided not to pick up the option on your contract."

I was taking off my shoes and my tie.

"I'm sorry, Frank—what?"

"It's not a position or a ploy, Mike. It's a final decision. I just wanted to make sure you were the first to know."

"Are you telling me that Westinghouse is canceling the show?"

"Oh God, no, Mike, they wouldn't do that. They're not crazy."

"Frank, you're not making any sense."

"They've decided to bring in a new host. Somebody younger. Don't take it personally. It's just business."

"They already have someone in mind, do they?"

"Yes. Yes they do. They've signed somebody."

"And who might that be?"

"Well Mike, they—John Davidson."

Frank stayed close to the door, just in case, but the entire conversation was held in the same tones as a discussion about the weather. I stared at Frank for a minute, then shrugged.

"Frank, I really have to get ready to do the show. Let's talk about this some other time, okay?"

"Sure. Sure, Mike. Anything you say. I—I just want to tell you that it's been an honor working with you."

"Thanks, Frank. Thanks. I really appreciate that."

Frank Miller and I never really spoke again. About anything. There wasn't anything else to say. That afternoon, the Group W guys began quietly approaching members of my staff while we were taping to make overtures about staying on to work for the new *John Davidson Show.*

The one thing that brings a smile to my face when I recall this difficult episode is the staff—our staff. Every one of them was offered an enhanced contract to stay with Westinghouse and John Davidson. Everyone was lobbied hard. Everyone knew there was nothing at all certain about any kind of Mike Douglas show being on the air anywhere in just a few short months. Thirty-nine out of forty turned down the offer and stayed with us.

For me, it was a bitter pill to swallow. The company that had built its powerhouse entertainment division on our show and had put hundreds of millions of dollars into its coffers over the course of our twenty-year joint venture had closed us down without a second thought. Before I was even told of their unilateral decision, Westinghouse headquarters issued a press release claiming that Mike Douglas had "decided to retire" and trumpeting John Davidson's anointing as his successor. It was a sorry attempt to eliminate me as potential competition, keep me from continuing with another syndicator or independently. In the ensuing weeks, I never received a single word of thanks or apology from the company, only a formal offer for a formidable, lump-sum payment if I would stay off the air.

We had six months left on our contract, six months of obligation to fulfill with partners who had now proclaimed themselves our enemy. I don't mind telling you, they were the darkest days of my life.

Doing a show every day awash in conflicting emotions and plagued by troubling questions wasn't easy. Should I hang 'em up or try to go on? Were they right? Not yet sixty, was I too old for the TV generation of the 1980s? Could we survive without Westinghouse? Was it possible to re-create the show? What to do? Where to go? Who to turn to?

To Gen. It was Gen who dismissed Westinghouse as "shortsighted." It was Gen who rallied our staff and foretold a bright future for all of us. It was Gen who urged us to develop a survival strategy and go for it. Six months later, as we bid farewell to Westinghouse, we were welcomed back on the air by over a hundred stations who had signed on to broadcast the new *Mike Douglas Show* through independent syndication.

For Gen and me, it was a particularly sweet victory. For years we continued to entertain the daytime audience that had become old friends. It was the same format, the same staff, the same innovations, and the same energy. Only this time, we were the Mom and Pop who owned the candy store. We tried not to gloat when the *Davidson Show* was canceled after a brief run. Reporters ran to us with the news and we had no comment, but it wasn't easy trying to keep the knowing smiles off our faces.

When we finally decided that, like all good things, our wonderful run on television had to come to an end, it was on our own terms. It was the right time and the way it was meant to be, with lots of remembering, celebrating, a few tears and hugs all around. Like Bob Hope says, thanks for the memories.

And thanks for my Gen. Since our departures, dozens of similar shows have come and gone. Many had almost an identical format, several had talented hosts, and some spent millions of dollars in a vain attempt to capture that vast but elusive audience that makes daytime a potential bonanza for would-be broadcast impresarios with dollar signs in their eyes. So many have tried. So few succeeded. Every now and then, an enterprising TV journalist will call and ask why—why don't these star-laden, lavishly produced, heralded new shows make the cut? What did we have that they don't?

That's easy. They don't have Gen.

*

Back to 1995. The memories and reminiscing helped, all right, but not nearly as much as the first words from that same young doctor after Gen emerged from surgery. I saw him coming, walking down that corridor, peeling off his gloves and mask, the messenger from heaven or hell, I didn't know which. I held my breath.

"Everything went fine, Mr. Douglas. Better than we expected. She's going to be all right."

I don't know that young man very well, but I love him dearly.

*

Today, I have my health, I have my girls, my sons-in-law, my grandchildren and great-grandchildren, and I have my Gen. I don't take any of them for granted anymore.

Gen and Mike

We spend our days with family and friends, people we love. We haven't forgotten the simple lessons of Mother Teresa and we try to do something every day that is of some small benefit to someone else. We owe so much to so many, it's the least we can do.

Once in a while, I'll do a guest shot on one of the current shows, like Regis & Kathie Lee or Rosie or Geraldo, but it's kind of unsettling. In my day, they poured water on my head and hit me in the face with pies. Now, they treat me with such courtesy and respect, I start to wonder who they're talking about. When I was on Howie Mandel's show last year, he thanked me for boosting his career, then Jay Leno walked in as a special surprise to thank me for boosting his career. I was blushing. C'mon, you guys. I paid you a couple hundred bucks to come on my show and boost *my* career.

Of course, it's not as good as the heyday when *The Mike Douglas Show* ruled daytime. It's really not. It's better. I don't have to worry about ratings or schedules or guests. If the show isn't going very well, all I have to do is reach for the remote.

Hey, we've got a lot more to talk about but two of the great-grandkids are here and I promised them we'd spend some time outside. Do you mind?

You know the routine. Think of it as a commercial. Get a quick snack if you want, make yourself comfortable, and don't worry—I'll be right back.

Index

Page numbers in *italics* refer to illustrations.

Photo Credits

Many thanks to Bernie Rich and Michael Leshnov, the fine *Mike Dougas Show* photographer who chronicled our two-decade run from the first days in Cleveland through Philadelphia to the last act in L.A. Their contribution to the show means more to me now—the gift of thousands of memories.

Mike Douglas Show photos courtesy of Eyemark Entertainment.

Cleveland State University Archives, photo collection: pages 20, 25, 50, 55, 66, 95, 105, 108, 112, 121, 123, 127, 129, 134, 142, 146, 148, 151, 161, 187, 189, 192, 193, 203, 205, 254.

Michael Leshnov/Lost Archives © 1999 Michael Leshnov: pages 45, 48, 51, 52, 58, 63, 64, 69, 73, 74, 76, 78, 83, 84, 86, 89, 90, 94, 98, 99, 100, 103, 107, 109, 115, 116, 118, 128, 131, 133, 135, 138, 139, 140, 153, 155, 164, 169, 170, 173, 175, 176, 190, 191, 195, 202, 218, 221, 223, 226, 229, 234, 237, 238, 241, 244, 248, 252, 257, 259, 264, 271, 272, 284.

Bernie Rich/Score Photography collection © Bernie Rich: pages 29, 61, 72, 145, 152, 275, 278.

Oprah Winfrey courtesy of Harpo/King World (Paul Natkin): page 274.

Rosie O'Donnell courtesy of *The Rosie O'Donnell Show:* page 280.

All other photos from the personal collection of Mike Douglas: pages 17, 29, 40, 117, 120, 179, 198, 201, 206, 214, 250, 293, 294, 297, 298, 304.